ALBERT B. COOK III, Ph.D., Western Reserve University, is Associate Professor of English at the University of Kansas. He formerly taught at Northern Michigan University.

INTRODUCTION TO THE
ENGLISH LANGUAGE

• STRUCTURE AND HISTORY

ALBERT B. COOK III

THE UNIVERSITY OF KANSAS

THE RONALD PRESS COMPANY • NEW YORK

Library of Congress Catalog Card Number: 69–12922
PRINTED IN THE UNITED STATES OF AMERICA

To

Dr. Russell Thomas

Professor of English Emeritus
and Chairman of the Department of Language and Literature
at Northern Michigan University from 1939 to 1962,
whose lifetime work exemplifies the essential relationship
between linguistics and literary scholarship:

He wæs godsibb ðisse bec.

Preface

This is an introductory textbook intended for the student who is new to systematic language study. It is meant not to make a "little linguist" out of him, but rather to increase his understanding of this fundamental human phenomenon, as exemplified by English, and introduce to him the structure, capabilities, history, and variety of his native language. I have therefore done my best to eliminate unnecessary technical terminology and to define carefully the new terms which had to be included.

The book is designed for a very full one-semester course introducing the student to the total area of English language study. Used in this manner, it would prepare the student for more advanced courses in a variety of special fields, including grammatical theory, philosophy of language, dialectology, modern English grammar, and history of the English language. However, it may also be used in the latter two courses over a two-semester period, supplemented by more advanced books, if the instructor chooses.

As an introductory work, this book includes the material most relevant to the beginning student. Such details as West Germanic vowel gradation or Old English weak neuter nouns are reserved for advanced courses or for graduate study, where they properly belong. In this book, the student is introduced to the phenomenon of language itself, to a discussion of the important features of grammatical theories old and new, and to an integrated description of modern English, using whichever theory applies most directly to the descriptive problem at hand. An inductive approach is used throughout the book, and thus the textbook narrative is purposely minimized. The student is asked to work out many of the details for himself in the discussion questions and exercises.

The discussion of the history of the English language is handled in reverse chronological order, beginning with Early Modern English and working backward to Old English. Although this has the disadvantage of disrupting the continuity of the phonological change from one period to another, it has the offsetting advantage of enabling the student to begin with that which is relatively familiar and work back to what is basically a foreign language to him. It is particularly important that the student do the exercises for this section carefully and conscientiously, either for class discussion or for course papers. With this background, he will be better equipped for one of the more advanced and detailed studies in the history of English, to say nothing of advanced courses in Middle English and Elizabethan literature.

One area which is given rather minimal attention is phonology. There is always time later, I feel, to cover this field more thoroughly, to involve the student in some of the disputes over rival phonemic systems. In fact, the system employed here is essentially a compromise which works well both for modern English and for the earlier states of the language. If the instructor wishes, however, he can supplement this as he sees fit, just as he is free to add to or disagree with any other part of the book.

In a field which is moving and changing as rapidly as linguistics, any undergraduate textbook is vulnerable to change. Chomsky's theory of generative grammar, for example, has changed considerably in the ten years since the publication of *Syntactic Structures*. In this book, stratificational grammar is still a footnote; tomorrow it may supersede everything else. It is also possible that a completely new system might arise, or an amalgamation of systems, and push the rest aside. I have tried to arrange this text to give the instructor room to work up his course in his own way, taking issue where he will, developing some parts further than I have done. Nothing demeans an instructor more than having a textbook which is intended to do his work for him, or which limits his freedom to expand and develop new ideas, thereby making him a mere adjunct, an arm of the author. I do not believe that any instructor will be tyrannized by this text, or straitjacketed by its contents or arrangement.

It is a pleasure to acknowledge here the help given me by so many colleagues and friends. David W. D. Dickson, now at Federal City College, Washington, D.C., and Arthur E. Pennell encouraged my efforts to try new directions in my courses and to write this book. Obviously, a good deal of thanks goes to several hundred English majors and minors who had perforce to submit to this experimentation and who offered many suggestions for improvement. My Northern Michigan University colleagues John VandeZande, John J. Filor, and Frank Bartol read and commented upon portions of the preliminary manuscript. A special measure of appreciation goes to Professor J. N. Hook of the University of Illinois, who read the manuscript in its various stages of completion and offered many necessary criticisms and useful comments. Naturally, none of these people should be held accountable for errors or lapses in the book.

It has been a tradition for writers to append a note of appreciation to their wives, "without whom . . . ." In my case, this is no empty courtesy, for my wife Jeanne audited my course, offered constant suggestions for its improvement, typed drafts and final manuscript, and acted always as a court of final appeal—all this in addition to her full-time duties as wife and mother. Truly, without her, this book would never have been written.

ALBERT B. COOK III

Lawrence, Kansas
March, 1969

Contents

INTRODUCTION TO THE

ENGLISH LANGUAGE

• STRUCTURE AND HISTORY

I

Introduction

LINGUISTICS

Language and the Discipline of English

The teacher of English, on whatever level, is involved in a discipline which includes language, composition, and literature, three areas which are seldom interrelated. In fact, the normal arrangement of the subject matter automatically makes these areas discrete and unrelated, despite recent concerted efforts to treat them as interconnected parts of a unified discipline. This division is evident even in the choice of a vocation. Ordinarily, English teachers become English teachers because they enjoy reading or have some facility in writing, usually creative writing. They virtually never are attracted to the profession because of their public school exposure to language—usually subsumed under the term *grammar*. Many students tend to equate "English" with grammar, a subject usually so grimly presented that they come to loathe it, even though they love to read and often are led to try their hand at writing as a result of their reading.

Several factors contribute to this antipathy toward language studies, one of the biggest being a widespread misunderstanding on the part of public school teachers and administrators of the work being done in the field today. Although this situation is certain to change in the near future, it is probably true that most college students interested in English teaching as a possible vocation had never heard of the work of **linguists** or of the general discoveries in the field of **linguistics,** or **linguistic science,** when they declared a major. The major purpose of this book is to introduce students to the field of linguistics and to show how its findings, as applied to English, can be of more than peripheral importance to them as they continue to specialize in English or in the collateral fields of speech, foreign languages, and dramatics.

The Linguist

To many people, a **linguist** is the same as a polyglot, one who can speak several languages fluently. For this reason, specialists in the field of linguistics have intermittently been looking for a better occupational word, though without success.[1] In professional usage, the **linguist** is a scholar who studies language objectively, observing it scientifically, recording the facts of language, and generalizing from them. The use of the term *scientific* should perhaps be soft-pedaled, because language is a human phenomenon which cannot be subclassified so neatly as the natural phenomena of the scientist; but so far as one is able to be scientific *vis-à-vis* human conduct, the linguist certainly adheres to the scientific method. The facts of language which he may observe include its sounds, forms, and syntactic arrangement, and from these he formulates general rules which describe how a specific language is actually used. In addition, the linguist can observe the facts of a language for the purpose of describing its historical development (historical linguistics), its regional and social differences (linguistic geography, or dialectology), its relationship to other languages (comparative linguistics), or its application to other fields, particularly education (applied linguistics). Because the field is so broad and touches so many facets of human conduct, it is a shame that so little real awareness or understanding of it has managed to percolate down to the schools.

[1] The term *linguistician* has been suggested, but it is usually shouted down by those who feel that it it is too fancy, or too much like "mortician." Occasionally the expression *linguistic scientist* is used interchangeably with *linguist*, but to the layman it is too close to the laboratory and the test tube.

The Linguist and His Co-workers

The linguist, primarily concerned with describing the language as it is, should be differentiated from certain other scholars who are also involved, at least peripherally, in language, and usually in the field of English. These include the rhetorician, who is primarily interested in effective written or spoken communication, and the literary critic, who makes value judgments about the worth and effectiveness, the literary merit, of the works of a writer's creative imagination. It sometimes happens that an English teacher can wear all three of these hats. Your instructor in this course, insofar as he assists you in objectively viewing your language, is a linguist. But if he teaches freshman composition, too, he is a rhetorician, using in part the findings of the linguist about social reactions to language to demonstrate to his writers how best to order their prose. Finally, if he also teaches a sophomore literary survey course, he is a critic, using as the basis of his subjective judgments on literature some of the opinions of the rhetorician on what constitutes good writing. Unfortunately, the relationships aren't always this simple, for even in the most enlightened English departments, when specialization is the natural order of things the communication between the linguist and his colleagues sometimes breaks down because of misunderstanding.

Part of the misunderstanding comes from the failure of the linguist (and his lay supporters) to make completely clear his attitude toward language. Too often, he is viewed as one who believes that "everything goes" in language, that "one expression is as good as another," especially in relation to such shibboleths as *ain't*. Actually, he tries to show that in certain communities, under specified conditions, *ain't* (originally a contraction of *am not*, and thus as respectable in its parentage as *isn't* or *aren't*) is in perfectly good spoken usage by all the leading citizens. Some people, unfortunately, see red where *ain't* is concerned, and they won't wait to hear the full explanation: the linguist isn't sanctioning the use of this heinous four-letter word in communities where the leading citizens abjure it; he is simply describing the facts. Other colleagues, depressed by the linguist's descriptions of the grammatical facts of a language, feel that he is complicating things unnecessarily, particularly when they feel they themselves have a sufficient grasp of the "grammar" they learned in school. Besides, they add, with his objective views on usage and his formulaic statements of grammar, the linguist is doing great violence to the language handed down to us from Shakespeare, Milton, and Wordsworth. Finally, there are those colleagues, more amused than alarmed, who profess themselves nonplussed by the preoccupation of some linguists (particularly those who are affiliated with the anthropology departments of major universities) with the "savage tongues" of the American Indians, or of Africa and the Far East. How, they ask, can one take techniques devised to analyze "inarticulate babblings of savages" and use them in the same way on the civilized languages of the West?

This situation is not as pervasive as it was even ten years ago, but there is still a great need for all educators, and laymen as well, to understand more thoroughly the work of the linguist, even if they cannot bring themselves to approve of it. Currently, this need is greatest amongst the English teachers in the public schools, who need to be shown how new language discoveries can benefit them. One place to start is with the future teachers, and the best possible footing comes from knowing what the linguist means when he uses such terms as *language, dialect,* and *grammar,* terms which have suffered from multiplicity of meaning, thereby causing more confusion among the already confused laity.

Definitions

For a start, consider the term **language.** Even though this might seem silly, try to give your definition of it. Here is a word that all of us have used without a second thought, a term which is so obvious that we feel we "know" its "meaning" without inquiring further. Consequently, by now you have probably come up with an answer very much like:

(1) Language is a means of communication.

If we consider this definition for a moment, we must agree that it is just a little bit circular. Furthermore, what is the medium of this "means of communication"? We could name a variety of ways by which communication is carried on: noises in the throat, scribbles on paper, scratches on stone, semaphore, wigwagging flags, smoke signals, Morse code, hand-and-arm signals, deaf-and-dumb signs, and anything else which might "communicate something."

It is a mistake to say that everything on this list is a summation of the instances of language. Consider, first of all, something of the matter of precedence. Some means of communication are less important than others, or are based directly upon them. After pondering this list for a moment, you have probably concluded that all of the various code and signaling devices are secondary to writing—and you are right. The Morse code, for instance, is a system of dots and dashes which is based directly upon the alphabet, and thus could not be devised without the clear and familiar presence of an alphabet system. It is true that before the era of the automatic writing machines, experienced telegraphers had devised a rather large inventory of abbreviations and short-cuts for the commonly used words and expressions in their work, but most of us have never gotten beyond a rather rudimentary knowledge of the Morse system, acquired in our Boy Scout days. At any rate, we can agree that these systems are dependent upon writing, and only a rather obvious sort of hand-and-arm signal could be used with any ease by anyone who was illiterate.

Consequently, we are left with only two means of communication which might be judged primary: noises we make with our throats (speaking) and scribbles we make on a surface (writing). Which is primary? The answer, you would say, is very simple. Remembering that the great tradition of Chaucer, Shakespeare, Milton, the Bible, the whole of literature, is handed down to us in writing; remembering that your basic medium of learning is the written textbook; remembering all of the agony you and your composition teacher put into your written work; perhaps remembering the old injunction to "put it into writing" so that you (or someone else) will remember it—you will immediately leap to the conclusion that:

(2) Language is a *written* means of communication.

Let's look at that a little more closely. Already we can probably frame some rather vague objections to this conclusion. For instance, there are hundreds of different groups of people who have no writing system whatsoever. It is very easy to dismiss them as ignorant, primitive, savage groups, of little account in the modern world, but is it fair to say that they have no language? On the contrary, they probably communicate with one another quite as easily as we do.

Just to make the situation a little plainer, consider the following pieces of information.

1. Mankind was speaking long before the dawn of recorded history. Writing, as we shall see in Chapter 6, is a relatively recent discovery. It is unfortunately true that we know very little about the peoples who leave behind only bits of tools or shards of pottery for archaeologists to uncover, and that "finds" like the Dead Sea Scrolls are far more spectacular, but this does not alter the historical precedence of speech over writing.

2. It is easy to be misled by the emotional appeal of great literature. Yet we must consider that such masterpieces as *Beowulf*, the Norse sagas, the Homeric epics, the "fairy tales" collected by Grimm, even a goodly part of the Bible, were all handed down intact in an oral tradition before someone decided to set them down in writing. Great literature was conceived and passed on without the benefit of writing, and it should also be remembered that the rime and rhythm techniques of poetry (and also of Elizabethan drama) were devised originally as aids to memory.

In connection with this, have you ever had the experience of reading to a young child one of his favorite stories? If, in the course of your reading, you skipped a passage or simply substituted a word, the chances are that you were promptly corrected. The truth of the matter is that all preliterate societies and peoples have remarkable memories and are quite able, even willing, to correct the storyteller who alters the story. Storytellers themselves were not selected for their memories—everyone had a good memory— but rather for their storytelling ability. Today, the sad truth probably is that because of our reliance upon writing, we have allowed a good portion of our faculties for memorization to atrophy.

3. But, you will argue, speech is lost the instant it is uttered by the speaker, whereas there is something permanent and lasting about writing. *Littera scripta manet*, as the old expression goes: "The written word remains." There is no denying this; but unfortunately there is a lot of writing left in the world which is scarcely more than scribbling or ornate carving, simply because there is no one around to decipher it for us. In the last chapter of his book *Lost Languages*, P. E. Cleator describes several of these written remains which give every indication of remaining unknown to us: the Cretan Linear A script, the so-called Eteocyprian script of Cyprus, the Etruscan inscriptions, the Mayan glyphs in the Yucatan, and the *rongo rongo* script of Easter Island, to name a few.[2] Those who could speak the languages inscribed have long since departed, taking with them their knowledge of the correspondence between sound and marking. Indeed, only the written word remains.

4. Finally, those of us who are poor spellers are ruefully aware of the imperfect correspondencies between our alphabet and our language. We have heard of writing systems commonly called "phonetic" in which there is a close correspondency between the letter and the sound. The systems of Spanish and Finnish come most readily to mind. But even here, the relationship is imperfect. And of course in English, there is a good deal of meaningless variation, exemplified by the diverse spelling of the *sh* sound as in *mission*, not to mention the pedantic superfluities in such spellings as *debt*, *psychology*, *knight*, and *phthisic*.

By now, I trust that you are convinced of the actual primacy of speaking over writing, and are willing to alter our definition to:

(3) Language is a *vocal* means of communication.

Thus we show that writing is a secondary language form based upon speech, and that Morse code, semaphores, Navy signal flags, deaf-and-dumb signals are all of them tertiary, based upon writing.

[2] (New York, 1959), pp. 161–77.

But still the definition is incomplete. What, for instance, is it that we are vocalizing? We don't just make a lot of noises; everything we utter is set forth in a meaningful order which we have somehow learned, and from which we depart only within narrow limits, lest we fail to communicate. In order to have communication, we must have system; otherwise we are simply making noises to no purpose. Thus we amend our definition:

(4) Language is a vocal *system* of communication.

The noises in our throats must adhere to some preconceived order and arrangement. All languages have system; the reason why languages other than our own sound like gibberish is because we have not mastered the complexity of their systems. In addition, this system has a framework of ideas built up within it, so that every utterance we make communicates these ideas to the auditor, who in turn responds by framing the same ideas, assuming we have communicated properly. Some of these ideas are lexical, conveying "dictionary" meaning, while others are grammatical, serving only the purpose of maintaining the system. We will call the former **symbols,** and the latter **grammatical signals,** both of which we must first learn in order to react to them or utter them. Thus we can further revise the definition to read:

(5) Language is a system of vocal *symbols and grammatical signals* used for communication.

Now let's further consider the nature of the "vocal symbols" in our definition. Take for example the semantic unit *dog*. We are all agreed that this word represents for us the general idea of *Canis domesticus*, with some emotional overtones, depending upon whether we remember a faithful pet, or were bitten once by one of those snarling creatures. Now, to make the problem more complex, consider as well the semantic units *chien, Hund, perro,* which represent respectively the French, German, and Spanish equivalents of our word *dog*. Some might notice that French *chien* seems to be derived from Latin *canis* and will likewise agree that German *Hund* is cognate with the English *hound*; but beyond that no one really can see how any one of these four words innately represents an idea of "dogginess," except that the speakers of the respective languages have all agreed arbitrarily upon the relationship of utterance and concept. In fact, one might almost argue that on the face of it, the infant's spoken *bow-wow* is ideationally more meaningful than *dog*.[3] Be it as it may, *dog* is in English the adult term, and in recognition of the fact that it is only our tacit agreement of utterance and idea at work here, and not any innate relationship bound up in the utterance, we can further alter our definition:

> (6) Language is a system of *arbitrary* vocal symbols and grammatical signals used for communication.

We have now built up the first part of our definition sufficiently well to make that last part seem weak. What is it that this system of arbitrary vocal symbols and grammatical signals can do? We have already listed communication, which suggests the imparting of ideas. But we don't simply listen passively to ideas all the time. Rather, we often find ourselves called upon to lend a helping hand, to assist in an enterprise, to rouse ourselves to action. Thus language is called upon not only for communication, but also for interaction.

But this isn't all. So far we have only implied that this is a human action. What of the so-called language of monkeys, for instance, or dolphins? Apparently they are able to communicate ideas, admittedly rather simple, and interact by means of an arbitrary vocal system. We are told that monkey colonies have signals which seem to mean danger, or food, or a predator. How does human language differ from these rude animal noises? The difference lies in the fact that whereas the monkeys can signal to one another the general concept of *food*, they are unable to communicate information and ideas which they might have acquired about the particular food in question. On the other hand, humans are able to say, "Don't eat that, it's poisonous!" (based upon the recollection of someone's sad experience, or what one has been told about someone who allegedly ate the food); or,

---

[3] It is instructive to note that even these onomatopoetic representations differ from language to language. See Noel Perrin, "Old Macberlitz Had a Farm," *New Yorker* (January 27, 1962), 28–29; with additions in the February 24, 1962, issue, p. 125.

"Don't eat that, it's not good for you" (in the situation of parent to child with a hunk of candy only a few minutes before dinner); or, "Eat that, it's good for you" (any parent speaking to any child about spinach, about which we have acquired a dubious, but time-honored notion of nutritious goodness); all the way through a scale of associations. We thus have passed on a whole complex of ideas, some of which are the result of personal experience, others of hearsay, and still others of cultural transference, even taboo. This is what makes language a purely human phenomenon, and thus we are ready to add to our definition:

> (7) Language is a system of arbitrary vocal symbols and grammatical signals used for communication, *interaction*, and *cultural transmission*.

This seems pretty good, but it is still a little bit impersonal. Who, we might ask, uses this instrument for communication, interaction, and cultural transmission? Obviously, the speakers of the language, but to refer to them in this way will force us to use in our definition the very word we want to define. Perhaps we should take our hint from Leonard Bloomfield: "Within certain communities successive utterances are alike or partly alike. . . . Any such community is a *speech community*."[4] Thus we can complete our definition both by making it less impersonal and by specifying the users:

> (8) A language is a system of arbitrary vocal symbols and grammatical signals by means of which *the members of a speech community* communicate, interact, and transmit their culture.

Our definition follows that of Edgar L. Sturtevant,[5] with the addition of the phrase *transmit their culture*, which, as we showed, makes explicit the human quality of language; and the phrase *grammatical signals*, ·which clarifies the difference between the lexical inventory of the language and the nonlexical portion which orders and regulates the system of the language. We can

---

[4] "A Set of Postulates for the Science of Language," *Language*, II (1926); reprinted in Martin Joos (ed.), *Readings in Linguistics* (3d ed.; New York, 1963), p. 26.
[5] *An Introduction to Linguistic Science* (New Haven, 1947), pp. 2–3.

quote several other definitions as well as for the sake of comparison:

> Language is a purely human and non-instinctive method of communicating ideas, emotions, and desires by means of a system of voluntarily produced symbols. These symbols are, in the first instance, auditory and they are produced by the so-called "organs of speech."
>
> EDWARD SAPIR, *Language* (1921)

> A language is an arbitrary system of articulated sounds made use of by a group of humans as a means of carrying on the affairs of their society.
>
> W. NELSON FRANCIS, *The Structure of American English* (1958)

> [Language is] a system of arbitrary vocal symbols by which thought is conveyed from one human being to another.
>
> JOHN P. HUGHES, *The Science of Language* (1962)

Whatever the definition, it must include directly, or by close implication, all of the following attributes of language:

1. Language has system.
2. Language is vocal.
3. Language is arbitrary.
4. Language is a human activity.
5. Language is noninstinctive.
6. Language is a social activity.
7. Language is related to culture.

Dialect and Language Change

There is still one attribute of language which falls outside of our definition:

8. Language changes.

About language change as a historical phenomenon we will have much to say later, especially as it involves English; but there is another aspect of language change, often misunderstood, which we should clarify now. This is the aspect of change over geographical territory, or between social groups, at a single period of time, generally referred to as **dialect.**

We should note that language, even as we have defined it, is a relatively abstract concept. Where, for example, should we go to find the English language? England? Scotland? Ireland? Canada? Australia? Perhaps America—but if so, where in America? New England? New York? Texas? California? It is obvious that nowhere in the world is spoken anything which all speakers of English can agree upon as *the* English language. Wherever one goes, one finds a dialect of English, but not "English" itself. The English language, insofar as it has any real existence at all, consists of an abstract system of correspondencies which all the so-called speakers of English adhere to more or less faithfully, and it is the relatively frequent occurrence of these correspondencies which permits, for example, an American President and a British Prime Minister to communicate one to another on perplexing international problems without the aid of interpreters. Whenever the members of a speech community depart significantly from these language correspondencies, they no longer speak a dialect of language X, but what instead becomes the nucleus of a new language, Y.

This is difficult for many people to understand. Somehow the idea of dialect connotes to them the idea of substandard, or at least different, speech. It's hard for them to realize that they, too, speak a dialect, differing from other regional and social dialects in its sound inventory, its grammatical forms, and its lexicon. They resemble the lady from Fort Worth who was heard to comment, during the 1964 Presidential campaign, "It's nice to have someone in the White House who doesn't speak with an accent." This is an old story; everyone speaks a dialect except me.

Dialect, then, is the concrete manifestation of the abstraction *language*. In fact, it is entirely possible to argue that dialect is only somewhat less abstract than language, that someone with sharp enough ears could note minute differences in the speech of individuals within the same community. This is certainly true, and the term for the dialect of each individual speaker is **idiolect.** It could even be said that each speaker's *idiolect* is the only concrete manifestation of human speech. However, this complicates matters unnecessarily, and for our purposes, we will consider *dialect* to be the concrete manifestation of the abstraction *language*. What is important here is the realization that *dialect* means simply the regional and social variation of language, and that every utterance represents a concrete instance of that language.[6]

Some might object that the language exists in concrete form in writing, where dialect differences scarcely show up at all, unless the author is consciously trying to re-create them in dialogue. This objection fails to take into account the nature of writing as a conventional system, rather than as a faithful reproduction of speech. In particular, the spelling is here confused with the sounds of the language system. Besides, we have already noted that writing is a secondary form, based upon speech. We will discuss later how writing developed and how we have crystallized it into a system which now tends to follow the spoken system at a respectful distance.

GRAMMAR

The Four Meanings

Before we go on to examine English at close hand, we need to consider one more term which we will be using throughout this book. This term, every bit as ambiguous in its unspecified state as the others we have examined, is **grammar.**

To practically everyone, the word *grammar* recalls language workbooks, sentence diagramming, and worry about *will* vs. *shall* and the preposition at the end of the sentence. All of these

---

[6] Some will perhaps note here a variation of the system devised by the Swiss linguist Ferdinand de Saussure in a sequence of lectures at the University of Geneva in the first decade of this century and published after his death as *Cours de Linguistique Générale*. Saussure posited the division of *le langage* (human speech) into two mutually sustaining parts, *langue* (language) and *parole* (speaking). *Langue* is the essential institution of speech, the social, established system; whereas *parole* is the individual act, accidental, dependent upon the immediate situation. *Langue* can exist without *parole*, as in such "dead" languages as Latin, but the reverse cannot be true. Thus the individual speaker relies upon his intuitive understanding of the system (*langue*) in making his individual utterances (*parole*); but if a significant number of speakers depart in any particular way from the system, the system must be tacitly altered to conform to the alteration, lest a new system be adopted in its place. The presentation which we have made here differs in that by working vertically from the abstraction *language* to the concrete *dialect* (or to *idiolect*, if you prefer) we have considered a situation more in keeping with the reader's experience.

impressions presuppose the notion of an absolute correctness in language, of "right" and "wrong," "good" and "bad." Insofar as we learned anything at all from these exercises, we learned what was considered the proper use of language. Thus we come to the first consideration of grammar: grammar as linguistic propriety, as in the commonly heard expression, "He doesn't use good grammar." This concept of grammar is usually represented by handbooks of proper usage, such as those often used in the schools or nationally advertised as aids in overcoming one's sense of linguistic inferiority. Thus the first level of the term *grammar* is based upon the concept of language etiquette.

But there are English grammars which are not primarily concerned about the goodness and badness of certain expressions. Such works as those by Henry Sweet and Otto Jespersen make few value judgments, but consist of a detailed description of the language under consideration. In this light, then, we can define the next level of the word *grammar*: a formal description, relatively complete and exhaustive, of a language.

Formal descriptions of languages, however, do not arise out of nothing, *sui generis*. They are developed out of a consistent theory which outlines the descriptive method. Thus, the third level of the term: a theory on which formal descriptions of languages are based. From this level of grammar come such expressions as *descriptive grammar*, *functional grammar*, and *transformational grammar*.

But description would be impossible if there was no inherent system to be described. Thus we come to the fourth and most abstract level of all: grammar as the system inherent in any language. It is this system which all speakers of a language learn at an early age while scarcely realizing that they are, whether or not a formal description of that language exists. When we speak of the grammar of language X, we are using this particular meaning of the word.

A Look Ahead

Throughout this discussion of the English language, we will concentrate primarily upon a clearer understanding of the second and third levels of meaning of the word *grammar*. Consequently, we will first examine various theories of grammar upon which formal descriptions of the English language have been built to see what they can tell us about the system within the language itself. Afterward, we will trace the history of the English language to note how the system of Modern English evolved. We will then study something of the dialects of English, particularly the regional variations which are in the system. But it must always be understood that the fourth level of meaning of the word *grammar* is ever-present in our discussions—underlying our whole framework, necessary as a basic conception of our purpose—to understand more fully the system implicit in present-day English and in its historical development.

QUESTIONS AND EXERCISES

A note on the discussion questions and exercises: The discussion questions and exercises which are appended to this and succeeding chapters are not to be thought of as supplementary material, but as integral parts of this text. They are intended to help you understand the material more clearly and often to apply the discursive portions of the text to new problems and considerations. At no time should they be considered mere busy-work. Even those questions which are intended to be aids for review should lead you beyond the material presented in the body of the chapter.

Some of the questions and exercises can be answered with little trouble; others will perhaps provide a useful basis for class discussion. There are some which would prove suitable topics for course papers. But none of them should be passed over. Together with the material in the body of each chapter, they make up the total subject of this text.

The following quotations illustrate instances of fallacious thinking about language. Discuss the fallacy direct or implicit in each quotation, suggesting reasons for the rise of each erroneous impression and whether or not it is still current.

    1. My lord, I do here, in the name of all learned and polite persons of the nation complain to your lordship . . . that our

language is extremely imperfect: that its daily improvements are by no means in proportion to its daily corruptions; that the pretenders to polish and refine it, have chiefly multiplied abuses and absurdities; and that in many instances it offends against every part of grammar . . . and these corruptions very few of the best authors in our age have wholly escaped.

JONATHAN SWIFT, *Proposal for Correcting, Improving, and Ascertaining the English Tongue*

2. Dante created the Italian language; Martin Luther created the German language; Chaucer and Shakespeare created the English language.

3. The methods by which one examines the babblings of a few hundred illiterate savages cannot be used for the serious study of a tongue which the people of a great nation have used to record their spiritual experience in immortal literature.

4. We are told that the new Oxford Dictionary will contain a quarter of a million words. Does any one of us know 250,000 English words? I doubt it. It is extraordinary how many words this small brain of ours will hold, but there are limits to everything. In China a young man receives his first or second class in examination, according to the number of words he can read and write. But in order to obtain the place of an imperial historian, a candidate is not required to know more than 9,000. *We* do more than this. Most of us can read Shakespeare's plays, and in order to do that, we must know about 15,000 words. But though we understand most of these words (there are only about 500 to 600 words in Shakespeare which may justly be called obsolete), there are many we should never think of using ourselves. Most of us, I believe, never use more than 3,000 or 4,000 words, and we are assured that there are peasants who never use more than 300 or 400. This does not mean that they would not understand more than that number, for the Bible which they hear in church contains about 6,000 words; these they would understand more or less accurately, though they would never think of using them.

F. MAX MÜLLER, *Three Lectures on the Science of Language*

5. There are other traits [of language] whose importance can with greater ease be made evident to anyone possessed of a normal ear.

To bring out clearly one of these points I select at random, by way of contrast, a passage from the language of Hawaii: "I kona hiki ana aku ilaila ua hookipa ia mai la oia me ke aloha pumehana loa." Thus it goes on, no single word ends in a consonant, and a group of two or more consonants is never found. Can any one be in doubt that even if such a language sound pleasantly and be full of music and harmony the total impression is childlike and effeminate? You do not expect much vigour or energy in a people speaking such a language; it seems adapted only to inhabitants of sunny regions where the soil requires scarcely any labour on the part of man to yield him everything he wants, and where life therefore does not bear the stamp of a hard struggle against nature and against fellow-creatures. In a lesser degree we find the same phonetic structure in such languages as Italian and Spanish; but how different are our Northern tongues.

> OTTO JESPERSEN, *Growth and Structure of the English Language*

6. A physician, of good general background and education, who had been hunting in the north woods, told me that the Chippewa language contains only a few hundred words. Upon question, he said that he got this information from his guide, a Chippewa Indian. When I tried to state the diagnostic setting, the physician, our host, briefly and with signs of displeasure repeated his statement and then turned his back to me. A third person, observing this discourtesy, explained that I had some experience of the language in question. This information had no effect.

> LEONARD BLOOMFIELD, "Secondary and Tertiary Responses to Language," *Language*, 20 (1944)

7. *Commencement* for *Termination.* A contribution to our noble tongue by its scholastic conservators, "commencement day" being their name for the last day of the collegiate year. It is ingeniously defended on the ground that on that day those on whom degrees are bestowed commence to hold them. Lovely!

Dépôt for *Station.* "Railroad dépôt." A dépôt is a place of deposit; as, a dépôt of supply for an army.

Dilapidated for *Ruined.* Said of a building, or other structure. But the word is from the Latin *lapis*, a stone, and cannot properly be used of any but a stone structure.

Electrocution. To one having even an elementary knowledge of Latin grammar this word is no less than disgusting, and the thing meant by it is felt to be altogether too good for the word's inventor.

Honeymoon. Moon here means month, so it is incorrect to say, "a week's honeymoon," or, "Their honeymoon lasted a year."

AMBROSE BIERCE, Write It Right

8. La famille indo-européenne est celle à laquelle étaient réservées dans l'histoire les destinées les plus hautes. Elle a créé les formes linguistiques les plus achevées, expressions des littératures les plus belles et les plus riches, instruments des civilisations qui ont conquis le monde; les langues indo-européennes se sont ainsi répandues dans la presque totalité de l'Europe et de l'Amérique, dans une grande partie de l'Asie et de l'Océanie, dans une partie notable de l'Afrique.

A. MEILLET ET MARÇEL COHEN, Les Langues du Monde

9. It is unfortunately fashionable in a few linguistic circles to regard literature as something set apart from language, to play up the spoken, popular tongue to the detriment of the written, literary language, and to view as "language" *par excellence* that form of speech which is most out of accord with the literary tradition—colloquialisms, vulgarisms and slang. That this attitude is a reaction against an earlier point of view which regarded literature and its language with undue veneration is beside the point.

Language and literature are fundamentally one. Speech gives rise to writing, granted. But once writing has come into being, the written form begins to affect the spoken tongue, stabilize it, mold it, change it, give it a more esthetically pleasing form, endow it with a richer vocabulary.

Attention has been focused upon the fact that the literary language exerts a restraining, conservative influence upon speech. This is largely true, and to the extent that it is true, is also desirable. Were the spoken language not so restrained, it would change at too rapid a rate. Permanent records of civilization's evolution could be kept only with the greatest of difficulty, while mutual comprehension between different areas and different periods would grow even more complex than it is.

MARIO PEI, The Story of Language

10. The American Negro cannot pronounce *r* in such words as *father, park, bird, beard,* and *hoarse* because his vocal organs are shaped differently from those of the white man.

BIBLIOGRAPHY

There are many popular introductions to the study of language crowding our library shelves today, and the reader is warned that a good many of them, despite the publishers' pious disclaimers, are either undigested puffs of enthusiasm or misguided potshots at the so-called structural linguists. The following list, though uneven, gives the interested neophyte the best overview of language study in general and some details of specific modern linguistic schools in particular.

Hall, Robert A., Jr. *Linguistics and Your Language.* Garden City, N.Y.: Double-day and Company, Inc.; second revised edition of *Leave Your Language Alone!* Ithaca, N.Y.: Linguistica, 1950.

Ornstein, Jacob, and Gage, William W. *The ABC's of Languages and Linguistics.* Philadelphia: Chilton Books, 1964.

Quirk, Randolph. *The Use of English.* New York: St. Martin's Press, 1962.

Sapir, Edward. *Language.* New York: Harcourt, Brace & World, Inc., 1921.

Whatmough, Joshua. *Language: A Modern Synthesis.* New York: St. Martin's Press, 1956.

The books by Hall, Ornstein and Gage, and Quirk are all intended for the general reader. Some may find the first too polemical for their taste and the other two too thin, but all three are sound introductions. The volume by Whatmough is harder reading. Sapir's book is a classic in the field which should be in the library of every student contemplating a career in language teaching.

2

Theories of Grammar: Background

SCHOOL GRAMMAR

Before we can begin to discuss modern theories of grammar, we must understand something about the language concepts out of which they developed or from which they departed. We cannot assume that modern theories grew out of a vacuum. Furthermore, the language attitudes of the past often pass for current today not only among the uncritical, but also among those who do not care to understand the work of linguistic science in the twentieth century. Consequently, it is important that we view the background of modern language study in its proper perspective.

A commonplace among linguists often assigns the findings and pronouncements of all students of language before the twentieth century under the general heading of "traditional grammar." This is actually an oversimplification, because it lumps together two entirely different strains of language speculation—one ultimately becoming the grammatical norm taught in the public schools, the other stemming from the work in historical and comparative philology in nineteenth-century Europe, especially Germany. To underline this distinction, we shall consider each system separately, assessing its contribution to contemporary linguistic thought.

The Roots

School grammar, though much modified, is ultimately derived from the philosophical speculations of the ancient Greeks, for whom it was largely a stepping-stone to more elevated concerns. Philosophers inevitably must define their terms, and thus arose a spate of interest over whether a work was innately connected with its significant or was merely an arbitrary designation for it. Out of this perfunctory examination came relatively sketchy descriptions of Greek parts of speech and syntax, later applied to Latin, and even to Hebrew. Unfortunately, Latin did not fit easily into the Greek straitjacket: for example, unlike Greek, it had no articles. But the fit was close enough, and where there were any serious differences, alterations were made to accommodate them. Through the Middle Ages, grammar was studied from two descriptions of Latin written early in the Christian era, and thus it happened that down through the Renaissance, *grammar* and *Latin* became synonymous.

By the end of the Middle Ages, however, Latin (like Classical Greek and Hebrew) was a dead language; that is, it was no longer in common use, save in liturgy and possibly diplomacy, and thus incapable of change. Therefore, the descriptive statements of the Latin grammarians took on an aura of being eternally true, the final say on all aspects of the language. Furthermore, with the rediscovery of Classical Latin (and later, Classical Greek), the learned began to make value judgments about the superiority of classical models over Vulgate and Medieval Latin, thus mixing the functions of the rhetorician and the critic, to the total exclusion of the linguist. Grammar, therefore, became an eminently practical study, in an impractical sort of way: a total concern for writing what was considered the very best Latin prose and verse, the actual application of which few cared or dared to question. And all this time the languages which everyone actually spoke, and in which some of the greatest monuments of literature were being written, were of no scholarly interest whatever.

Among the general public, a practical interest in the modern languages soon developed, spurred on at first by a widespread desire to learn them for business or social reasons. Consequently these languages became a subject for grammatical analysis, with the system for this analysis close at hand: the time-tested Latin grammar. Without bothering to consider the implications of what they were doing, the schoolmen simply placed English, for instance, into the same framework as Latin, blithely classifying the English noun into nonexistent dative, ablative, and vocative cases, and trying to categorize the verbs in paradigms parallel to the inflected Latin system. When they could not find a like system in English, as, for example, a highly inflected adjective declension, its absence was explained away as "degeneration." Frequently, when faced with duplications of form, they made value judgments as to the superiority of one over the other by appealing to logic, as in the instance of the double negative, or simply devised rules by magisterial fiat, as in the famous case of *will* and *shall*. Because Latin was immutable and unchanging, they assumed that their descriptions of English were likewise permanent. And always, in writing up their rules of language, they tacitly assumed that English was derived from Latin, Latin from Greek, and Greek from Hebrew.[1] This was the situation of popular grammar early in the nineteenth century, when it was adopted unquestioningly by the schools, usually as a preparation for the rigors of Latin. Small wonder then that one can still hear, "I never really understood English grammar until I took Latin."

Formal Analysis

Oddly enough, the ancients were often more scrupulous in their descriptions than we have given them credit for being. In defining the noun, the Greek *Techne Grammatike* of Dionysius Thrax (first century B.C.) stated: "A noun is a part of discourse having cases, indicating a body or a thing, and is used in a common or specific [we would say 'proper'] way." This definition is oversimplified but it at least defines by form as well as meaning. Through successive applications first to Latin and then to English,

---

[1] This assumption led to the formation of usage rules still given lip-service today. We must never split infinitives or end sentences with prepositions because the Romans never did. The *a priori* derivation of English from Latin automatically eliminated any possibility of seeing that the English infinitive and verb-plus-particle constructions were basically different from the Latin.

it was watered down to our present school grammar definition: "A noun is the name of a person, place, or thing." This notional or meaning-based definition is essentially useless: it does not explain the noun to the schoolchild who has not already learned somehow what a noun is, and those who *do* know don't need it and never use it, not even for that grade school exercise in underlining the nouns once and the verbs twice.

Other criteria of the ancients underwent similar successive mutation. The listing of the parts of speech changed bit by bit, increasing or decreasing in number according to the caprice of the grammarians, who finally hit upon the magic number *eight*. Thus present-day school grammars list as the eight parts of speech nouns, pronouns, verbs, adverbs, adjectives, prepositions, conjunctions, and interjections. This list mixes together recognizable parts of speech (nouns, verbs, adjectives, adverbs), subcategories (pronouns), function words (prepositions and conjunctions), and nonwords (interjections). Furthermore, these "parts of speech" are as erratically defined as was the noun: sometimes notionally, sometimes syntactically, never formally, always incompletely.

Thus we find that school grammar, still widely taught, is uncritically derived from Latin grammar. It oversimplified the findings of the Latinists and passed them on without examination. The school grammarians jumped to untenable conclusions, as, for example, appealing to logic, and they promulgated a doctrine of absolutes in correctness. They established improper bases by mixing the notional with the syntactic. They failed to develop any consistent structural concepts and apply whatever might be useful to the problems of composition and literature. Consequently, school grammar, in derivation and in practice, is not a theory of grammar at all, but simply an accretion which has too often been given the status of a dogma, both for those who teach it and those who had to learn it so arduously.

Syntactical Analysis

We can see how school grammar works beyond the level of workbook rules and parts of speech exercises by examining its explanation of English syntax. Here, reasonably enough, the basic unit is the sentence, notionally defined as "a group of words expressing a complete thought." As has been pointed out many times, "a complete thought" virtually defies description or identification, and thus any student who is having trouble with his sentence structure is as much in the dark as before. The school grammar sentence is classified structurally into simple, compound, complex, and compound-complex categories, each of them circularly defined according to their components: "A complex sentence consists of a dependent clause and an independent clause. A dependent clause is one which cannot stand alone . . . ." Again, the student who needs most to understand the rhetorical implications of these classifications cannot possibly grasp them from such criteria. The sentence is further classified syntactically into declarative, interrogative, exclamatory, and imperative categories, all of them notionally defined. Rarely are hints ever given as to how these might be formed, and thus exercises in identification are largely self-defeating.

Until recently, the standard exercise in sentence analysis was "parsing," ticking off each word of a sentence one by one, identifying its part of speech and its use in the sentence. It was limited primarily to individual word analysis, seldom analyzing whole units larger than prepositional phrases, and completely neglected syntactic relationships between units within the sentence. This exercise, usually performed orally, has been relegated to Limbo along with the spelling bee and the birch rod, the now familiar Reed–Kellogg diagramming system having taken its place.[2]

Briefly, this diagramming system sets out to illustrate how the core of the sentence, starkly set forth on a horizontal line, is acted upon by a succession of modificational elements. This can be illustrated using a relatively uncomplicated sentence: "Some of my old friends gave me a birthday present yesterday." This system has certain advantages, notably the intuitive functional division of the sentence into "subject" and "predicate," which all linguists today recognize to be syntactically valid in

[2] Linguists owe a debt of gratitude to Harold A. Gleason, Jr., for uncovering the origin of this system of syntactical analysis and for showing that in its inception it was academically more respectable than successive watered-down modifications have made it. See his *Linguistics and English Grammar* (New York, 1965), pp. 142–51, 300–11.

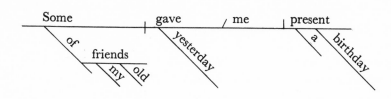

English. But other than this, it would seem to have many disadvantages. For one thing, it completely obscures any indication of word order, which in English is the primary syntactic marker. Despite considerable attempts to modify it, this system cannot in actual practice accommodate all of the features of the sentence. It is particularly weak in illustrating the structural relationships of so-called complex sentences. Finally, the various alterations by different textbook writers do not agree. Some would place *me* in our illustration below the verb in a phrase diagram with an "understood *to*." Actual practice with the system, using sentences taken from current writing, demonstrates its basic unworkability, and it is instructive to recall that most diagramming exercises are done with sentences carefully worked out in advance.

Although many students get some enjoyment out of working these puzzles, the more perceptive quickly notice areas where the diagrams have built-in weaknesses. For instance, it could be argued that in the above example *friends* rather than *some* ought to be the subject of the sentence, but the rules of diagramming permit no other way of handling the preposition *of*. Further, the building up of modificational elements seems too simple: the assumption of "my friends, old friends" or "a present, birthday present" doesn't seem real or natural. Handling *birthday* as a modifier—perfectly valid here—contradicts the notional definition of a noun. Finally, there seems to be something vaguely unnatural about *yesterday* modifying *gave*. True, the rule states that an adverb "modifies a verb, adjective, or another adverb," and *yesterday* qualifies as an adverb that "asks the question

'When?' " But the implication that the sentence could read "yesterday gave" or "gave yesterday me" doesn't accord with the student's sense of style or sentence form. Thus diagramming becomes a purely mechanical exercise, a word puzzle of dubious usefulness, but still repeated over and over again, often into high school.

Deficiencies

School grammar has consistently been justified as a means of improving the student's writing. Even the most vehement critics of the public schools concur in this when they cry for more grammar, by which they mean school grammar, whenever they find widespread evidence that our students can't write. The justification presupposes an automatic movement from the linguistic level of language description to the rhetorical level of well-ordered writing, but in school grammar the two levels are hopelessly mixed and no means is provided by which a class might apply the lessons of grammatical study to the creation of new sentences. Descriptive in purpose, school grammar is pre-scriptive in actual practice, simply because the average teacher does not understand language except in the incomplete terms of the system being taught.[3] Good students will go along with it, applying their previously acquired understanding of English to prickly problems; poor students will be alienated by the whole business. All in all, this is a sorry picture of an important part of the school curriculum, repeated year after year, taking up valu-able time better spent in reading and composition.

[3] I do not intend this statement to be a mass indictment of our public school teachers. On the contrary, I can only praise their efforts and accomplishments against the overwhelming disadvantages of too much to do, too little time, and great snarls of administrative red tape. They deserve much more recognition for their services than a gold watch presented at a retirement banquet.

On the other hand, one's respect becomes diminished somewhat when a teacher continues to give the same course for thirty years, inevitably resisting any suggestion of change in the interim. One has even less respect for those administrators and school board members who contribute to this teacher's failure by not giving their faculty members opportunities to keep up with their fields, plan their courses, or reflect upon the subject matter (summer school is a poor substitute!)—and are them-selves proof against any attempts to change.

HISTORICAL AND COMPARATIVE PHILOLOGY

At the beginning of the nineteenth century, while the prescriptions of the school grammarians were rapidly being incorporated into the curriculum, another group of scholars was beginning work along a different line of reasoning. By the middle of the century, this group had established the study of **historical and comparative philology** on the continent of Europe, especially in Germany. These scholars were primarily engaged in tracing the histories of the languages of Europe and setting up correspondencies between related languages, their ultimate purpose being to infer from the detailed correspondencies and historical descriptions the nature of the original languages from which the various families of languages were derived, particularly the Indo-European family.[4]

Looking back upon their work with the knowledge accumulated over a century and a half, one is tempted to treat the philologists and their findings somewhat patronizingly, just as people now think of the early airplanes and automobiles as quaint creations. But reviewed in the context of their times, their conclusions were not naive, but rather the result of careful, detailed accumulations of data leading to well-considered approximations of what the original languages must have been like. Their work was especially detailed in the matter of sounds and sound changes and to a lesser degree in the grammatical forms of the languages; unfortunately, they made little progress in syntax. At any rate, the conclusions they built up over the years have held up well, and it is certainly unjust to combine the scholarship in comparative and historical philology with the prescriptions of the school grammarians under the broad heading of "traditional grammar."

The Accomplishments of the Philologists

It is not necessary here to give a detailed survey of the work of the philologists, which is readily available for the interested

[4] The Indo-European family, sometimes called *Indo-Germanic* or *Aryan*, includes most of the major languages of Europe, plus a number in the Middle East. It is subdivided into nine groups: Indo-Iranian (including modern Persian and Hindi), Slavonic, Hellenic, Romance, Celtic, Germanic (which includes English), Albanian, and the extinct Hittite and Tocharian. Prominent omissions from this listing are Finnish, Estonian, and Hungarian (Finno-Ugric languages); Turkish (Ural-Altaic); Basque; and modern Hebrew and Arabic (Semitic languages).

student. Instead, simply a capsule discussion will summarize some of the most important results of a century of effort.

Hypothesis of an Indo-European family of languages

Even before the generally accepted beginning of the philological tradition, roughly 1800, it had become evident that the theories proposing a Hebraic or Hellenic origin of all extant languages were untenable. Even after the renewal of interest in Sanskrit, the ancient liturgical language of India, in the later eighteenth century, the philologists did not succumb to the temptation to make it the ancestor of the modern European languages. Rather, based upon correspondencies too regular to be coincidental, they saw that Sanskrit, Greek, Latin, the Germanic languages, Celtic languages, and Slavonic languages had all developed from an *Ursprache*, a common ancestor, no longer extant.

Comparative studies

Working from a variety of recorded sources, comparative philologists began to accumulate evidence which gave further credence to the notion of a common ancestor. In particular, they built up details of regular sound changes, and, to a lesser extent, changes in grammatical forms, the end result being the careful placement of each language or language state into a specific position relative to all other Indo-European languages.

Sound "laws"

From the detailed evidence of certain sound shifts, the philologists began to formulate inductively conclusions about the regularity of such shifts. Perhaps the most famous of such statements is that which has come to be called "Grimm's Law," a description of sound-shift correspondencies first noted in 1814 by the Danish scholar Rasmus Rask, but which was first given detailed codification by Jacob Grimm.[5] This "law" demonstrates

[5] Grimm also received lasting fame as the man who, with his brother Wilhelm, compiled the pioneering collection of folklore based on scholarly principles, *Kinder- und Hausmärchen*, popularized as the "fairy tales." We should add here that in his

how certain consonants of the original Indo-European, still observed in other Indo-European languages, underwent a change in the Germanic languages, and how another shift took place at the division of Germanic into High German and Low German. It is the most spectacular (and for English, the most important) of hundreds of like sound shifts which occurred when languages gradually changed or broke off from their parent languages.

The neo-grammarians

As the philologists gathered their evidence and reasoned out sound-shift correspondencies, they frequently found a certain number of forms which did not, on the face of it, follow the regular patterns and as a consequence had to be set aside as exceptions to the rule. This state of things could not last for long, and soon others were sifting the "exceptions" to see if they did not work according to some logic of their own. In the instance of the exceptions to "Grimm's Law," it was demonstrated that the sound-shift pattern was forestalled by a shift of stress in the words involved. This discovery, by analogy called "Verner's Law" after its discoverer, started the controversy of the so-called *Junggrammatiker*, or neo-grammarians, who adopted as their article of faith the doctrine that sound-shift changes admit of no exceptions, that what appear to be exceptions to a sound-change pattern actually operate under another, perhaps undiscovered, pattern of their own. The controversy this doctrine generated has not yet been completely resolved.

The formal classification of languages

As the work in philology spread into other language families, there developed a strong desire to classify all of the languages

---

philological studies he gave full credit to Rask for his discovery; its assignment to Grimm and the coinage of the title "Grimm's Law" was the work of F. Max Müller, a British popularizer of philology in the latter half of the century. Calling this sound shift a "law" is, of course, sheer nonsense, for sound changes occur in each instance but once, as historical events, and are not constantly in operation, as are the phenomena described by the laws of physics. A brief statement of Grimm's sound-shift discoveries may be found on p. 249n.

according to their basic structural features. Probably the best-known effort in this direction is the classification of languages into the categories of isolative, agglutinative, and flexional. **Isolative** languages are those without inflections of any kind, relying entirely on word order to show grammatical relationships. Chinese is the most commonly cited example. **Agglutinative** languages are those which attach inflections to words as affixes to show grammatical relationships, the theory being that the inflectional affixes were themselves at one time individual words. Turkish is the usual instance given of this category. Finally, **flexional** languages are those in which the words undergo interior changes in addition to inflections to show their structural patterns, Latin and Greek being the most familiar examples. In some philological circles, the hypothesis was advanced that languages passed from one stage to the next in the order given here, the flexional languages being the "most highly developed." These classifications, as well as this hypothesis, represent an oversimplified view of language, but they still occasionally crop up in studies in historical linguistics. English illustrates the weakness of this classification. Insofar as it relies upon word order, it is isolative; because it uses inflections for the most part added to words as grammatical signals, it is agglutinative; when it resorts to internal alteration of sounds in "irregular" forms, it is flexional. Which category, then, does it fall under?[6]

Synthesis

This kind of theorizing, though often discredited today, had the advantage of leading others into attempting a synthesis of the work done up to then. Though the synthesizers were sometimes led themselves into the blind alleys of Hegelian cyclical theories, Comtian positivism, and psychological enthusiasm, many of their conclusions, notably those of Hermann Paul and Otto Jespersen, have acted as a springboard to modern linguistic study.

---

[6] Recent field work in American Indian languages has made necessary a fourth category—*polysynthetic*, in which syllables are the units of both lexical and grammatical meaning and are the bases upon which complicated word compounds are built.

The Contributions of the Philologists to Modern Linguistics

Our debt to all these men is great, and modern linguists too often forget that they work today on the basis of principles first established by the philologists. Enthusiasts and critics are both guilty of attributing these principles to the so-called structural linguists, an attribution which the structuralists are the first to deny. But as we list these principles, we must also take note of the weaknesses of the philologists, who in practice sometimes tended to vitiate what they had developed:

1. *Language is speech.* Because they usually worked from manuscripts, a necessity in historical studies, the philologists failed to distinguish clearly between sounds and their graphic representations, and thus their comparisons are often between letters rather than sounds. For example, Grimm's crucial 600-page chapter in which he formulated his famous "law" is entitled *Die Lehre von den Buchstaben*, "The study of the letters."

2. *Language has system.* Unfortunately, the description of the components of the system became an end, rather than a means to a generalization about the system. Except for now-discredited Hegelian cyclical theories, popularized by August Schleicher, the philologists were rarely able to generalize: the details got in the way.

3. *Language has variety.* But like true children of their times, they tended to over-romanticize dialects, seeing in them something of the Good Old Speech before it became sophisticated. This attitude was expressed in its earliest form by Johann Gottlieb Herder and was picked up later by Grimm (and by the poet Goethe).

4. *Language changes.* Because they were working back to the origins of language, theorizing about the *Ursprache*, the philologists ended up studying change for change's sake, not for the purpose of giving the world a truer, more realistic picture of the nature of this change and its present implications. On the other hand, some philologists, notably Otto Jespersen, viewed historical change in a spirit of progressivism: that change leads to constant improvement. Today, it seems more truthful to say that change is simply change, no more.

For our present purposes, perhaps the greatest contribution of the philologists, and at the same time their most conspicuous failure, rests with the compendious, multi-volumed grammars of English which appeared in the early decades of the twentieth century. These enormous storehouses of facts and examples by such great names as Poutsma, Kruisinga, Jespersen, Sweet, and Curme, and the one-volume works which epitomized them, are descriptive of every facet of English usage, with an eye to historical development. Following the principles established by the philologists who preceded them, these grammarians described the language as they found it, without condemnation, without making value judgments about usage. However, their devotion to the collecting of data virtually ruled out any formulation of a theory of language, save in describing for description's sake. With their attention to the detail, they were unable to see beyond it to the generalizations about the overall working of the very language they described.[7] Yet their work has remained significant, for they gave to modern linguistic science the raw materials upon which to construct workable grammatical theories.

QUESTIONS AND EXERCISES

1. The following statements were extracted from the teacher's manuals accompanying the eleventh-grade volume of five different English grammar series currently on the textbook market. What common patterns do they show concerning their awareness of modern linguistic theories and their incorporation of them into their school grammar approach?

> a. It is no longer a secret that the traditional grammar inherited from eighteenth-century England does not perfectly picture the structure of our language. Modern linguists have nearly completed a quite different picture. They have not yet agreed, however, upon a terminology suitable for use in secondary schools.

[7] For a detailed criticism of these grammars, and especially of their syntactic descriptions, see Eugene A. Nida, *A Synopsis of English Syntax* (Norman, Okla., 1960), pp. 12–39.

Meantime, English teachers have two alternatives. They may scrap traditional grammar entirely and use those elements of linguistic analysis that can be explained simply. Or they may modify traditional grammar where it is most obviously out of joint with the language and use many of the significant insights of structural linguistics. The second alternative is the course chosen by the authors of [this text].

In each of the textbooks for grades nine through twelve, a special chapter presents some of the most interesting and useful concepts of linguistics.[8]

b. The grammar taught and used throughout [this text] is traditional grammar. This point must be made, now that linguists have presented us with several other ways of describing our language. In the opinion of the authors, the new grammar is not yet clearly enough defined for general use in the schools and neither are the schools prepared to adopt it completely as a replacement for the traditional. Unless our goal is chaos, we had better bear those ills we have than fly to others that we know not of. Teachers who wish to experiment with the new grammar, however, will find in the *Teacher's Manual* for Book 11 a series of ten grammar lessons based on the structural linguists' description of English.[9]

c. These days new theories of English teaching and new materials come with bewildering rapidity. It is clearly impractical and unwise to attempt to ride every new hobby-horse. The English teacher must be resourceful, flexible, able to blend "the best of the old and the best of the new."

[This text] shows how some of the newer concepts may be blended with the old. It provides a workable transition from the grammar of the past to the grammar of the future. It indicates how teachers may use some of the newer concepts without throwing out everything of value from the past.

There is danger in thinking that some new grammatical "discovery" is a remedy for all ills. Uninformed persons who make wildly enthusiastic claims embarrass the scholars in the

[8] Thomas Clark Pollock, Marion C. Sheridan, Dorothy Williams, and Charles Stone, Teacher's Manual for *The Macmillan English Series*, Book 11 (New York: The Macmillan Company, 1964).

[9] John E. Warriner, Joseph Mersand, Helen Townsend, and Francis Griffith, *English Grammar and Composition*, Book 11 (rev. ed.; New York: Harcourt, Brace & World, Inc., 1965).

field. The newer grammar studies can make valuable contribu-
tions. They provide no magic shortcuts, however, no substitutes
for practice and more practice. The area they deal with is a
relatively small one in the total language arts field. . . .

If you, as classroom teacher, wish to try some additional
materials suggested by recent studies in grammar, try the suggestions in the following pages. The lesson plans that follow show
how certain insights of modern grammarians can be brought
into play in the English classroom without discarding the traditional nomenclature and approach. If you wish to do your own
experimenting, you can add to the body of information and help
chart the road ahead.[10]

d. In this fourth edition, the authors and publishers of [this]
series reaffirm their conviction that effective instruction in
English must be founded upon a basic-skills approach. Each
book in this edition has been expanded by 64 pages, thus en-
riching the features that have made the series a consistent leader
since its inception, notably in the important area of composition.
Of course, parts of each book have required practically no change.

Valuable new opening and closing sections on "The English
Language" and "Linguistic Grammar" have been added, both
written and supervised by authorities in the field. These new
units have been so planned that they may be studied separately,
if desired, without disturbing the basic continuity of the
text.[11]

e. The nomenclature employed in this unit on grammar is
conventional. There is no introduction of new terms to confuse
students already brought up on traditional grammar. The
purpose of this unit is to make those traditional terms and their
applications clear and understandable to eleventh-grade students.
The authors of [this text] have thought it wise to preserve the
fundamental outlines of traditional grammar, at the same time
recognizing many of the principles of the new approaches to
grammar wherever possible. The aim has been to give a solid
body of information about the language and to create a solid
background upon which later studies of linguistics can be based.[12]

---

[10] H. I. Christ and A. E. Terino, *Modern English in Action* 11 (Boston: D. C. Heath
and Company, © 1965).

[11] Mellie John and Pauline M. Yates, *The New Building Better English*, Book 11
(4th ed.; New York: Harper & Row, 1965).

2. The following is an extract from the September 19, 1691, issue of the *Athenian Mercury*, a popular question-and-answer broadside sheet published in London during the last decade of the seventeenth century. Analyze the question and its answer carefully, to determine which comments reflect attitudes leading to the establishment of school grammar, and which ones anticipate the formulations of the philologists.

> Quest. 5. Whether there's any such thing as the perfection of a Language, and wherein it consists, and whether our Language is now in its heighth, or when it was so?
>
> *Answ.* This may be a more difficult question than at first it appears. All Languages are in a continual flux, one Age making still Additions to the past, or at least altering or taking away many Words from it; that Comparison of the Poets being extreamly apt—that *Words* are like *Leaves*, the Old still wearing off and *New* springing up in their rooms. The Grammarians, whose unenvy'd Business 'tis to *Beat Languages*, as *Oldham* calls it, have almost demonstrated that the *Phoenitian* is only a Corruption or Dialect of the *Hebrew*, the *Greek*, and perhaps many other Languages[,] of the *Phoenitian*, the old *Roman* of the *Greek*, the very Characters being the same, as may be seen in old Inscriptions and Monuments. On the other side, the modern *Greek* and *Russian* from the antient Classic *Greek*, the *Italian*, *French*, *Spanish*; *Portuguese* from the Corruption of the *Lattin*, and its adulterous mixtures with several barbarous Languages, every one of which daily alter, and are still like to do so as long as the World lasts; and when they are so much alter'd that the greatest part of the Words come to be chang'd, it's probable enough that these will still be call'd New Languages. Thus 'twas here in *England*; the old *Saxon* is undoubtedly the proper *English* Tongue, our very Countrey taking its last and most famous Name from those *Angli*; and yet our present *English* is as absolutely a different language from it as the old *Greek* is from the *Roman*. But still, which is more to our present purpose, old *Chaucer*, *Gower*, and their Contemporaries were call'd great Refiners of our *English*

---

[12] John E. Brewton, R. Stanley Peterson, B. Jo Kinnick, Lois McMullan, and Marion L. Street, *Using Good English* 11 (teachers' ed.; River Forest, Ill.: Laidlaw Brothers, 1966).

Language, and undoubtedly were thought to have brought it to as great a Perfection by their Contemporaries, as we say a *Waller*, a *Dryden*, a *S[wif]t* or a *B[urne]t* have in our age brought it. And 'twas just the same Case with *Ennius* and *Lucilius* in their times, who were thought as well of by others, and spoke as ill of their Language who went before 'em, as *Horace* or any of the Critics of *Augustus* his Court who came after 'em. But the mentioning his Court recalls to mind the Notion of some Men, and we think the most common of any other, concerning the Perfection of any Language: *That the Court is the Standard of a Language, all own*, that then the Language is in perfection when the Empire is in perfection, and the Court at the greatest heighth, is generally held, and an Instance given thereof is that of *Augustus Caesar*. But still the difficulty seems to recur—is not this a begging the Question! and how know I that the Language of the *Romans* was in greater or more proper Perfection at that time than 'twas in the Reign of *Augustus*, or in the greatest heighth of what is call'd Barbarism? or is there any reason that he who conquers most, his Language must be best, which seems that Case of *Augustus*—if so, the barbarous *Goths* and *Hunns* had afterward as good a Title to *Purity of Language* as the *Romans* before, the Romans being at first only colluvies of Robbers got together, and hardly of so honorable an original as those who afterwards turn'd 'em out, or became their Masters. Accordingly if it be said that then a *Language* degenerates when it comes to be mingled with any *barbarous*, that is, Foreign Words; it must at this rate be said, it always degenerates, because all Languages daily Enfranchize such *Foreign Words* as they find necessary or convenient. But this is only *Negative*, 'twill be still said we are never the nearer. Where shall we fix the Perfection? or is there any or No? We think there is, and in these two things it must be fix'd or no where—in the pleasingness and tunableness of the Accent, and the Expressiveness and Fulness of the *Language*—and if this may be the *Standard*, we are sure our *Language* is now at or near the Achme, and has not been so in *former Ages*.

3. The following extracts are taken from essays by Dr. Samuel Johnson, written in connection with his famous Dictionary. In the same manner as with the passage from the *Athenian Mercury* above, determine the areas where Johnson seems to be following

in the tradition of the school grammarians, and where he antici-
pates the principles formulated by the philologists. Study the
passages, too, to determine where he contradicts the opinions
expressed by the writer of the *Athenian Mercury.*

From *The Plan of a Dictionary of the English Language:*
  To the Right Honourable Philip Dormer, Earl of Chesterfield,
  one of His Majesty's Principal Secretaries of State (1747):

  . . . It was not easy to determine by what Rule of Distinction
the Words of this Dictionary were to be chosen. The chief Intent
of it is to preserve the Purity, and ascertain the Meaning of our
English Idiom; and this seems to require nothing more than that
our Language be considered, so far as it is our own; that the
Words and Phrases used in the general Intercourse of Life, or
found in the Works of those whom we commonly style polite
Writers, be selected, without including the Terms of particular
Professions. . . .

  . . . The first Part of the Work to be considered is the Orthography, which was long vague and uncertain; which at last,
when its fluctuation ceased, was, in many cases, settled but by
Accident; and in which . . . there is still great Uncertainty
among the best Criticks: Nor is it easy to state a Rule by which
we may decide between Custom and Reason, or between the
equiponderant Authorities of Writers alike eminent for Judgment
and Accuracy.

  The great orthographical Contest has long subsisted between
Etymology and Pronunciation. It has been demanded, on one
Hand, that Men should write as they speak; but, as it has been
shown that this Conformity never was attained in any Language,
and that it is not more easy to persuade Men to agree exactly in
Speaking than in Writing, it may be asked, with equal Propriety,
why Men do not rather speak as they write. . . .

  When a Question of Orthography is dubious, that Practice
has, in my Opinion, a Claim to Preference, which preserves the
greatest Number of radical Letters, or seems most to comply
with the general Custom of our Language. But the chief Rule
which I propose to follow is, to make no Innovation, without a
Reason sufficient to balance the Inconvenience of Change; and
such Reasons I do not expect often to find. All change is, of
itself, an Evil, which ought not to be hazarded but for evident

Advantage; and as Inconstancy is, in every Case, a Mark of Weakness, it will add nothing to the Reputation of our Tongue. . . .

The present Usage of Spelling, where the present Usage can be distinguished, will therefore, in this Work, be generally followed; yet there will be often Occasion to observe, that it is, in itself, inaccurate, and tolerated rather than chosen. . . . It will likewise be sometimes proper to trace back the Orthography of different Ages, and show by what Gradations the Word departed from its Original.

Closely connected with Orthography is Pronunciation, the Stability of which is of great Importance to the Duration of a Language, because the first Change will naturally begin by Corruptions in the living Speech. The want of certain Rules for the Pronunciation of former Ages, has made us wholly ignorant of the metrical Art of our ancient Poets; and since those who study their Sentiments regret the loss of their Numbers, it is sure Time to provide that the Harmony of the Moderns may be more permanent.

A new Pronunciation will make almost a new Speech; and therefore, since one great End of this Undertaking is to fix the *English* Language, Care will be taken to determine the Accentuation of all Polysyllables by proper Authorities, as it is one of those capricious Phænomena which cannot be, easily, reduced to rules. . . .

By tracing . . . every Word to its Original, and not admitting, but with great Caution, any of which no Original can be found, we shall secure our Language from being overrun with Cant, from being crouded with low Terms, the Spawn of Folly or Affectation, which arise from no just Principles of Speech, and of which therefore no legitimate Derivation can be shewn.

When the Etymology is thus adjusted, . . . we are to examine by what Rules [the words] are governed, and how they are inflected through their various Terminations. The Terminations of the *English* are few, but those few have hitherto remained unregarded, by the Writers of our Dictionaries. Our Substantives are declined only by the plural Termination, our Adjectives admit no Variation, but in the Degree of Comparison, and our Verbs are conjugated by auxiliary Words, and are only changed in the Preter Tense.

To our Language may be, with great Justness, applied, the Observation of *Quintilian*, that Speech was not formed by an Analogy sent from Heaven. It did not descend to us, in a state of Uniformity and Perfection, but was produced by Necessity, and enlarged by Accident; and is, therefore, composed of dissimilar Parts; thrown together by Negligence, by Affectation, by Learning, or by Ignorance.

Our Inflections, therefore, are by no Means constant, but admit of numberless Irregularities, which, in this Dictionary, will be diligently noted. . . .

Thus, my Lord, will our Language be laid down, distinct in its minutest Subdivisions, and resolved into its elemental Principles. And who, upon this Survey, can forbear to wish, that these fundamental Atoms of our Speech, might obtain the Firmness and Immutability of the primogenial and constituent Particles of Matter, that they might retain their Substance, while they alter their Appearance, and be varied and compounded, yet not destroyed.

But this is a Privilege which Words are scarcely to expect: For, like their Author, when they are not gaining Strength, they are generally losing it. Tho' Art may sometimes prolong their Duration, it will rarely give them Perpetuity; and their Changes will be almost always informing us, that Language is the Work of Man, of a Being from whom Permanence and Stability cannot be derived.

* * *

From *Preface to the English Dictionary* (1755):

When I took the first survey of my undertaking, I found our speech copious without order, and energetic without rule: wherever I turned my view, there was perplexity to be disentangled and confusion to be regulated; choice was to be made out of boundless variety, without any established principle of selection; adulterations were to be detected, without a settled test of purity; and modes of expression to be rejected or received, without the suffrages of any writers of classical reputation or acknowledged authority.

Having therefore no assistance but from general grammar, I applied myself to the perusal of our writers; and noting whatever might be of use to ascertain or illustrate any work or phrase, accumulated in time the materials of a dictionary, which, by degrees, I reduced to method, establishing to myself, in the progress of the work, such as experience and analogy suggested to me; experience, which practice and observation were continually increasing; and analogy, which, though in some words obscure, was evident in others.

* * *

As language was at its beginning merely oral, all words of necessary or common use were spoken before they were written; and while they were unfixed by any visible signs, must have been spoken with great diversity, as we now observe those who cannot read to catch sounds imperfectly, and utter them negligently. When this wild and barbarous jargon was first reduced to an alphabet, every penman endeavored to express, as he could, the sounds which he was accustomed to pronounce or to receive, and vitiated in writing such words as were already vitiated in speech. The powers of the letters, when they were applied to a new language, must have been vague and unsettled, and therefore different hands would exhibit the same sound by different combinations.

From this uncertain pronunciation arises in a great part the various dialects of the same country, which will always be observed to grow fewer, and less different, as books are multiplied; and from this arbitrary representation of sounds by letters proceeds that diversity of spelling observable in the *Saxon* remains, and I suppose in the first books of every nation, which perplexes or destroys analogy, and produces anomalous formations, which, being once incorporated can never be afterward dismissed or reformed.

* * *

Such defects are not errors in orthography, but spots of barbarity impressed so deep in the *English* language, that criticism can never wash them away: these, therefore, must be permitted to remain untouched; but many words have likewise been altered by accident, or depraved by ignorance, as the pronunciation of the vulgar has been weakly followed; and some still continue to be variously written, as authors differ in their care or skill. . . .

In this part of the work, where caprice has long wantoned without control, and vanity sought praise by petty reformation, I have endeavoured to proceed with a scholar's reverence for antiquity, and a grammarian's regard to the genius of our tongue. I have attempted few alterations, and among those few, perhaps the greater part is from the modern to the ancient practice; and I hope I may be allowed to recommend to those, whose thoughts have been perhaps employed too anxiously on verbal singularities, not to disturb, upon narrow views, or for minute propriety, the orthography of their fathers. It has been asserted, that for the law to be *known*, is of more importance than to be *right*. "Change," says *Hooker*, "is not made without inconvenience, even from worse to better." There is in constancy and stability a general and lasting advantage, which will always overbalance the slow improvements of gradual correction. Much less ought our written language to comply with the corruptions of oral utterance, or copy that which every variation of time or place makes different from itself, and imitate those changes, which will again be changed, while imitation is employed in observing them.

This recommendation of steadiness and uniformity does not proceed from an opinion that particular combinations of letters have much influence on human happiness; or that truth may not be successfully taught by modes of spelling fanciful and erroneous; I am not yet so lost in lexicography as to forget that *words are the daughters of earth, and that things are the sons of heaven.* Language is only the instrument of science, and words are but the signs of ideas: I wish, however, that the instrument might be less apt to decay, and that signs might be permanent, like the things which they denote.

. . . Those who have been persuaded to think well of my design, will require that it should fix our language and put a stop to those alterations which time and chance have hitherto been suffered to make in it without opposition. With this consequence I will confess that I flattered myself for a while; but now begin to fear that I have indulged expectation which neither reason nor experience can justify. When we see men grow old and die at a certain time one after another, from century to century, we laugh at the elixir that promises to prolong life to a thousand years; and with equal justice may the lexicographer be derided, who being able to produce no example of a nation that has preserved their words and phrases from mutability, shall imagine that his dictionary can embalm his language, and secure it from corruption and decay, that it is in his power to change sublunary nature, and clear the world at once from folly, vanity, and affectation.

With this hope, however, academies have been instituted, to guard the avenues of their languages, to retain fugitives, and repulse intruders; but their vigilance and activity have hitherto been vain; sounds are too volatile and subtile for legal restraints; to enchain syllables, and to lash the wind, are equally the undertaking of pride, unwilling to measure its desires by its strength. . . .

Total and sudden transformations of a language seldom happen; conquests and migrations are now very rare: but there are other causes of change, which, though slow in their operation, and invisible in their progress, are perhaps as much superior to human resistance, as the revolutions of the sky, or intumescence of the tide. Commerce, however necessary, however lucrative, as it depraves the manners, corrupts the language; they that have frequent intercourse with strangers, to whom they endeavour to accommodate themselves, must in time learn a mingled dialect, like the jargon which serves the traffickers on the Mediterranean and Indian coasts. . . .

There are likewise internal causes equally forcible. The language most likely to continue long without alterations, would be that of a nation raised a little, and but a little, above barbarity, secluded from strangers, and totally employed in procuring the conveniences of life; either without books, or, like some of the *Mahometan* countries, with very few: men thus busied and unlearned, having only such words as common use requires, would perhaps long continue to express the same notions by the same signs. But no such constancy can be expected in a people polished by arts, and classed by subordination, where one part of the community is sustained and accommodated by the labour of the other. . . .

. . . As politeness increases, some expressions will be considered as too gross and vulgar for the delicate, others as too formal and ceremonious for the gay and airy; new phrases are therefore adopted, which must for the same reasons be in time dismissed. *Swift*, in his petty treatise on the *English* language, allows that new words must sometimes be introduced, but proposes that none should be suffered to become obsolete. But what makes a word obsolete, more than general agreement to forbear it? and how shall it be continued, when it conveys an offensive idea, or recalled again into the mouths of mankind, when it has once become unfamiliar by disuse, and unpleasing by familiarity?

* * *

The great pest of speech is frequency of translation. No book was ever turned from one language into another, without imparting something of its native idiom; this is the most mischievous and comprehensive innovation; single words may enter by thousands, and the fabric of the tongue continue the same; but new phraseology changes much at once; it alters not the single stones of the building, but the order of the columns. If an academy should be established for the cultivation of our style—which I, who can never wish to see dependence multiplied, hope the spirit of *English* liberty will hinder or destroy—let them, instead of compiling grammars and dictionaries, endeavour, with all their influence, to stop the license of translators, whose idleness and ignorance, if it be suffered to proceed, will reduce us to babble a dialect of *France*.

If the changes that we fear be thus irresistible, what remains but to acquiesce with silence, as in the other insurmountable distresses of humanity? It remains that we retard what we cannot repel, that we palliate what we cannot cure. Life may be lengthened by care, though death cannot be ultimately defeated: tongues, like governments, have a natural tendency to degeneration; we have long preserved our constitution, let us make some struggles for our language.

* * *

4. The two documents extracted above represent two different stages in Johnson's compilation of his dictionary, the first being a procedural statement written shortly after he had begun work in earnest; the second, a retrospective *apologia* written after his work was completed. What statements in the first are modified or

changed in the second, and how significant are these differences? What did Johnson discover about language in the course of his work?

BIBLIOGRAPHY

An attempt at an objective view of school grammar is Harold A. Gleason, Jr., *Linguistics and English Grammar* (New York: Holt, Rinehart and Winston, Inc., 1965), chaps. 1 and 4. The rest of the book, which covers the grammatical theories in our next chapter, is pretty rough going.

The definitive study of historical and comparative philology is Holger Pedersen, *Linguistic Science in the Nineteenth Century*, trans. John W. Spargo (Cambridge, Mass.: Harvard University Press, 1931). Less detailed introductory accounts are Otto Jespersen, *Language: Its Nature, Development and Origin* (New York: The Macmillan Company, 1922), chaps. 1–4; and John T. Waterman, *Perspectives in Linguistics* (Chicago: University of Chicago Press, 1963), chaps. 1–3. Both Waterman and Pedersen include opening chapters on classical and medieval language study. A good recent historical account of language study is R. H. Robins, *A Short History of Linguistics* (Bloomington: Indiana University Press, 1968). Selections from the most important works of the philologists mentioned in this chapter are conveniently collected in *A Reader in Nineteenth-Century Indo-European Linguistics*, edited and translated by Winfred P. Lehmann (Bloomington: Indiana University Press, 1967).

The following is a representative list of compendious, detailed English grammars:

Curme, George O. *A Grammar of the English Language*: Vol. II, *Parts of Speech and Accidence*; Vol. III, *Syntax*. Boston: D. C. Heath and Company, 1931, 1935. (Volume I, planned as a history of the language, was never published.)

Jespersen, Otto. *A Modern English Grammar on Historical Principles*. 7 vols. Heidelberg and Copenhagen, 1909–1949.

Kruisinga, E. *A Handbook of Present-Day English*. 2 vols. Utrecht and Groningen, 1925–1932.

Poutsma, H. *A Grammar of Late Modern English*. 4 vols. Groningen, 1904–1926, 1929.

Sweet, Henry. *A New English Grammar*. 2 vols. Oxford: The Clarendon Press, 1900–1903.

The following are worthy examples of shorter English grammars compiled on the same basic principles as the above:

Curme, George O. *Principles and Practice of English Grammar*. New York: Barnes and Noble, Inc., 1947.

Jespersen, Otto. *Essentials of English Grammar*. New York: Henry Holt and Company, 1933. Reprinted, 1964, by University of Alabama Press.
Long, Ralph B. *The Sentence and Its Parts*. Chicago: University of Chicago Press, 1961.
Roberts, Paul. *Understanding Grammar*. New York: Harper & Row, 1954.

The Roberts book is particularly recommended for English teachers, in that it reveals in detail the weaknesses of school grammar definitions and procedures, and offers viable alternatives which would work well in the classroom.

For collections of essays which reveal varying attitudes toward the English language through the years, mostly, but not exclusively, in the school grammar vein, see Susie I. Tucker (ed.), *English Examined: Two Centuries of Comment on the Mother Tongue* (Cambridge: Cambridge University Press, 1961); and W. F. Bolton (ed.), *The English Language: Essays by English and American Men of Letters 1490–1839* (Cambridge: Cambridge University Press, 1966).

3

Modern Theories of Grammar

DEVELOPMENT OF LINGUISTIC SCIENCE

From Philology to Linguistics

We have seen how the historical and comparative philologists, in the course of tracing the correspondencies between related languages and in attempting to get some idea of what the primordial *Ursprache* might be like, came to formulate certain principles which have helped to guide linguistic science ever since. Unfortunately, the more tangible side of their work took the form of multi-volumed accumulations of language data which, though they still provide fine resources for linguists today, do not really help us to understand the language being described; nor does minute comparative study really help us to understand language in general. Hence, these detailed grammars of English and this philological inquiry have become a mixed blessing, and it finally became evident to those who began studying languages during the final period of philological synthesis that there was a great need to find new methods and directions.

One of the first to see this need was the Swiss linguist Ferdinand de Saussure, who was briefly mentioned in Chapter 1. Saussure began his studies in the mainstream of the philological tradition—

his first important work is entitled *Mémoire sur le Système primitif des Voyelles dans les Langues indo-européennes* (1879). But he quickly became dissatisfied with what he felt to be undue concentration on the fortunes of the Proto-Indo-European *a* sound, and he consequently devoted the rest of his life to a reconsideration of both the theory of language and the way it actually operates. As was stated in footnote 6 of Chapter 1, the result was a series of classroom lectures which were posthumously published as *Cours de Linguistique Générale* (1915).[1] This work, with its now famous division of *le langage* into *langue* and *parole*, generated much excitement, especially in Europe, and has led to the principal divisions today of the various linguistic "schools" or "circles" on the continent.[2] Saussure's main interest was in the *langue* portion of *le langage*, and those in Europe who came after him have generally followed his philosophical bent.

The Background of American Descriptive Linguistics

In America, however, it was the *parole* side of the equation which almost by accident captured the interest of the language scholars, not yet designated "linguists." At the turn of the century, after decades of neglect alternating with policies of savage extermination, the United States government, acting through the Bureau of Indian Affairs, began to develop a kind of hindsighted interest in the vanishing Indians. Under the leadership of the German scholar Franz Boas, a group of cultural anthropologists began to work with the relatively few remaining tribesmen who retained the original Indian culture, trying to learn all they could before these pitiful remnants of a proud race died and their descendants gradually became assimilated into the white man's culture.

[1] Translated from the French by Wade Baskin as *Course in General Linguistics* (New York, 1959).

[2] Chief among these are the Genevan School, in direct line of descent from Saussure, the Copenhagen "Glossematic" School, the Prague Circle, and the British Firthian School. See the articles on these groups in *Trends in European and American Linguistics 1930–1960*, edited on the occasion of the Ninth International Congress of Linguists by Christine Mohrmann, Alf Sommerfelt, and Joshua Whatmough (Utrecht and Antwerp, 1963); and the companion volume, *Trends in Modern Linguistics*, edited by Mohrmann, F. Norman, and Sommerfelt. See also Francis P. Dinneen, *An Introduction to General Linguistics* (New York, 1967), chaps. 7, 10, 11.

But before one can understand any culture well, he must first learn the language. For some of the Indian languages, dictionaries, grammars, and Bible translations were available, but many of these were found to be incomplete, inaccurate, or based upon the old false premise of the universality of Latin grammar. Out of necessity, therefore, Boas and the pioneers who worked with him or followed in his steps gradually developed the principles for uncovering the language forms and syntax of hitherto unknown systems, principles which now make up the basic tenets of **descriptive linguistics.**

Thus it is that the basis for descriptive linguistics is anthropological, originally the starting point for an intensified study of "primitive" cultures. Even today, much of the best work in descriptive studies of unknown languages and dialects is being done by field workers under the auspices of the American Bible Society, whose ultimate aim is to make Bible translations available to missionaries in Mexico and Central and South America. This is probably the reason for the cries of anguish when these principles were first applied to English. Somehow, laymen seemed to feel that English, and the languages of other "civilized" societies, should not be treated in the same way as the gibberish of "primitive" savages.[3]

However, the adaptation of the principles of descriptive linguistics to English did not happen overnight. Until World War II, most of the descriptive linguists moved in their own circles and were pretty much disregarded by the language and literature fraternity. Even after the founding of the Linguistic Society of America in 1925, with the quarterly publication thereafter of its

---

[3] I use the quotation marks on purpose. By now, all of us should be aware of the cultural relativity between the various beliefs and observances of different societies in the world, even though it is probably natural that each man assumes the intrinsic "superiority" of his own social codes, including his language. Along the same line, we should not confuse the merits of a language with the cultural level of those who speak it. There is no "primitive" language; every language is completely adapted to the society of its speakers and is fully able to handle their communication needs. Simply because one cannot discuss nuclear physics in Bantu, it does not follow that Bantu is inferior to English. If the time ever comes when the speakers of Bantu need to discuss nuclear physics, they'll find a way, just as the American colonists found ways of speaking about the strange flora and fauna of the New World—by borrowing and lexical transfer.

journal *Language*, the important theoretical work of the members went unnoticed, except when the rhetoricians stirred up the Great Usage Controversy.[4] But when the United States became involved in World War II, the descriptive linguists quickly found themselves Very Important People.

Before the war, the foreign language program in America was a relatively unimportant adjunct to the educational process. Those who "took" foreign languages did so for the cultural veneer they offered, or to pass reading examinations for the doctorate. If anyone needed a speaking knowledge, he very practically enrolled in a Berlitz school. But when the United States government found itself in need of people who were fluent speakers not only of French, Italian, and German, but also of such hitherto exotic tongues as Russian, Hindustani, and Japanese, it called upon those experts in Athabaskan and Nahuatl to work up crash programs for interpreters and military government teams. There is no need here to go into the Armed Forces Language Program.[5] It is sufficient to say that at the end of the war, even those who were unimpressed by the program found themselves strongly affected by it, and it was not long afterward that more descriptive linguists turned their attention to English, motivated in good part by a strong desire to improve the quality of English instruction in the public schools.[6]

DESCRIPTIVE GRAMMAR

Basic Tenets

Before we can see how the descriptive techniques apply to English, we must first of all enumerate the basic tenets of descriptive theory. The descriptivists began by completely accepting the

---

[4] See Chapter 6.

[5] For a good summary, see William G. Moulton, "Linguistics and Language Teaching in the United States 1940–1960," pp. 82–109 of *Trends in European and American Linguistics*, previously mentioned.

[6] Let me note in passing my preference for the terms *descriptive linguists* and *descriptivists*, rather than the commonly used *structural linguists* and *structuralists*. The former seems to me to be more general and all-inclusive; and the latter tends to raise the ire of wrong-headed lay critics.

principles formulated by the historical and comparative philologists. These principles, briefly stated, are:

1. Language is primarily speech.
2. Language has system.
3. Language has variety.
4. Language changes.

We have already mentioned that both friend and foe tend to credit these basic principles to the descriptivists, but they actually antedate descriptive linguistics, and today linguists of whatever persuasion are pleased to attribute them to the philologists, to whom they owe so much as groundbreakers.[7]

Second, because the tenets of descriptive linguistics involve uncovering the system of a specific language, the descriptivists carefully stipulate their basic procedure. They approach the language to be described without preconceptions of any kind. In its basic sense, this means that they must study it *for itself*, without trying to make it conform to any other known system; and in its strictest sense this means that the linguist should not have reviewed any previous descriptions, lest they prejudice his view. In his actual uncovering process, the linguist assumes that the native speaker is capable of making utterances which conform to the system of the language, and which are amenable to analysis. On the basis of such recorded utterances, the linguist makes a step-by-step analysis which exhaustively covers, in order, the phonology, the morphology, and the syntax of the language. **Phonological analysis** is the complete record of the sounds of the language, **morphology** is the study of its units of meaning, both lexical and grammatical, and **syntax** is the study of its systematic arrangement. Each of these steps is done independently, without reference to the next higher step—this is the procedure which the orthodox descriptivist insists upon.

From this step-by-step procedure, the ultimate aim of the linguist is to devise a consistent description complete enough to

---

[7] For a relatively recent statement, see James B. McMillan, "Summary of Nineteenth-Century Historical and Comparative Linguistics," *College Composition and Communication*, V (1954), 140–49.

satisfy the basic requirements for learning the language. From this descriptive grammar, the learner would first master the sound patterns of the language, re-enforced by some common idioms. From there he would learn the grammatical patterns, with a concurrent increase in the vocabulary, and finally he would graduate to the more complex, often "irregular" features of the language, always learning the patterns and superimposing new lexical features and additional patterns upon the basic forms.

One point more needs to be made. In working up his descriptions of a language, the descriptivist relies upon the forms of the language themselves as his grammatical base, not upon notional meanings for these forms. This point is frequently misunderstood. It does not mean that the descriptivist has thrown meaning out entirely. On the contrary, lexical as well as grammatical meaning forms the basis for the second step in his procedure for uncovering the grammatical system. What it *does* mean is that each group of like forms is described *functionally*, that is, by the way it actually operates in the sentence. The descriptivist does not define his formal groups notionally, the trap in which the school grammarians were snared. Obviously, it is necessary that the description include a lexicon, or word list; and once the forms have been described grammatically, their employment can then be notionally described, often with very subtle distinctions.

Procedural statements, however, are not very enlightening by themselves. In order to clarify them, we should briefly show how these procedures can be used with English.

Phonological Analysis

The basis for a phonological analysis of any language is a close **phonetic** transcription taken directly from the freely uttered speech of one or more informants. This task has, of late, been made immeasurably easier by the tape recorder, but it still requires close attention to all of the nuances of speech to isolate each individual sound unit or **phone.** The fieldworker making the transcription must listen closely to the speech of his informants to catch differences in articulation which to the ordinary listener would pass unnoticed. This very close transcription forms the basis for an analysis to determine the *significant* sounds of the language. The *phones* of a language can number well into the hundreds, some of them differing very minutely, but the significant sounds, the **phonemes,** rarely add up to more than fifty.

In determining the **phonemic** inventory of a language, in our case English, the linguist studies closely all sounds which are *phonetically similar* to determine, in consultation with his informants, what kind of distributional pattern they might have. For example, in an extensive phonetic transcription of English, he might find the sound combination *lull*, phonetically transcribed [ləł].[8] He has already noted that both the initial and final sounds are **laterals;** that is, they are articulated by a flow of air off the side of the tongue. However, in the articulation of the initial sound [l], the tip of the tongue is placed against the alveolar ridge, just in back of the upper front teeth; whereas the final consonant sound [ł] is made by raising the back of the tongue toward the soft palate. The former is called the "clear *l*"; the latter, the "dark *l*." After checking such other sound combinations as *let, life, lit, lack; full, pool, yell, roll,* and with the same or similar phones in medial positions, *fellow, pillar,* and after conferring with his informants to make sure that native speakers of the language consider the sounds to be "the same," he concludes that they are positional variants of the phoneme /l/, with the "clear *l*" occurring initially, and the "dark *l*" occurring finally and medially.[9] Since the "clear *l*" and the "dark *l*" do not infringe upon each other's territory, they are said to be in **complementary distribution,** and thus make up two **allophones** of the phoneme /l/.[10]

In this same manner, the descriptivist analyzes every sound in his close phonetic transcription, gradually building his phonemic

---

[8] The phone [ə], often called "schwa," is the final vowel sound in *sofa*. For a list of the *phonemes* in English, see Chapter 4, pp. 78–81.

[9] In some dialects, he would also note the "voiceless *l*" [l̥], which occurs in consonant clusters following a voiceless consonant, as in *fling, clay*. Voiceless sounds are those uttered with the vocal cords held open, and thus not vibrating.

[10] Note that we customarily enclose phonetic transcriptions between brackets [], and phonemic transcriptions between slants or virgules //.

inventory of the language. Ultimately, this inventory will consist of a description of the phonemes, including the careful notation of the positional variations of their allophones.

Morphological Analysis

We have so far considered the individual significant sound units of English, the phonemes. Insofar as each of them is treated separately and distinctly, the descriptivist has only the basis for the sound elements of the language. But when, as part of the next step in language discovery, he places sound units together to form clusters or continuous patterns of sound, he gets not just more sound, but meaning. The study of the individual units of meaning of a language is called **morphology,** and any indivisible unit of meaning is called a **morph.**

It is tempting to equate the morph with the old-fashioned, everyday "word," but this just doesn't work out in actual practice.[11] Although it is true that what are normally called words may also be morphs—*home, cat, man*—there are many other words which consist of two or more morphs. For example, *unmanly,* though one word, contains three morphs. The **base form,** or nuclear morph, rendered phonemically, is /mæn/. In addition, there is the adjectival morph /-li/ added as a suffix, plus the negative prefix morph /ən-/. Morphs, by the way, are typically written in phonemic transcription. Because the morph /mæn/ can stand alone, it is called a **free form.** The others, because they must occur in combination with other morphs, are called **bound forms.** Bound forms can occur with free forms, as in our example above, or with other bound forms, as in *receive,* in which /-siv/, though a bound form, is also the base. Most bound forms, though, operate as affixes (prefixes and suffixes in English) or as grammatical inflections.

---

[11] It is the usual naive practice to think of a word in the context of writing: a cluster of letters surrounded by white space. A better definition, more in keeping with the spoken nature of language, would be, "a base form, with or without one or more inflections or affixes, capable of standing alone." The last part is needed to avoid sanctioning *ceiving. (The asterisk marks any form which is in violation of the language system and is, in the broadest sense, ungrammatical.)

The morph is defined as any indivisible unit of meaning; in the same manner as in phonology, we look for the unit of meaning which the speakers of the language actually detect and understand. This unit of significant meaning is called the **morpheme,** by analogy with *phoneme,* and, continuing the analogy, it is made up of one or more **allomorphs.** The allomorph is defined as one of a group of morphs which are lexically identical and phonemically similar. Like the allophone, allomorphs occur in complementary distribution.

To clarify this sudden burst of technicality, let's consider the following morphs: /ro/, /læd/, /roz/, /kæt/. Because these are the sole forms of these morphs, they become the lone allomorphs of their respective morphemes. We indicate morphemes by writing them in standard orthography and placing them between braces, thus: {row}, {lad}, {rose}, {cat}. So far, there is nothing complicated about it, but suppose we add to each of them the inflection in English for plurality. Phonemically, we would have: /roz/, /lædz/, /rózəz/, /kæts/. In short, plurality is indicated by the following inflectional forms: /-z/, /-əz/, /-s/. If we placed this evidence with other instances of plurality, we would find that these morphs do not occur at random, but are in fact allomorphs of the noun plural morpheme, arbitrarily indicated as {-Z$_{pl}$}, each in complementary distribution with the others. The form /-əz/ occurs after bases ending in sibilants and affricates; /-z/ after all vowels and other voiced consonants; and /-s/ after other voiceless consonants. Obviously, these allomorphs are lexically identical and phonemically similar.[12]

In general, the plurals of the English nouns are formed in this manner, with one of these three allomorphs. There are, however, always exceptions. Take for instance the morpheme {elf}. We would expect that the combination of it with the plural morpheme is rendered /*ɛlfs/, but in actuality, it is /ɛlvz/. We must then say

---

[12] If the forms are absolutely lexically identical, it isn't necessary to insist that they be phonemically similar. Certainly the /-ən/ allomorph in *oxen* is every bit the indicator of plurality as /-s/ in *cats.* As for the phonological terminology in the preceding sentences: *voiced* consonants are sounded with the vocal bands held close, causing vibration; *sibilants* are, roughly speaking, *s* sounds; and *affricates* are sounds which begin with complete closure, released slowly as a sibilant, like both *ch* sounds in *church.*

that the morpheme {elf} consists of two allomorphs: /ɛlf/ is the regular free form, while /ɛlv-/ is the bound form which occurs only in combination with the /-z/ allomorph of the morpheme {-Z$_{pl}$}. Keeping track of all of these allomorphic combinations is the province of **morphophonemics.**

Because English is a language which has borrowed widely, it does require a certain degree of sophistication to perform morphological analysis on some of the Latin, French, and Greek derivatives. Often the bound affixes are "dead," like the Latin forms {per-} and {e-}, as in *persuade* and *evade*, and are never used to form new words. Rather narrow analysis is therefore needed to determine whether or not to include them as divisible units of meaning. For instance, there is that old demon of the spelling bees, *antidisestablishmentarianism.* It is simple enough to work out some of the morphemes in this word: one can readily divide off {anti-}, {dis-}, {ment}, {-ary}, {-an}, {-ism}. But one still has the base *establish* to consider. It might be possible to divide it as either *e-stablish* or *e-stabl-ish*, and there are good etymological arguments for them both, but the most sensible analysis is probably to think of it as a single morpheme.

Even with native English words, there are certain problems. For example, the simple word *daisy* evolved from the Anglo-Saxon equivalent of "day's eye." A morphologist who was aware of the word's etymology could consider it to be a combination of the three morphemes {day}, {-Z$_{gen}$},[13] and {eye}. The average speaker of English, however, probably thinks of the word *daisy* only in reference to the flower, neither knowing nor caring about its metaphorical origin. Consequently, we would not be doing linguistic science a disservice if we analyze it as a single morpheme.

This points up the basic difficulty with morphemic analysis in English. Quite often, the analysis will vary with the sophistication of the analyst, his knowledge of foreign languages, and his etymological awareness. The most important and most valid portion of morphology is in finding and analyzing the *grammatical* forms of the language under consideration. Too narrow an analysis of the lexical forms can lead to absurdity.

---

[13] {-Z$_{gen}$} is the arbitrary designation for the possessive, or genitive, morpheme.

Syntactical Analysis

So far, there would be very little disagreement among linguists about the basic findings of the descriptivists. Possible differences of opinion would center on matters of detail: the precise number and nature of the phonemic inventory of a language, for example, or the manner of dividing certain combinations into morphemes, as outlined in the last few paragraphs. But in general, all linguists agree as to the basic methodology of phonological and morphological analysis, though there is room for argument about the particulars.

Disagreement becomes more fundamental when one comes to the problem of syntactical analysis, which should be the capstone of the linguist's description. For a long time, there were no really precise procedures to follow in this respect, as evidenced by the many descriptions of newly recorded languages in which the phonological and morphological analyses were full and complete, but in which the syntactical analysis, the study of the arrangement of the morphemes, was limited to a handful of not very useful generalizations on about the same level as the elementary *subject-verb-object* arrangement of English. Thus, students using these descriptions had only very simple arrangements to work with and still be sure about, and they were therefore forced to spend a good deal of time having to learn syntactic specifics on the spot, equivalent to "getting the feel of the language."

Immediate Constituent Analysis

One early form of syntactical analysis was the theory of the **immediate constituent** (**IC**). In this analysis, individual elements were coupled together in pairs, the nature of the relationship being described in terms of the function of these elements, or *constituents*. According to the theory, there could be five types of relationships:

1. Predication—between subject and predicate.
2. Complementation—between verb and complement.
3. Coordination—between equivalent constituents.

4. Subordination—between a subordinator (a preposition, for instance) and the phrase or clause pattern which follows.

5. Modification—between a head and a modifier.

This analysis, which was developed primarily out of an attempt to deal with English syntax, can be illustrated with the following sentence:

The boys and girls read their books in the house.

In this illustration, predication describes the relationship between *the boys and girls* and *read their books in the house.* In like manner, *read* and *their books* illustrate complementation, *boys* and *girls* illustrate coordination (with the relationship further cemented by the conjunction *and*), and *the* and *boys and girls* and *their* and *books* illustrate modification. Finally, *in* and *the house* stand in subordinate relationship to one another (and *in the house* itself is related to *read their books* by modification). In each of these instances, the relationships are between immediate constituents.

In this analysis, the relationships can be illustrated graphically by means of an IC diagram:

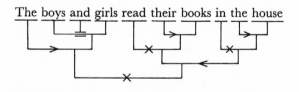

In this diagram, each immediate constituent pair is connected by means of tying lines. Further, the relationship between constituents is specified on each horizontal line. Because their relationship is **exocentric**—that is, the whole unit does not function in the same manner as its immediate constituents—predication, complementation, and subordination are all indicated by means of the **X** on the line. The two **endocentric** relationships, modification and coordination, are specified individually, in the former by means of the arrow, always pointed in the direction of the head, and in the latter with the equal sign, the conjunction, if any, tied directly into it, as in our illustration.[14]

What the immediate constituent analysis reveals, at least for English, is that the relationships are basically **binary;** that is, with one possible exception, the relationships are in pairs. The exception is coordination; here, there can be three or more constituents in the relationship, exclusive of the conjunction, as in:

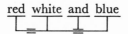

Further, the IC diagram can be used to indicate more fully the relationships between the constituents and their nature. One can place on the vertical lines the names of the constituents and on the horizontal lines the designation of the relationship. Thus, in our illustration:

[14] The IC diagram was first introduced in Eugene A. Nida, *A Synopsis of English Syntax*, pp. viii–lviii. It might be preferable to differentiate between the exocentric relationships by means of letters, with *P* for predication, *C* for complementation, and *S* for subordination. The arrow for modification and equal sign for coordination are sufficiently self-explanatory to leave alone. Thus:

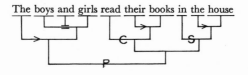

For a somewhat different (and earlier) method of illustrating IC relationships, that of enclosing the related constituents in "Chinese boxes," see W. Nelson Francis, *The Structure of American English* (New York, 1958), chap. 6. This method is not recommended simply because the confusion of lines causes an optical sensation not unlike that of Op Art. Whichever IC diagramming method is used, the biggest advantage over the Reed–Kellogg system is that it does not obscure word order.

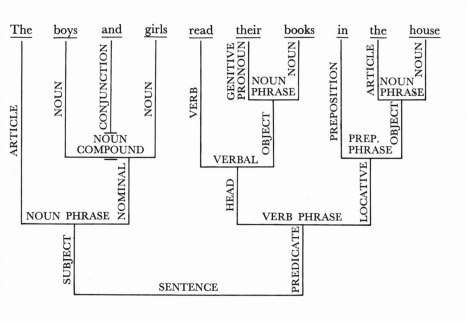

Shortcomings of IC Analysis

I have not gone over this analysis step by step, nor have I given a very detailed account of it, because it is, in several respects, unsatisfactory. For one thing, the basic relationships between constituents have to be changed considerably from language to language. There is nothing very "universal" about any of the relationships, which here were indicated for English. Second, the analysis becomes less satisfactory when one attempts to work with more complex sentences, just as in Reed–Kellogg sentence diagramming. Third, the binary nature of IC analysis really shows us nothing about the general nature of syntactical relationships. Although it helps us to analyze structures which are already formed, it does not show us how to form new structures, unless we reach the untenable conclusion that new utterances are made by superimposing new forms over the old. Finally, the relationships depend too much upon intuition. There are too many situations in which defining the relationship would be a matter of faith rather than of scientific description. There has to be, in short, a form of descriptive syntactical analysis both general enough and yet useful enough to show us how morphemes may be put together to make meaningful utterances.

Tagmemic Analysis

The key to a more meaningful syntactical description might be related to the fundamentals of phonological and morphological analysis. Those who were dissatisfied with IC analysis reasoned that there must be syntactical units analogous to the phoneme and the morpheme, made up of elements equivalent, on a different level, to the allophone and the allomorph. Constant reflection upon this consideration led to the "discovery" of the **tagmeme,** the significant unit of grammatical relationships.

To see how this concept works, we can take a rather common and familiar structural instance, the noun phrase. As an example, we can select from our IC exercise *their books*, a single structural occurrence, or **tagma** (analogous to the *phone* or *morph*), consisting of a genitive pronoun plus a noun plus $\{-Z_{pl}\}$, the latter an optional item which doesn't have to be added. We can then list other similar instances:

John's books	genitive proper noun plus noun (plus $\{-Z_{pl}\}$), placed in parentheses to show that it is optional
the books	definite article plus noun (plus $\{-Z_{pl}\}$)
a book	nondefinite article plus a noun (this time a noun without a plural inflection: **a books* is ungrammatical)

None of these instances can work in combination with one another. We cannot say, for example, **the a book* or **a John's book*. Thus we can say that they make up part of an inventory of **allotagmas** of the **tagmeme** which describes a basic noun phrase pattern: the determiner plus a noun. This pattern is sometimes called a **slot,** and the forms which can be used in the slot are called **fillers.** Thus, in our example the determiner slot can be filled with a definite article, a nondefinite article, a genitive pronoun, or a genitive proper noun. All of this is by way of elementary explanation; we shall see in the next chapter how this slot-and-filler approach can be expanded for the noun phrase.

The tagmemic principle works on several *levels*. At the highest level, the sentence, it is used to describe the elements making up what have been traditionally called compound and complex sentences. The other levels might be called the clause level (in which the elements would most commonly be the subject-verb-object pattern in English); the phrase level, as in the example just cited above; and the word level, in which the inflectional morphemes are put together, as *they* + {-Z_{gen}} to form *their*, or *book* + {-Z_{pl}} to form *books*. In the next chapter, we will go over these levels in more detail, examining the slot-and-filler analysis of the sample sentence used in IC diagrams.

The concept of the tagmeme answers some of the basic objections to IC analysis: it works readily with complex sentences; it explains easily and in generalized terms how morphemes may be strung together into structural relationships, rather than how words are connected into surface relationships; and it can be employed in any language under investigation, even though the designations of both slot and filler differ radically from one language to another. It might also be added that some descriptivists see the tagmemic principle as a device for teaching composition and as an aid to stylistic analysis in literary criticism.

Summary

Essentially, then, descriptive grammar is a theory which is based on a discovery procedure. It presents a viable, consistent pattern for describing a hitherto unrecorded language and for teaching it to others. And though a complete descriptive grammar of any language is itself a complex and difficult (some would say impossible) accomplishment, the fact remains that the description is internally more reliable than are the massive accumulations of data which came out of the philological tradition.

GENERATIVE-TRANSFORMATIONAL GRAMMAR

Origin of Transformational Grammar

When we mentioned earlier that a general dissatisfaction over IC analysis led to the formulation of the tagmemic procedures briefly outlined above, it should be understood that the discontent came from more than one quarter. Tagmemic procedures still operate within the basic theoretical framework of descriptive grammar. However, there has been developed within the past ten years a radically different set of procedures based upon another theory of grammar (and ultimately, of language). This theory is called generative-transformational grammar (usually shortened to transformational grammar), and the basic position was first outlined by Noam Chomsky in *Syntactic Structures*, a monograph published without fanfare in The Hague, Netherlands, in 1957. Since then, with the work of a good many others, the procedural specifics of transformational grammar have been altered and revised, some rather extensively, but the basic theory remains the same.

Objections to Descriptive Theory

Chomsky begins by positing several arguments and objections to the theory and methodology of descriptive grammar. First of all, he questions the usefulness of discovery procedures as a means either of language learning or of grammatical description, once the basic field work has been completed. In particular, he is dubious about the need to continue following the step-by-step procedures of phonology, morphology, and syntax, without mixing them, in formulating a description. This, he argues, tends to make field work methodology an article of faith. It should be added here, however, that several reasonably orthodox descriptivists had made the same objections, and today this argument is equivalent to flogging a dead horse.

The second objection, however, is more cogent. Chomsky turns here to the problem of the descriptivist's corpus, the detailed language transcription on which his description is based. However long the corpus, Chomsky argues, there is always the danger of serious omission, which could make the description partially, or even totally, invalid. Further, harkening back to Saussure's basic formulation, this puts too much emphasis upon an informant's *parole*, without making due allowance for *langue*. Or, putting it in terms which the transformationalists themselves have given currency, this credits too much the informant's **performance** without giving consideration to his **competency,** his capacity—and ultimately the capacity of all users of the language—for forming or understanding any grammatical utterance which has never been spoken before.

A third objection is closely related to this. What means does the descriptivist have to verify whether or not his informants are making grammatical utterances? In the last analysis, the rueful answer must be that he has none, short of reading back his corpus to another informant. And herein lies the point: though there is no indication that any speaker of a language will utter only grammatical sentences (and there is every indication that the reverse may be true), that speaker is nonetheless able to tell whether or not any given utterance is grammatical—that is, whether it conforms to the inherent system of the language.

The transformationalist's objections, then, concentrate on this basic point. The descriptivists have devised a reasonably good set of procedures for language discovery, but they have not given us the means whereby we are able to come up with entirely new utterances outside of the corpus, unless they hold to intuition or the superimposition of new utterances upon old, both of which conclusions are untenable. This is similar to the basic objection of the adherents of the tagmemic school, who were formulating their alternatives at about the same time that Chomsky's monograph appeared. He and his followers, however, preferred to develop a wholly different approach.

Principles of Transformational Grammar

Basically, transformational grammar is a set of procedures for forming an infinite number of grammatical sentences in a given language. Hence, the *grammar* is the process by which any grammatical sentence is formed; and a *sentence* is defined as the end result of the application of all pertinent procedures. These definitions are unavoidably circular, for they are based upon the procedures of transformational grammar; and because the number of possible sentences in a given language is infinite (though any given sentence is itself finite), there's just no other way to make a useful definition.[15] It should be noted that the basic difference between descriptive grammar and transformational grammar rests in their intended purposes. The former sets out to *describe*, as completely and yet as generally as possible, a given language in terms of a corpus—in short, from what has already been uttered. The latter proposes to *generate* an utterance or group of utterances from the moment of its vague conception in the speaker's thought processes, down to its finite, specific grammatical form—in other words, to form new utterances from their first inception, the **deep structure,** down to their concrete form, the **surface structure.**

The transformationalist begins by generating the **kernel sentence** from a relatively small set of procedures.[16] To form these kernel sentences, he makes use of three different kinds of procedures: **phrase structure procedures,** which define the abstract processes by which the sentence is formed; a **lexicon,** which lists the words which fit each abstract category; and **morphophonemic procedures,** which designate the way in which morphemes are combined in actual speech.[17] The systematic application of these generative procedures results in a *kernel sentence*, a rather basic utterance—active, simple, indicative.

---

[15] Given the basic end of the transformationalists, to say that a sentence consists of a subject, a verb, and an object does not help us to form new sentences never before uttered; and the school definition that a sentence is "a group of words expressing a complete thought" is absolutely worthless.

[16] I prefer the term *procedure* over *rule*, the former tending to be less inflexible than the latter. Should I be forced to use *rule* for reasons of style, bear in mind that I do not intend it to mean something rigidly permanent.

[17] Morphophonemic procedures are those which indicate how combinations of morphemes are sounded. An alternate set of procedures which indicate how these combinations are written is called *morphographemic*. The former term is used in a general sense to cover both areas, though those of a puristic bent may wish to discriminate.

A Sample Generative Grammar

Though we will delve more deeply into transformational grammar as applied to English in the next chapter, it wouldn't hurt to present here a sample grammar, drastically oversimplified, to illustrate how a kernel sentence might be generated.

Phrase structure procedures:

(1)   S → NP + VP

(2) NP → det + Noun

(3) VP → Verb + NP

These phrase structure procedures set up basic abstract categories which go from the very general S, or sentence, all the way down to the surface specifics of the utterance. They are often called "rewrite rules." The first can be read, "A sentence is rewritten as a noun phrase plus a verb phrase." This statement does not mean that all sentences, in their final form, consist of a noun phrase followed by a verb phrase, nor does it give credence to the concepts of "subject" and "predicate." Many sentences, as uttered, do not have noun phrase "subjects"—commands, for example; on the other hand, sentences in answer to a question may consist only of a noun phrase ("Who broke the window?" "John."). What the first rewrite procedure indicates is that *underlying* any given utterance in its final form is the deep structure notion which is arbitrarily labeled NP + VP.

By following the above procedures faithfully, we can ultimately come up with the following consecutive sequences;

(1) S

(2) NP + VP (rule 1)

(3) det + Noun + VP (rule 2)

(4) det + Noun + Verb + NP (rule 3)

(5) det + Noun + Verb + det + Noun (rule 2)

It is also possible to illustrate these generative procedures by means of a "branching tree" diagram, thus:

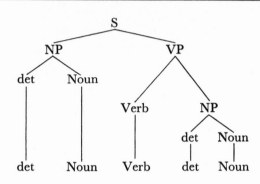

Either way, and I recommend simply following out the procedures by simple steps rather than by diagrams, we have moved from the deep structure of the utterance to its surface structure, with this **terminal string** as the end result:

det + Noun + Verb + det + Noun

Since no more phrase structure procedures apply, we now consult the lexicon to fill in these abstract categories.

Lexicon:

(1) det → the, a

(2) Noun → man, boy, horse, dog

(3) Verb → saw, looked at

These procedures give us some choices, and thus our kernel sentence might end up as:

the + boy + saw + a + man

Our oversimplified grammar has no morphophonemic procedures, but if, in a somewhat more complex grammar we ended up with the combination *see* + {-D$_{past}$}, we would need the following:

see + { $-$D$_{past}$} $\rightarrow$ saw[18]

Finally, assuming a final procedural step which would allow us to remove the plus signs, capitalize the first word, and put a period at the end, we have the sentence "The boy saw a man." It is possible from this sample grammar to generate forty-eight kernel sentences.

Even if we were given a set of generative procedures far more complex than this, we would by no means have covered the field of possible utterances. Hence, the grammarian must devise a set of **transformational procedures,** which systematically rearrange one or more kernel sentences into a more complex form, called a **transform.** These procedures, for example, would transform the kernel sentence generated above into a passive construction:

A man was seen by the boy.

Or a question requiring a simple affirmative:

Did the boy see a man?

These are only a few of the possible transformations which can be applied to the kernel sentence. We will examine more of them in detail in Chapter 5. What is important to note is that they rearrange only the surface structure of the kernel sentences; the deep structure of the kernel is unchanged.

Another Look Ahead

In the first part of the preceding chapter, we broke down pretty definitively the basic premises of school grammar, so much so that perhaps some of you were tempted to ask, "Do we need any grammar at all?" By outlining briefly two contemporary grammatical theories, I have tried to show here that it is possible

---

[18] Notice that morphophonemic procedural statements have two or more forms to the left of the arrow and only one to the right, whereas phrase structure rules, being definitions, have only one form to the left of the arrow and one or more to the right. {-D$_{past}$}, by the way, is the past tense morpheme.

to postulate an intellectually honest, self-consistent grammatical description. In the next chapter we will begin to apply them both in analyzing the structural patterns of modern English, and I will be shamelessly neutral in my presentation. In the recent past, a portion of the academic world has become an arena for a genteel battle between the descriptivists and the transformationalists; but for our own purposes we will adopt the best that each has to offer and consider how each might offset the weaknesses of the other. This is an ecumenical age, and there is no reason why we cannot achieve some kind of synthesis which is pertinent to our principal objective—the better understanding of our language.

QUESTIONS AND EXERCISES

1. Discuss the following as a review of this chapter:

    a. What generalizations pertaining to descriptive theory are subsumed under the expressions -*eme* and *allo-* ?

    b. Explain the statement that the potential number of sentences in a language is infinite, but the individual sentence is finite. Why doesn't the fact that you can always add or insert another word or phrase to any given sentence invalidate the latter part of this statement?

    c. What aspect of language is implied in naming the end product of the phrase structure rules a "terminal *string*" ?

    d. Why do you suppose that the term *phrase*, as used both in tagmemics and transformational grammar, presents an obstacle to many students? What, therefore, is the unspoken assumption in the often-heard statement that the transformationalists employ the terminology of traditional grammar?

    e. Why might some people be troubled by the circularity of the transformationalists' definitions of *sentence* and *grammar*? Are these definitions really very different from those found in a standard dictionary? What assumptions does the dictionary editor make about the background of the dictionary user in formulating his definitions? Do these assumptions help to make more meaningful the definitions mentioned here? What is the basic fallacy in the school grammar definition of the sentence?

f. How do descriptive grammar theory and transformational grammar theory complement one another? What do you think is the basic reason for the antagonism between the two camps?

2. Work out the following morphological exercises:

a. What must be added to the inventory of allomorphs making up $\{-Z_{pl}\}$ in order to accommodate the following nouns: *ox, child, sheep, deer, foot, man, woman?* *Note*: It might be useful to devise an inventory of allomorphs for some of these nouns in the manner of {elf}, then posit a ø ("zero") allomorph of $\{-Z_{pl}\}$.

b. What are the allomorphs making up the negative prefix {in-} (as in *inability*) which accommodate prefixing it to *material, logical, numerable, practical?* *Note*: Don't be misled by the spelling.

c. What allomorphs make up the morpheme $\{-Z_{gen}\}$? In what ways do they parallel those making up $\{-Z_{pl}\}$? In what respects do they differ?

d. With perhaps some assistance from your instructor, list the allomorphs making up $\{-D_{past}\}$, with their distribution.

3. We have mentioned that our sample generative grammar of the sentence presented in this chapter is grossly oversimplified. Name some elements which might be added to it (other than lexical forms) which would enable you to generate more kernel sentences.

4. Study carefully the following quotation from one of the classic works in linguistics:

The multiple expression of a single concept is universally felt as a source of linguistic strength and variety, not as a needless extravagance. More irksome is a random correspondence between idea and linguistic expression in the field of abstract and relational concepts, particularly when the concept is embodied in a grammatical element. Thus, the randomness of the expression of plurality in such words as *books, oxen, sheep,* and *geese* is felt to be rather more, I fancy, an unavoidable and traditional predicament than a welcome luxuriance. It is obvious that a language cannot go beyond a certain point in this randomness.

Many languages go incredibly far in this respect, it is true, but linguistic history shows conclusively that sooner or later the less frequently occurring associations are ironed out at the expense of the more vital ones. In other words, all languages have an inherent tendency to economy of expression. Were this tendency entirely inoperative, there would be no grammar. The fact of grammar, a universal trait of language, is simply a generalized expression of the feeling that analogous concepts and relations are most conveniently symbolized in analogous forms. Were a language ever completely "grammatical," it would be a perfect engine of conceptual expression. Unfortunately, or luckily, no language is tyrannically consistent. All grammars leak.[19]

How does this statement point up the difficulty of formulating a complete description of English grammar, regardless of the grammatical theory? What other considerations stand in the way of completeness? Do you think a complete description of English grammar, or the grammar of any language, is possible?

BIBLIOGRAPHY

One of the problems facing the beginning student is that there are very few treatments of descriptive grammar theory which were written especially for the beginner. Most of the established works in the field are intended for the graduate student or the practicing linguist; and all of them face the problem of being superseded, in whole or in part, a few years after publication. The best place to begin is probably with journal articles intended for the general reader: W. Nelson Francis, "Revolution in Grammar," *Quarterly Journal of Speech*, XL (1954), 229–312; and a series by George P. Faust, "Basic Tenets of Structural Grammar," "Terms in Phonemics," and "Something of Morphemics," *College Composition and Communication*, IV (1953), 122–25; V (1954), 30–34, 65–69. These are reprinted in several collections of readings in linguistics, of which the best are Harold B. Allen (ed.), *Readings in Applied English Linguistics* (2d ed.; New York: Appleton-Century-Crofts, 1964); and John A. Rycenga and Joseph Schwartz (eds.), *Perspectives on Language* (New York: The Ronald Press Company, 1963). These and many other articles are also available in the Bobbs-Merrill reprint series in *Language and Linguistics*. The student should also sample other likely articles in these collections. Another fine introductory essay is William G. Moulton's "Linguistics," in James Thorp (ed.), *The Aims and Methods of Scholarship in Modern*

19 Edward Sapir, *Language* (New York: Harcourt, Brace & World, Inc., 1921).

Languages and Literatures (New York: Modern Language Association of America, 1963), pp. 1–21.

The following is a list, by no means exhaustive, of English grammars based on descriptive theory which contain general introductory chapters repaying close, careful reading:

Francis, W. Nelson. *The Structure of American English.* New York: The Ronald Press Company, 1958.

Hill, Archibald A. *Introduction to Linguistic Structures.* New York: Harcourt, Brace & World, Inc., 1958.

Hockett, Charles F. *A Course in Modern Linguistics.* New York: The Macmillan Company, 1958.

Whitehall, Harold. *Structural Essentials of English.* New York: Harcourt, Brace & World, Inc., 1951.

Two texts along the same line, but not primarily limited to English, are Harold A. Gleason, Jr., *An Introduction to Descriptive Linguistics* (rev. ed.; New York: Holt, Rinehart and Winston, Inc., 1961); and Robert A. Hall, Jr., *Introductory Linguistics* (Philadelphia: Chilton Books, 1964). All of the books cited here can be read through with profit, provided that the reader remembers that linguistics is a field subject to change.

Descriptive grammar theory is all predicated upon the landmark publication of Leonard Bloomfield's *Language* (New York: Henry Holt and Company, 1933); and, more recently, George L. Trager and Henry Lee Smith, *An Outline of English Structure* (Washington: American Council of Learned Societies, 1957). Both are extremely difficult, and though seminal, are still subject to supersession. Franz Boas' "Introduction" to *The Handbook of American Indian Languages*, Bulletin 40, Part I (Washington: Smithsonian Institution Bureau of American Ethnology, 1911), still interesting and pertinent reading, was reprinted in 1964 by the Georgetown University Press.

Tagmemic theory is presented most definitively in Kenneth L. Pike, *Language in Relation to a Unified Theory of the Structure of Human Behavior* (rev. ed.; The Hague: Mouton and Company, 1967). However, this is an extremely difficult work for the neophyte; a less compressed discussion is contained in Benjamin Elson and Velma Pickett, *An Introduction to Morphology and Syntax* (Santa Ana, Calif.: Summer Institute of Linguistics, 1965), Part II.

Even more acute is the problem facing the beginning student looking for basic source explanations of generative-transformational grammar. Here, virtually all the journal articles on the subject seem directed at fellow linguists. Probably the least difficult short introduction is John Viertel, "Generative Grammars," *College Composition and Communication*, XV (May, 1964), 65–81. The best textbook introduction to the subject is contained in Owen Thomas, *Transformational Grammar and the Teacher of English* (New York: Holt, Rinehart and Winston, Inc., 1965), especially Chaps. 1–3. Also useful are the first two chapters of Emmon Bach, *An Introduction to Transformational Grammars* (New

York: Holt, Rinehart and Winston, Inc., 1964). Among the most recent books on the subject, Ronald W. Langacker, *Language and Its Structure* (New York: Harcourt, Brace & World, Inc., 1968), is a general overall introduction to transformational theory; and Roderick A. Jacobs and Peter S. Rosenbaum, *English Transformational Grammar* (Waltham, Mass.: Blaisdell Publishing Co. 1968), though specifically concentrating upon English, presents a good summary of transformational theory in sections 1 and 2, and in an "Epilogue" by Paul M. Postal.

The shifting field of transformational grammar is still too young to develop any "classics," other than Noam Chomsky's *Syntactic Structures*, cited earlier, and this work has been partly superseded as the result of newer studies by Chomsky and his colleagues. The most recent, as of this writing, *Aspects of the Theory of Syntax* (Cambridge, Mass.: The M.I.T. Press, 1965), contains a reasonably complete bibliography of studies published up to then. Jerry A. Fodor and Jerrold J. Katz (eds.), *The Structure of Language: Readings in the Philosophy of Language* (Englewood Cliffs, N. J.: Prentice-Hall, Inc., 1964) is the most comprehensive collection of readings on transformational theory, but it, like the Chomsky writings, is hard going. There simply is no royal road to grammatical theory.

4

Basic Units of the Sentence

This chapter and the one which follows are both intended to introduce to you the grammar of modern English, the recurring patterns of the language which we as native speakers actually use in our daily communication. They are meant to reveal the system which underlies the utterances we make, using that grammatical theory which seems most capable of illuminating the specific area. However, it seems best at the beginning to point out the drawbacks of this description, so that you will not be misled into jumping to the wrong conclusion.

To begin with, there is no complete grammar of a living language, and this description is, of course, no exception. Living languages are slippery beasts; even though ninety per cent of the utterances in a given language may conform to the grammarian's description, there is still that ten per cent which either is undergoing change anew or hasn't yet conformed to the main body of the language patterns. Thus every language description has some measure of built-in obsolescence. Even the multi-volumed descriptions of Jespersen or Poutsma have this disconcerting feature. They describe the language patterns of yesterday, but not necessarily of today.

This leads us to the second point. Nothing which is offered in these chapters is to be given the sanctity of Holy Writ, nothing here is to be taken as authoritative. All of it, or any part of it, can change tomorrow. This is a defect not so much in the grammatical theory or presentation as simply in the nature of language. To assert that these descriptions are not susceptible to change or alteration is to fall into the dogmatic snare of the school grammarians.

Finally, it must be admitted that anything presented in these chapters can be argued and debated. The presentation here is eclectic, making use of whatever grammatical theory seems to work best in clarifying that aspect of English grammar which is under scrutiny at the moment. This will obviously not appeal to those who feel duty-bound to defend one theory against another. Undoubtedly, too, they will be able to make their theory elucidate the salient features of English every bit as well as the presentation here. There is also the possibility that a new grammatical theory can come along at any time to supersede the descriptions here.[1]

All of this can be most disconcerting to the person who wants the Truth all nicely pinned down, to be his into perpetuity. Yet this state of flux is the constant rule in all of the sciences, and even in the arts we have changes in artistic fashions, changes in taste, even changes in critical approaches. The purpose of education is not to dogmatize, but rather to make the educated man aware of the fact of change in his universe. Your duty in this course is precisely that of the educated man in any discipline. You should question every statement, check it against your own observations, advance counterproposals of your own. At no time should you accept anything passively. Out of this changing discipline you

---

[1] At this writing, there is emerging a new grammatical theory called *stratificational grammar*, which appears to be (at least from a very superficial overview) based on a re-evaluation of Chomsky's generative grammar, using the glossomatics theories developed by the Danish linguist Louis Hjelmslev. It is at the moment too new, too technical, and too generalized to be applied to our study—though it may perhaps be applied before long to just such problems. The basic study is Sydney M. Lamb, *Outline of Stratificational Grammar* (Washington, 1966), supplemented by several articles in the journals.

should, hopefully, select that medium which best suits your purposes, whether they be in teaching or in scholarship, at the same time constantly seeking a better medium.

THE PHONEMES OF MODERN ENGLISH

Review of Phonemics

Before we begin an analysis of the syntactic patterns of modern English, it would be well to cover first of all the sounds, or phonology, of our language. Then, with this rather basic unit out of the way, we can go on to cover noun and verb structures and, in the next chapter, the arrangement of the sentence.

The systematic basis of phonological analysis was previously covered in the discussion of the methodology of the descriptive linguist in Chapter 3. There we noted that the linguist begins with the *phones*, the single isolated units of sound, which he then analyses into *phonemes*, the significant units of sound, noting as part of his analysis the distribution of the *allophones* which make up each significant unit. In every phase of his analysis, he must pay particular attention to the so-called organs of speech.

The Organs of Speech

Phonologists refer to the *so-called* organs of speech for a very simple reason. The parts of the body which are used in articulating speech sounds are not primarily intended for this purpose; rather, they perform the more basic function of sustaining life itself, as through breathing or ingesting food. In English, the following organs are used to produce speech sounds, usually in combination:

lips (labial)
teeth (dental)
tongue, *divided into*
   tip
   blade
   front
   back

tooth ridge (alveolar)
hard palate (palatal)
soft palate (velar)
pharynx (pharyngeal)
larynx, sometimes called the *vocal cords* or *vocal bands*
lungs

In parentheses are the descriptive terms used to designate each separate sound. Because all speech in English is initiated by exhaling, there is no need to mention in each instance the action of the lungs. The action of the larynx is designated in terms of whether the vocal bands vibrate or not: in the former instance, the sound is **voiced** (abbreviated *vd.*); in the latter instance, it is **voiceless** (*vl.*). The difference can be noted very plainly if you pronounce the sound represented by the letters *f* and *v* in *focal* and *vocal*, at the same time holding your fingers on your "Adam's apple." You will notice that both sounds are articulated identically, by the placement of the upper front teeth on the lower lip, the only difference being that for the *v* there is a vibration caused by the vocal bands. Thus, the *v* would be designated as the *voiced labio-dental*, and the *f* the *voiceless labio-dental*. Most of the consonantal sounds in English occur in pairs like this, the only discernible difference being the voicing.

The English Consonants

Figure 4–1 lists the twenty-four phonemes making up the inventory of consonants in English, together with examples of their occurrence initially, medially, and finally, and their articulatory description, giving both the articulator and point of articulation. They are further grouped by articulatory classes. The **stops** are characterized by the momentary holding back of the air flow before release (or *plosion*). The **fricatives** (sometimes called **continuants** or **spirants**) do not hold back the flow of air, but cause it to pass through a channel, thereby setting up audible friction. The **nasals** are characterized by the passage of air through the nose, which passage is permitted by a lowering of the *uvula*, an appendage at the end of the soft palate. The **semi-vowels** are those sounds which glide into or out of a vowel sound.

Stops:

/p/	pat, happy, lip /pæt, hǽpi, lɪp/	vl. bilabial
/b/	bat, rabbit, club /bæt, rǽbɪt, kləb/	vd. bilabial
/t/	teen, cutter, hat /tin, kɔ́tər, hæt/	vl. tip-alveolar
/d/	dig, ladder, rid /dɪg, lǽdər, rɪd/	vd. tip-alveolar
/k/	kid, nickel, back /kɪd, níkəl, bæk/	vl. back-velar
/g/	give, ragged, bag /gɪv, rǽgəd, bæg/	vd. back-velar

Fricatives:

/f/	feet, coffee, laugh /fit, kɔ́fi, læf/	vl. labio-dental	
/v/	vat, lover, have /væt, lɔ́vər, hæv/	vd. labio-dental	
/θ/	think, ether, bath /θɪŋk, íθər, bæθ/	vl. tip-dental	
/ð/	then, either, bathe /ðɛn, íðər, beð/	vd. tip-dental	
/s/	sit, masses, miss /sɪt, mǽsəz, mɪs/	vl. blade-alveolar	⎫
/z/	zoo, visit, was /zu, vízət, wəz/	vd. blade-alveolar	⎬ sibilants
/š/	ship, mission, wish /šɪp, míšən, wɪš/	vl. front-alveolar	⎪
/ž/	measure, rouge /méžər, ruž/	vd. front-alveolar	⎭
/č/	church, nature /čərč, néčər/	vl. front-alveolo-palatal	⎫
/ǰ/	judge, agent /ǰəǰ, éǰənt/	vd. front-alveolo-palatal	⎬ affricates

Nasals:

/m/	man, hammer, ham /mæn, hǽmər, hæm/	vd. bilabial
/n/	nip, manner, can /nɪp, mǽnər, kæn/	vd. tip-alveolar
/ŋ/	singer, ring /síŋər, rɪŋ/	vd. back-velar

Semivowels:

/r/	row, merry, bar /ro, méri, bar/	vd. retroflexive glide
/j/	yet /jɛt/	vd. linguo-palatal glide
/w/	wish /wɪš/	vd. labio-velar glide

Lateral and Pharyngeal:

/l/	let, mellow, pal /lɛt, mélo, pæl/	vd. alveolar lateral
/h/	have /hæv/	vl. glottal fricative

Figure 4–1. English Consonant Phonemes.

Subcategories of the *fricatives* are the **sibilants,** or *s* sounds, and the **affricates,** stops with slow fricative release.[2]

[2] The convenience of having typewriter keyboard letters handy for some of these phonetic symbols has led to a small modification of the International Phonetic Alphabet. In particular, most phonologists now use /š, ž, č, ǰ/, in preference to the old IPA /ʃ, ʒ, tʃ, dʒ/, respectively.

The English Vowels

The vowel sounds differ from the consonants in that they are formed only through an oral modification, without either obstructing or channeling the flow of air. The oral modification is caused by the relative closeness of the front, the midpoint, or the back of the tongue to the roof of the mouth. The relative closeness is classified by **high, mid,** and **low;** the position points, by **front, central,** and **back.** This classification can be determined by reference to Figure 4–2, the tongue-position rectangle; thus, when

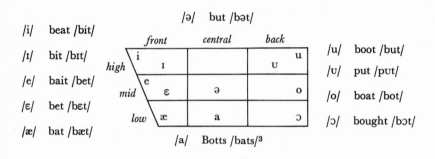

/i/	beat /bit/
/ɪ/	bit /bɪt/
/e/	bait /bet/
/ɛ/	bet /bɛt/
/æ/	bat /bæt/

/ə/   but /bət/

	front	central	back	
high	i		u	
	ɪ		ʊ	
mid	e			
	ɛ	ə	o	
low	æ	a	ɔ	

/a/   Botts /bats/[3]

/u/	boot /but/
/ʊ/	put /pʊt/
/o/	boat /bot/
/ɔ/	bought /bɔt/

Figure 4–2. English Vowel Phonemes.

we speak of the *mid-back* vowel, for instance, we refer to the /o/ as in *boat.* All vowel sounds in normal English speech are voiced. Furthermore, all English back vowels are accompanied by lip-rounding, whereas the front and central vowels are unrounded.

Close phonetic transcription is considerably more difficult for the vowel sounds than for the consonants. Because the tongue position does not call for an exact point of articulation, there are probably thousands of possible oral vowel phones. The transcriber must indicate their relative lowering and raising, fronting and retracting, from some sort of predetermined norm, usually his

[3] Again the typewriter keyboard causes us to modify to /a/ the old IPA symbol /ɑ/, though in handwritten transcription the latter is used because it's easier. In close *phonetic* transcription, [a] represents a fronted low-mid vowel, halfway between [æ] and [ɑ], but this need not concern us here.

own pronunciation. In addition, some vowel phones are lengthened, also to relative degrees. Fortunately, these minute differences of fronting, retracting, raising, lowering, and lengthening
are usually the result of environmental influences of consonant
sounds preceding or following the vowel or from the stress pattern
of the overall utterance. Thus, the determination of the vowel (or
vocalic) phonemes becomes fairly simple when the transcriber looks
for significant vowel contrasts. The vowel contrasts in the tongue-
position rectangle (Figure 4–2) with the accompanying list of
sample instances, are those represented in the writer's own
pronunciation, the Northern dialect of the Great Lakes area.

Some students who have taken courses in phonetics will perhaps be puzzled by the absence of the phone [ʌ], which most
phonetic textbooks designate as the *stressed* mid-central vowel,
contrasting with the unstressed mid-central vowel [ə]. The illustrative word for this contrast usually is *above* [əˈbʌv], as it is
recorded in the "broad" phonetic transcription of the textbooks.[4]
However, because the difference is one of stress, they can be considered allophones of /ə/, and we can transcribe *above* /əbə́v/. In
like manner, we have excluded the stressed and unstressed central
retroflex vowels, respectively [ɝ] and [ɚ], as contrasted in
further [ˈfɝðɚ]. Again, we will consider these as stress variants,
and indicate the sound diphthongally as /ər/, the vowel sound
gliding off into the retroflexive semivowel. Thus it is analogically
akin to the situation in *dear, pair,* and *four,* phonemically /dir, per,
for/.

Some of these vocalic phonemes diphthongalize; that is, they
pair up in contrastive situations. The following are the significant
diphthongs in the writer's own speech:

/ai/ bite /bait/
/au/ bout /baut/
/oi/ boy /boi/ (sometimes /ɔi/ : /bɔi/)
/iu/ abuse /əbiús/ (n.), /əbiúz/ (vb.)

The /iu/ diphthong in an initial position usually becomes /ju/, as
in *use* /jus/ (n.), indistinguishable from the semivowel on-glide. In

---

[4] In fact, most of these courses in phonetics ordinarily offered by speech or
English departments are for all practical purposes courses in *phonemics.*

dealing with diphthongs it should be remembered that they occur as the nucleus of a single syllable, and do not form two separate syllables. Thus we differentiate between *mare* /mer/ and *mayor* /méjər/.

Suprasegmental Phonemes (Stress)

Thus far we have discussed the so-called *segmental* phonemes of English, those which can be individually analyzed as segments and sequentially arranged in a linear string of sounds. Mention should be made here of the **suprasegmental** phonemes of stress, the relative loudness which is superimposed over a sequence of segmental phonemes, but unanalyzable as part of the linear sequence. We can recognize three such stress patterns: major stress, marked /ˊ/ over the vowel phoneme in the nucleus; minor stress, marked /ˋ/; and no stress, which is unmarked. Thus, for example, the stress markings for the word *elevator* would be *élevàtor*, showing major stress on the first syllable, minor stress on the third, and no stress on the second and fourth.

Summary

These phonemes represent the writer's own inventory, including twenty-four consonants, eleven vowels, and four diphthongs. Although there is not a set of exercises included here for transcription, it would be well for you to practice transcribing these sounds, both in isolated words and in clause combinations. Perhaps your instructor will give you a series of exercises along these lines. He might even want to modify somewhat the symbols used in transcribing, possibly introducing you to the Trager–Smith system of vowel analysis.[5] The possibility of variation should be

---

[5] The Trager–Smith system is based on nine vowel sounds, each representing one of the nine parts of the rectangle:

bit /bit/	i	i	u	put /put/
bet /bet/	e	ə	o	obey /obéj/
bat /bæt/	æ	a	ɔ	bought /bɔt/

But /bət/ — Botts /bats/

neither troublesome nor a proof of weakness. You are sure to find that other linguistic studies do not necessarily follow our particular system, which is not inviolable by any means; and in any event one can always refer to a key when in doubt. It should only be noted that I have found the system presented above to be useful both for historical and contemporary purposes, and we will be using it consistently throughout this text when it becomes necessary to refer to phonological patterns.

QUESTIONS AND EXERCISES—PHONOLOGY

1. How do the phonemes /ŋ/, /ž/, /j/, /w/, and /h/ differ from the other consonants in English?

2. Why is the expression "dropping one's *g*'s," as in *runnin'*, a misconception? What accounts for this popular misunderstanding? Explain what actually happens, making reference to phonemes.

3. What set of sounds do the nasals resemble? What are the principal differences?

4. Examine the vowel phonemes carefully in the light of your own pronunciation, especially the low vowels. What differences, if any, do you find? Can these differences be accommodated by the phonemic system here, or must you devise additional symbols?

5. Compare our English phonemes with those of any foreign language you have studied. What phonemes does the foreign language have which are lacking here? Conversely, which phonemes of English are absent from the phonemic inventory of the other language? How do you account for the difficulty which non-native speakers have with certain sounds in English? Do all non-native speakers have the same difficulties? Explain.

These are the "pure" vowels. All others diphthongalize, fronting with /-j/, retracting with /-w/, or centering with /-h/ or /-r/. Examples: *beat* /bijt/, *bait* /bejt/, *bite* /bajt/, *boy* /boj/, *butte* /bjuwt/ (actually a triphthong), *boot* /buwt/, *boat* /bowt/, *bout* /bawt/, further /fɔrðər/. The high-central /i/ is the vowel sound of *just* in "just a minute" /jist/, as opposed to "a just solution" /jəst/.

6. We have not included intonation, or pitch, in our discussion of suprasegmentals. This is characterized by the relative rise or fall of tone during an utterance. Thus a declarative statement, ^{2}*He is going*^{3} *home*^{1}↘, contrasts with a question, ^{2}*He is going*^{3} *home*^{3}↗ (the superscript numbers show relative pitch, with /^{1}/ being lowest and a hypothetical /^{4}/ highest, the arrows indicating falling and rising fade-out). What difficulties stand in the way of analyzing intonation in phonological terms? Why might intonation be more easily analyzed morphemically?

THE NOUN PHRASE

The English Noun

We are now ready to take a look at some of the principal structural features of Modern English. The first consideration is the expansion of what is called the **noun phrase.** It might seem odd to some of you to speak of the noun *phrase*, particularly when you tend to think of a phrase as a subordinate kind of modificational structure—specifically, a prepositional phrase. But when linguists speak of the *phrase*, they mean a cluster of words structurally grouped around a nuclear form—in the present instance, a noun. Thus they can examine the options which are open to the speaker when he comes to a noun phrase portion of an utterance, at the same time noting the specific ordering of these options, which is so important to Modern English.

But before we begin to look at the expansion of the nuclear noun into a noun phrase, we must be able to identify a noun in context. As we have noted before, the school grammar definition that a noun is "the name of a person, place, or thing" is of no actual use to anyone, first of all because it unconsciously presupposes that he can already identify nouns, and second because the definition itself must be expanded to accommodate all known notional concepts of nouns. We need to look in another quarter for our means of identification, and in turning to the actual formal occurrences of nouns, we have what is our best opportunity for determining that any given word is in fact a noun.

Noun Identification

There are four formal means of identifying nouns. In order of their importance, they are:

1. Proximity of **function words**—words with little or no lexical meaning of their own, used in the vicinity of the nuclear word.
2. **Grammatical inflections**—affixes (in English, suffixes), which add *grammatical* meaning to the word.
3. **Derivational suffixes**—bound morphs which, when added to another part of speech, turn it into a noun.
4. **Syntactic patterns**—when all else fails, the inspection of the word's syntactic position to see whether it conforms with observable patterns of known forms.

These are not foolproof, but it has been my experience that those students who are best able to identify parts of speech in school grammar exercises are actually applying these procedures, perhaps unconsciously.

For the noun, the commonest *function words* used with it are the articles, the definite article *the*, or the nondefinite article *a*, and its fellow, *an*. There are other function words—the demonstratives, for instance—but the articles occur most frequently (just notice how often *the* has occurred so far in this paragraph). There are only two *grammatical inflections* for the noun in English—$\{-Z_{pl}\}$, the plural morpheme, and $\{-Z_{gen}\}$, the genitive morpheme, both of which occur with relative frequency. On the other hand, there are many *derivational suffixes*: among the commonest are $\{-ness\}$, which turns an adjective into a noun; $\{-er\}$, which turns a verb into a noun; and $\{-ment\}$, which also turns a verb into a noun. You can detect more of these *nominalizing* suffixes simply by glancing at any printed page.

Syntactic patterns pose a certain amount of difficulty, in that technically one should not anticipate these patterns prior to formulating them. However, nearly everyone is sufficiently experienced with his native tongue to recognize the principal positions of any formal category. One means of identifying syntactically the English noun is to determine if the word fills the blank in a test frame like "The ———— is good," one of several such frames set up by Charles C. Fries.[6] Those with a reasonably good command of the structure of English can set up several functional positions for the noun. In general, the word is a noun if it functions as the principal nucleus of the subject of the sentence, the object of the verb, the complement of a copulative verb, or the object of a preposition. Unfortunately, if one is unable to identify these functional positions, he cannot apply these tests, and this is precisely why this fourth means of identifying nouns is the least satisfactory.

Nonetheless, despite a certain small amount of leakage, these remain the most satisfactory methods for determining whether any given word is a noun, or one of the other three parts of speech (verbs, adjectives, adverbs). *Man* is a noun. Why? Because you can say "the man," or "a man." You can say "men," or "man's." Further, it occurs predictably in "The man is good," or "I see the man," or "Give it to the man." However, its appearance in "The sailors *manned* the vessel" is the clearest indication that in this particular utterance it is neither inflectionally nor syntactically a noun, but something else.

This last point is important. No word out of context can be absolutely identified with assurance that it is one or another part of speech. Despite the fact that *green* and *red* generally occur as adjectives, in the sentence, "The *greens* are prettier than the *reds*," both occurrences are environmentally, inflectionally, and syntactically nouns. However, this fact does not keep linguists from making syntactical generalizations about English. We can therefore conclude that once a given word has been employed as a particular part of speech, it can be used predictably in the same manner again.

Slot-and-Filler (Tagmemic) Analysis

All this, however, is purely introductory. The main purpose here is to show how the immediate environment of the noun can be expanded into the noun phrase. And to this end, the best medium for the exposition of this linguistic phenomenon is that by-product

[6] See his *The Structure of English* (New York, 1952), chap. 5.

of tagmemics, the **slot-and-filler** approach. In the previous chapter, in which we reviewed some of the theoretical implications of this linguistic approach, it was stated that the analysis consisted of the revelation in a sentence of several layers, or *strata*, each of which had certain optional and mandatory slots which could be filled by specified forms. In general, there are five such levels, each of which uncovers the one beneath it. These five are:

sentence
clause
phrase
word
stem (primarily for derivational suffixes)

Each of these levels consists of both mandatory and optional slots that are filled by designated forms which reveal the level immediately beneath it. The slot generally names a grammatical function, and the filler supplies the forms which fulfill the function.

To forestall confusion, let's analyze a simple sentence similar to that which we used in the last chapter: *The boys read their books in the house.*[7] On the *sentence* level, we have a base slot, filled by an independent clause, plus the characteristic pitch pattern of the declarative sentence, the $/^{231}\searrow/$ pitch.[8] The *clause* level consists of a subject slot filled by a noun phrase, and a predicate slot filled by a transitive verbal, object, and locative. At this point, while still at the clause level, we have the phenomenon of **layering**: the setting of structures within structures. Here the object filler itself is filled by a noun phrase; and the locative filler is filled by a relator plus an object, which object itself is filled by a noun phrase. At the *phrase* level, each of the noun phrases consists of a limiter slot, filled by a determiner, and a head slot, filled by a count noun,

---

[7] This analysis is for illustrative purposes only. Ordinarily I do not recommend exercises which simply call for the reverse analysis of sentences already formed, a process ultimately as sterile as traditional diagramming. Slot-and-filler analysis, a branch of tagmemic theory, provides a revelatory system for the details of the theory, not a means for classroom exercises.

[8] The tagmemic formula would read, "Sentence = Base: Ind. Clause + $/^{231}\searrow/$"; that is, the sentence level consists of a base slot, filled by an independent clause and $/^{231}\searrow/$ intonation. Where later levels require choices and options, the formula shorthand includes the sign + for mandatory slots and fillers, and ± for optional ones.

Base: *Independent Clause* + /²³¹↘/ *Pitch*

Morpheme	Word (class)	Phrase element	Phrase	Clause element
The	Article	Limiter (Determiner)	Noun Phrase	Subject
boy	N	Head (Count Noun)	Noun Phrase	Subject
$-Z_{pl}$	No.	Head (Count Noun)	Noun Phrase	Subject
$-D_{past}$	Tense	Aux	Transitive Verbal	Predicate
read	Tr. Verb	Main Verb	Transitive Verbal	Predicate
they	Pron.	Limiter (Determiner)	Noun Phrase	Object (Predicate)
$-Z_{gen}$	Gen.	Limiter (Determiner)	Noun Phrase	Object (Predicate)
book	N	Head (Count Noun)	Noun Phrase	Object (Predicate)
$-Z_{pl}$	No.	Head (Count Noun)	Noun Phrase	Object (Predicate)
in	Pre-position	Relator		Locative (Predicate)
the	Article	Limiter (Determiner)	Noun Phrase	Locative Object (Predicate)
house	N	Head (Count Noun)	Noun Phrase	Locative Object (Predicate)
ø	No.	Head (Count Noun)	Noun Phrase	Locative Object (Predicate)

The + boy + Z_{pl} + $-D_{past}$ + read + they + $-Z_{gen}$ + book + $-Z_{pl}$ + in + the + house + ø

The   boys   read   their   books   in   the   house

Figure 4–3.

a category of nouns which can take the plural inflection. At this point, having gotten to the *word* level, a written description becomes confusing, and it is much easier to refer to Figure 4–3 for the complete slot-and-filler analysis.

As the diagram shows, the end result of the slot-and-filler analysis is a complete linear string of morphemes. In the present instance, the string would be {the + boy + -Z_{pl} + -D_{past} + read + they + -Z_{gen} + book + -Z_{pl} + in + the + house + ø}. Application of the necessary morphophonemic procedures would give us the original sentence which we set out to analyze.[9] The important factor here is the point that this analysis gives us the needed orderly arrangement of morphemes, the **string.** This end result underlines the importance of the order of forms in English, plus the perhaps self-evident point that the speaker *of any language* can make but one utterance at any given time, thus uttering what is in effect a linear string of morphemes. This analysis simply uncovers the linear arrangement of forms to which the speaker must adhere if he wishes to be understood. Though it is not shown in the diagram, a by-product of this analysis is a set of restrictions on certain fillers which are included or excluded by virtue of the selection of one specific kind of filler over another. For instance, the choice of a plural form with a count noun precludes the selection of *a* or *an* to fill the article slot of the determiner.

The Expansion of the Noun Phrase

This rather limited introduction to the slot-and-filler analysis of the sentence leaves a certain number of points unstressed. For instance, it does not show that the **determiner** filler of the limiter slot is the only category under the noun phrase, other than the noun nucleus itself, which is mandatory. And further, it does not show any of the optional slots and fillers at the phrase level. We need, therefore, to look more closely at the expansion of the noun phrase.

---

[9] The final string has the puzzling characteristic of listing the verb tense inflection before the verb. This strange state of affairs will be clarified in the next section, when we examine the verb phrase.

We can begin by taking the noun *book* as our nucleus and try to fill in the slots around it. The most obvious expansion which comes to our mind is the **article:** *the* book, or *a* book. However, we have already noted in the last chapter that there are other forms which can take the place of these articles. We can say *this* book, *that* book, *any* book, *his* book but we cannot say *a this book, or *the his book. All of these forms—articles, demonstratives, and nouns with genitive inflections—come under the general heading of *determiners*, and all are included in the class because they may be used interchangeably, but cannot be used in combination. Further, there are additional choices available when the optional plural ending is added to the noun head: *these, those, some*; though *a/an* is thereby eliminated from consideration.[10] Finally, this is the one noun phrase category which, as we said before, must be filled; all others, save for the nuclear noun itself, are optional.

Immediately, we can find what seem to be instances that contradict this last statement. There are many examples of nouns which seem to function without any determiner at all. For instance, we can easily make up such grammatical utterances as "I spent too much money on books." The fact is that *books* only appears to be without a determiner. In actuality, the speaker has made a subconscious decision to select what is called a "zero" determiner, symbolized by ø, which carries with it a kind of meaning of its own. Notice, for example, what would happen to the statement if we selected *my, the, these, those,* or *some*, rather than ø, in the sentence just cited. Thus, our statement stands: some form of determiner must fill the limiter slot in the noun phrase.[11]

Premodifier Slots

With this out of the way, we can turn to some other possible means of expanding the sequence. The next way that comes immediately to mind is by adding an **adjective:** "the *new* book." Note here that it is possible to add a long string of adjectives to the

[10] Even though $\{-Z_{pl}\}$ is contextually mandatory, it is always *grammatically* optional.

[11] Warning is hereby posted against trying to posit a ø form in any other positional filler under the noun phrase. Only with the determiner is any meaning gained by selecting the ø form.

noun phrase. We can say "the *new blue* book" or "the *beautiful new* book." Because we can add as many adjectives as we like, we say that this is the one slot under the noun phrase which is **recursive.**[12] Further, each adjective can be preceded by a **qualifier:** "the *rather* new, *deep* blue book." This is an optional instance of layering, not requiring a new slot. Finally, each adjective can be inflected comparatively (the morpheme {-er}, sometimes pre-empted by the qualifier *more*): "the new*er* book." But the adjective under this modifier slot cannot be inflected superlatively; that belongs to another slot.

Our sample noun phrase is further expanded by filling the **attribute** slot immediately before the noun head. This is filled with a noun; thus, "the new *history* book." If you feel that *history* is somehow adjectival, notice that one cannot say **the history new book*. The noun attribute is rather common in English, which makes rather foolish the often-heard prohibition that one shouldn't use a noun "to modify another noun." To begin with, the noun is used attributively, not as a modifier; and if there is something awkward about specific occurrences of the noun attribute + noun construction, the fault is stylistic, not grammatical.

Together, the modifier and the attribute slots make up the optional **premodifier** category on the phrase level. We have thus far shown only one of the *limiters*, the determiner. There are four other distinct categories which fill this slot, and it is best that we collect them all now.

Limiter Slots

We might consider first the role of the numerals. Though they are frequently thought of as a kind of adjective, they actually are part of the limiter fillers. In addition, there are two kinds of

[12] One point which still requires investigation is the precedence of the recursive adjectives in a string. We do not, for example, say **the blue new book*. Sometimes precedence is determined when the first adjective modifies all of the succeeding noun phrase, as in our second example above. On the other hand, precedence seems to be of little importance when each adjective independently modifies the noun head, as in *the beautiful, wonderful, adventurous book*. In a situation like this, each adjective is given equal stress when spoken, and in writing, each is set off with commas.

It would appear that the $N + -Z_{gen}$ filler for the determiner slot is recursive: "John's wife's cousin." Actually, this is another instance of layering, *John's* being the determiner filler for *wife*, and the combination being the determiner filler for *cousin*.

numerals, **ordinal** and **cardinal,** each making up separate slots. We can expand our noun phrase, therefore, to read "the *first three* new history books," with an ordinal numeral (including *last*) preceding a cardinal numeral. (Notice that filling these slots in this manner has forced the choice of the plural.) Another expansion is the **particularizer** slot, which can be filled either with a **specifier,** a limited category consisting basically of the words *other, same, chief, only, whole,* or with an adjective plus a superlative inflection (the morpheme {-est}, sometimes indicated by the qualifier *most*). This slot is not fixed; it can come either after the determiner or after the cardinal slot, but usually not both places at once. Thus we can further expand our sample phrase to "the first three *other* new history books," or "the *other* first three new history books." You will note that placement of the particularizer depends solely upon the presence of the ordinal and cardinal slots.

There is one more limiter, the **predeterminer.** This slot can be filled either by the words *both, all, half,* or by a quantity word or phrase plus *of.* A quantity word can be something on the order of *most, lots, four* (including the three just mentioned), among others, and a quantity phrase can include *a little, a great big bunch,* or the like. The important thing is that it expresses a quantity, whether definitely or by implication. Thus we can expand our sample phrase to read "*all (of)* the first three other new history books," the parentheses around *of* showing that for *all,* as well as *both* and *half,* it is optional. The fact of the predeterminer itself points back to a statement made in Chapter 2, when, in the course of discussing some of the weaknesses of school grammar, it was noted that in the sentence "Some of my friends gave me a birthday present yesterday," students have objected to the analysis of *some* as the subject of the sentence. We can see now that *some of* is the predeterminer, and the noun head is *friends,* with an optional plural contextually required in this instance—the selection of a predeterminer ordinarily forces the selection of the plural.[13]

---

[13] Part of the problem lies in the fact that the singular quantity word often governs the singular person marker in the present tense of the verb: "One of my students has the measles." Instances like this undoubtedly influenced the thinking of the school grammarians. However, this is not always the case: "A portion of my friends have new cars"; *but*, "A portion of his library was given away." Here the nuclear noun affects the person marker.

Postmodifier Slots

For the noun phrase, then, we have uncovered the following slots: a mandatory *limiter*, filled by a *predeterminer*, *determiner*, *ordinal*, *cardinal*, and *particularizer*, all optional save the determiner, and all in this order, except the unfixed particularizer; and an optional *premodifier*, filled by a *modifier* and an *attribute*; plus the mandatory *head*, of course, the nuclear noun. There is still one more category to be covered, the optional **postmodifier**, which follows the head. This category is much less definite as to the recursive features of its slots, but it can be filled by three successive slots: the **adverb**, normally a locative adverb, or adverb of place; the **phrase**, filled by a prepositional phrase, itself usually an adverbial of place; and a **clause**, filled with a relative clause. Thus we can finally expand our phrase to read, "all of the first three other new history books *there on the table, which I told you to take upstairs.*" Notice that to fill the phrase and clause slots, we must revert to the phrase and clause levels, another instance of layering.[14]

To understand the slot-and-filler order of the noun phrase, you might make reference to Figure 4–4, which shows both the phrase and the word level, with some of the fillers on the word level. The chart shows the rigid nature of English word order in the noun phrase, an order for which there is no logic, at least as we can see it, but which is, in its own way, rigorously absolute. Close study of the diagram will also reveal the *function* of each of the slots, which in standard tagmemic analysis is considered to be more important than their ranking. Be that as it may, the ordering of forms can itself be of importance and interest, especially to those of us so familiar with it as to be unaware of the system. The order is further clarified in the diagram by numbering each word slot by its relationship with the nuclear noun. What the diagram does not show, however, is the elimination of certain options when one selects a certain kind of nuclear noun.

---

[14] The same is true of the predeterminer slot, which can be filled with a quantity phrase, such as *a great big bunch of boys*, and thus constitutes yet another instance of layering.

Noun Phrase

Limiter				Premodifier			Head	Postmodifier		
Pre-determiner	Determiner	Ordinal	Cardinal	Particularizer	Modifier	Attribute	Nucleus	Adverb	Phrase	Clause
Quantity + of both all half	Article Demonstrative $N + \{-Z_{gen}\}$	Ordinal Numeral	Cardinal Numeral	Specifier Adjective + {-est}	Adjective (+ Adj . . .)	Proper Noun Count Noun Mass Noun	Proper Noun Pronoun Count Noun Mass Noun	Locative Adverb	Prepositional Phrase	Relative Clause
$N - 7$	$N - 6$	$N - 5$	$N - 4$	$N - 3$	$N - 2$	$N - 1$	N	$N + 1$	$N + 2$	$N + 3$

Note: The particularizer slot $(N - 3)$ may precede the ordinal slot $(N - 5)$. The filler for the modifier slot $(N - 2)$ is recursive.

Figure 4-4.

Restrictions on Selections

When one has selected a **proper noun,** for instance, like *John,* or *Salt Lake City,* or *England,* one's further choices are greatly reduced. The only limiters you can select are the predeterminer and the determiner ø. The selection of predeterminer is governed to a large extent by the geographical and physical properties of that symbolized by the nuclear proper noun. We can, for example, say "All of North Dakota is covered with snow," or "Half of England was destroyed by bombing," but it's hard to find a suitable sentence in which to place "Half of John . . . ." It is interesting to note that the clause, which is the sole postmodifier option for the proper noun, can only be what is called a **nonrestrictive** or **appositional clause.** Thus we say "John, who is my friend, . . ." or "Salt Lake City, which is the capital of Utah, . . ."—the clauses in both instances being no more than frosting on the cake. The proper noun, in any instance, is unique, hence able to get along without them.

The restrictions on the **pronoun** are almost as rigorous. Again, we must exclude the premodifiers, but in the limiter we can again select the predeterminer and the mandatory ø article of the determiner. If we select a predeterminer, we must, in addition, change the pronoun to its objective case form. Thus, *we,* but *some of us; they,* but *a certain number of them.* Unlike the proper noun, the pronoun can have any or all of the forms filling the postmodifier slot.

The **mass noun,** a category which includes words taken as uncountable quantities, like *sugar, salt, sand, grain, learning, people,* is considerably less restrictive in our choice of expansions.[15] In fact, the only slots which are denied the mass noun are the ordinal and the cardinal. All the others are open. However, there are some restrictions within the fillers: in the predeterminer, *both* and *half* cannot be selected; and in the determiner, we are limited to

---

[15] It should be noted that in certain contexts many mass nouns do become, after some change of meaning, count nouns. It is important to recognize the change of meaning. *Grain* in "The *grain* is in the bag" is a mass noun, but in "little *grains* of sand" it is a count noun. To save your sanity, it's best to think of such instances as two completely different forms which just happen to sound alike.

the articles ø, *the*, and *any*, the demonstratives *this* and *that*, and noun + {-Z$_{gen}$}.

All of the fillers of all the slots are opened to the **count noun,** though the selection of the plural makes some available (as the demonstratives *these* and *those*) which were not available to the base form. We might also note here that the selection of the article *a/an*, and such other nondefinite articles as *any* and *some*, forces a restrictive clause, should the clause slot in the postmodifier be selected.

There are other restrictions on certain selections, not to mention a few moot points, both of which will be taken up in the exercises. The important thing here, however, is to note the complete regularity of the slots under the phrase stratum, and to see the absolute necessity of this regularity. This ordering of the noun phrase comes with unconscious ease to the native speaker of English. In fact, it is so apparently self-evident to us that unless its complexity is consciously noted, we are not aware of the trouble which non-native speakers may have with it. Out of simple perplexity, the non-native will probably try to superimpose his own native pattern upon English, with results which are at best confusing, and at worst chaotic. Recognition of the patterning of the noun phrase, then, will help us to appreciate the complexity of our language, and to marvel at our ability to have learned it by the age of six. It also demonstrates the supreme importance of word order in the grammar of English.

QUESTIONS AND EXERCISES—THE NOUN PHRASE

1. In the preceding portion of this chapter, we have seen how the expansion of the noun phrase follows certain rigid patterns of word order. In particular, we have seen how the other parts of speech are ordered in this sequence around the nuclear noun, and how they function. How does this expansion of the noun phrase point out the insufficiency and incompleteness of the school grammar definitions of the noun, the pronoun, the adverb, and the adjective?

2. Some of you may have boggled a bit at the final result of the noun phrase expansion, and I have to admit at this point that it is not an especially elegant example of English prose. What problem does this illustrate which goes along with the expansion of the noun phrase? How does this account for the relatively few instances of a fully expanded noun phrase in contemporary English writing?

3. The explanation of the noun phrase should account for almost all of its occurrences that you will be likely to encounter. However, the English language is a changing phenomenon which refuses to be pinned down absolutely. Therefore, it should not be surprising if there are a few loose ends which are not accounted for in our description. Study the occurrences, or possible occurrences, of *few, some, no, (a) certain*. Where would you place them in the slot-and-filler system of the noun phrase, and what characteristics do they have which make their placement difficult? To what extent do they tend to invalidate our analysis?

4. What restrictions on your choice of fillers for other slots are laid down by the selection of a *singular* count noun? In like manner, what choices are gained and lost by the addition of $\{-Z_{pl}\}$ to a nuclear count noun?

5. We have shown how a nuclear proper noun, with the mandatory selection of the ø article in the determiner slot, forces a *nonrestrictive* clause in the optional clause slot; and we have made some tentative comments about the nondefinite articles forcing a *restrictive* clause if the clause slot option is taken. Test these two slots with other determiners to find what specific pattern emerges here. How do your findings help to clarify a minor, though knotty, problem in the teaching of composition?

6. In connection with exercise 2, chart the frequency of occurrences of the combinations of various fillers (e.g., non-definite article + count noun; predeterminer + definite article + adjective + count noun; etc.) as they occur over several pages of contemporary prose. Compare the usage of several different authors. Do any variations of patterns emerge which might help in forming generalizations about style? What is the frequency ratio of long expansions to relatively short ones?

7. Before going on to the next section of this chapter, list some of the specific means by which we can identify the verb in context, using the four devices which we used to identify nouns.

THE VERB PHRASE

Verb Identification

If you have done your assignments diligently up to this point, and specifically exercise 7 in the preceding section, you should be able to identify a **verb** in its context. To sum up, a verb may be inflected to show present or past tense, or past or present perfect forms (using school grammar terminology). It may be accompanied by function words normally called *auxiliaries* (we will call them *modals*, for reasons which will become apparent shortly), or *have* or *be*. Other parts of speech may become verbs by the addition of a derivational suffix, such as *-ize* or *-en*, and there is even a derivational prefix *en-*. And if all else fails, we can determine by analysis that the verb normally occurs after a noun phrase subject and before a noun phrase object. We can turn now to the analysis of the verb in its regular milieu, the **verb phrase.**

Generating the Verb Phrase

For the purposes of this phrase of our analysis, we shall use the generative portion of transformational grammar, by which we can *generate* the kernel sentence, with special attention to the verb phrase, from its deep structure generalities to its surface structure specificity. The basis of transformational grammar was outlined in the preceding chapter; what remains is to show how it operates, with reference to the verb phrase, and what it reveals to us about the verb phrase in the context of the kernel sentence. This is accomplished through nine procedural steps, which are not as difficult as they look, though they might appear forbiddingly formulaic at first. The transformational grammarian does not claim that we actually follow these procedures in forming grammatical utterances—no one really knows how these complex mental processes work—but these procedures do present an economical way of revealing how the sentence-forming operations can be done.

The first procedure is the one which we have already encountered:

(1) S → NP + VP

Plainly stated, this rule indicates that the most basic underlying concept of the sentence may be rewritten as a noun phrase plus a verb phrase. This does not mean that every sentence in its final form actually consists of a noun phrase and a verb phrase, in that order. What this basic statement does say is that *underlying* every sentence in its final form is the concept NP + VP, altered and shaped by succeeding procedural statements and transformations. In fact, some grammarians believe that this concept underlies all language, and may be taken as a linguistic universal. Some of you may be tempted to reread this statement as "S → Subject + Predicate," which is all right, provided that you realize that you are making a statement about the *function* of the elements in this procedure, and not the *structure* itself. It will be the structural hierarchy which will concern us here, not functional analysis.

We will not develop further the NP portion of our equation. There is a sequence of procedures by which we can generate the surface structure of the noun phrase, the end result of which is identical with our slot-and-filler analysis, with the exception of modification. To the thorough-going transformational grammarian, modification results from transformational operations upon a sentence embedded within the generated noun phrase. Thus, *the red barn* results from a series of surface rearrangements and deletions upon the terminal string "the barn (the barn is red) . . ." For purposes of the present analysis, however, we can consider every occurrence of NP to be ultimately identical with the end result of our slot-and-filler analysis.

With this in mind, we can now follow out the rewriting of VP. Thus our next rewrite procedure:

(2) VP → Aux + MV

Or, the verb phrase is rewritten as **auxiliary** plus the **main verb.**

There is a tendency to consider both of these concepts too narrowly. Students are apt to think of *auxiliary* solely in terms of the so-called auxiliary verbs, which our next procedure will prove false, and that the *main verb* is synonymous with "verb" itself. Granted that the terms seem to be imprecise, it should still be remembered that though they have been borrowed from school grammar, successive rewrite procedures will define them in quite a different way. Thus, we could rewrite VP as X + Y, so long as successive rewrite procedures lead us to generate a grammatical utterance. We prefer, however, to stick to terms which are familiar, but we must not permit our familiarity with them to obscure the fact that we are viewing them differently.

The Verb Phrase Auxiliary

Procedure (2) shows the basic division of the deep structure concept of VP into two parts, each of which needs to be redefined. We can begin with the auxiliary:

(3) Aux → Tn (M) (have + -D$_{\text{part}}$) (be + -ing)

This step seems formidably complex, and we do need to study it carefully, but in reality it elucidates rather neatly a very complicated aspect of Modern English. The elements closed in parentheses are optional; thus the one mandatory element is **tense.** If any or all of the optional elements are selected, they must occur in this order.

Before we can explain all of the ramifications of this procedure, we should pause for a moment to rewrite *tense*:

$$(4) \quad \text{Tn} \rightarrow \left\{ \begin{array}{l} \text{-Z}_{\text{pres}} \\ \text{-D}_{\text{past}} \end{array} \right\}$$

The braces indicate that a choice *must* be made between the elements enclosed, selecting one and only one of the possible choices. We see, then, that *tense* resolves itself into a choice between **present** and **past,** the former manifested structurally only in the so-called third person singular, present indicative inflection.

With this out of the way, we can resume our discussion of the definition of Aux. The procedure states that the auxiliary is rewritten as a mandatory tense (past or present) plus an optional *modal*, plus an optional *have* + -D$_{part}$ (sometimes called **phase**), plus an optional *be* + *-ing* (sometimes called **aspect**). A *lexical* rule will permit us to list the actual instances of the modal:

(3a) M → shall, will, can, may, must[16]

By arbitrarily (and momentarily) selecting *walk* as our MV, we can see how Aux might work out on the surface of language.

For instance, suppose that for Aux we took only the mandatory Tn and none of the options, and from the choices given for Tn we selected -D$_{past}$. Our terminal string would be:

—D$_{past}$ + walk

Already, we can see objections. We *know* that the tense inflection does not precede the verb. As it happens, the grammarians who perfected this system were aware of this, too, and they have devised a transformational rule which states, in effect, that every occurrence of Tn, -D$_{part}$, and *-ing* in the terminal string is reversed, *one time only*, with the verb form following it. The transformational procedure may be stated as follows:

af + v ⇒ v + af #[17]

where *af* stands for Tn, -D$_{part}$, or *-ing*; and *v* stands for a verb, M, *have*, or *be*. The double cross (#) acts as a barrier to prevent the procedure from occurring more than once with the same *af* or *v* elements. Where the need for it occurs, this transformational procedure is mandatory. Thus:

-D$_{past}$ + walk ⇒ walk + -D$_{past}$ # (walked)

No doubt you are thinking that this "flip-flop" is a stupid encumbrance, unnecessarily complicating things. I agree that its necessity might be unfortunate, but there seems to be no simpler way of rewriting Aux—and simplicity is fundamental in grammatical description. The problem evolves from the optional elements of the Aux. If there were only Tn, the rule could be written to show

---

[16] Some grammarians would add *ought to, need to, have to, be going to,* and perhaps *dare.* With *must* (and *ought to*) the Tn choice is limited to -Z$_{pres}$.

[17] The double arrow (⇒) indicates a transformational procedure, and can be read, "is transformed into." Owen Thomas (*Transformational Grammar and the Teacher of English,* p. 60) calls this the *flip-flop* rule, which is inelegant, but perfectly clear.

the tense element following its verb. However, the presence of M and the elements making up *phase* and *aspect* complicates the picture. The Tn, for instance, is always attached to the first verb or verblike element in the VP. Likewise, for *phase*, the element *have* requires {-D$_{part}$}, the past participle morpheme, to be attached to the verb or verblike element following; and in *aspect*, the element *be* requires the present participle morpheme {-ing} to be attached to the verb following. If all the elements in Aux were mandatory, the procedure for VP could read:

$$*M + Tn + have + be + -D_{part} + MV + -ing$$

But because all the elements of Aux are optional except Tn, such a procedural statement would require a good many further statements to attach -D$_{part}$, for instance, to the MV in place of- *ing*, if the *aspect* option was not taken, and so on. Further, we will later see that there are portions of the MV which cannot be followed by the affix elements of Aux. Consequently, procedure (3) seems to be the simplest way of rewriting Aux, despite the seemingly backward order and the extra need for the "flip-flop" transformation.

Now that we hopefully have clarified the order of the elements and the need for their rearrangement, we can test them with some other terminal strings, using some of the options available to us. Thus:

(a) Tn + M + MV
     -D$_{past}$ + shall + walk $\Rightarrow$ shall + -D$_{past}$ # walk
                                           (should walk)

(b) Tn + M + have + -D$_{part}$ + MV
     -D$_{past}$ + shall + have + -D$_{part}$ + walk $\Rightarrow$ shall
     + -D$_{past}$ # have + walk + -D$_{part}$ # (should have
                                               walked)

(c) Tn + M + have + -D$_{part}$ + be + -ing + MV
     -D$_{past}$ + shall + have + -D$_{part}$ + be + -ing + walk
     $\Rightarrow$ shall + -D$_{past}$ # have + be + -D$_{part}$ # walk
                           + -ing # (should have been walking)

By taking some of the options and omitting others, you can work out the other terminal strings generated by procedures (3) and (4).

The Elements of the Main Verb

Procedure (4) ends our consideration of the Aux portion of VP. With it, we come to the surface of that deep structure concept. We can turn now to the operations which generate the surface structure of MV.

$$
(5) \quad MV \rightarrow \left\{ \begin{array}{l} V \\ be + \left\{ \begin{array}{l} NP \\ Adj \\ Loc \end{array} \right\} \end{array} \right\} (Adv)
$$

This procedure gives us choices within choices. We must select either a **verbal,** which will be further defined below, or *be* plus either a **noun phrase,** an **adjective,** or a **locative.** We have already considered the NP, and the adjective is fairly self-explanatory. The *locative* is that element which, in school grammar terminology, answers the question "Where?" Thus, a lexicon for Loc would list such items as *there, upstairs, in the house,* etc. The selection of *be* plus one of the three further choices would result in something akin to the following structures, involving what is often called a **complement:**

(The boy) is a student. (NP)

(The boy) is handsome. (Adj)

(The boy) is in the house. (Loc)

Note that for either selection in the rewrite procedure for MV, we have the option of an **adverbial.** This must itself be further defined:

(6) Adv → (Loc) (Tm)

The **time** adverbial, again reverting to familiar terminology, answers the question "When?" Included in its lexicon would be such items as *tomorrow* and *in an hour.*

We must now pick up the concept *verbal* and follow its operation to conclude the discussion of the VP:

$$
(7) \quad V \rightarrow \left\{ \begin{array}{l} V_i \ (Man) \\ VT \\ VC \end{array} \right\}
$$

You have probably determined that these choices refer respectively to **intransitive, transitive,** and **copulative** verbs. When the classification is written as a subscript, as in V_i, it indicates that this is its surface state, and you need only to consult the lexicon to complete the terminal string. The intransitive verb choice completes the operation for that portion of VP, but procedures are still pending for VT and VC. The lexicon for V_i would include an almost inexhaustible list, from which *walk, talk, come* may be taken as typical. **Man,** the **manner** adverbial, optional after V_i, answers the question "How?"—as *hopefully, gladly, in a pleasant manner,* etc. Thus, a possible terminal string which included the Man option might be:

Tn + V_i + Man

-D_{past} + speak + hopefully $\Rightarrow$ speak + -D_{past} #

hopefully (spoke hopefully)

Or, if one included the Adv options from procedure (6):

Tn + V_i + Man + Loc + Tm

-D_{past} + speak + hopefully + at the office + yesterday

$\Rightarrow$ speak + -D_{past} # hopefully + at the office + yesterday

(spoke hopefully at the office yesterday)

There are all sorts of further combinations, including the optional elements of Aux.

It remains then to consider VT and VC in turn.

$$(8) \quad VT \rightarrow \left\{ \begin{cases} V_t \\ V_{oc} \end{cases} + NP \ (Man) \atop V_{mid} + NP \right\}$$

The lexicon for V_t should be examined a bit. In addition to the basic transitive verbs, as *read, write, drive,* etc., we can have such verb + **particle** combinations as *look over, turn on, bring in* and such verb + **preposition** combinations as *speak to* and *look at.* The difference between the particle and the preposition is that the former may be removed from its position immediately following the verb and placed at the end of the sentence; thus:

look over the assignment $\Rightarrow$ look the assignment over

turn on the motor $\Rightarrow$ turn the motor on

But we cannot say *speak me to* or *look me at*. Thinking in terms of verb + particle and verb + preposition helps to clarify a knotty problem of school grammar. We can differentiate between:

He *ran up* the bill (verb + particle)

and,

He *ran up the hill* (V_i + Loc)

The V_{oc}, or **objective complement** verb, consists of a rather unwieldy conflation in its lexicon. It would include *elect president* and *call a liar*. Note that the surface structure would usually call for a transformational rule reversing the position of the objective complement and the NP object:

elect president + John ⇒ elect John president

call a liar + John ⇒ call John a liar

The V_{mid}, or **middle verb** consists of a fairly limited number of what might be called quantitative verbs: *have, cost, weigh*, etc. Note that whereas all of the choices open to the VT must have a NP object, the V_{mid} cannot be followed by the Man option. ** The candy bar costs ten cents gladly* is clearly ungrammatical.

The following sample terminal strings summarize the basic possibilities of procedure (8):

(a) Tn + V_t + NP + Man

-D_{past} + see + the engine + clearly ⇒ see + -D_{past} #
the engine + clearly (saw the engine clearly)

with *verb + particle*:

-D_{past} + look + over + the engine + carefully
⇒ look + -D_{past} # over + the engine + carefully
(looked over the engine carefully) *or* look + -D_{past} # the
engine + over + carefully (looked the engine over
carefully)

with *verb + preposition*:

-D_{past} + look + at + the engine + carefully ⇒ look
+ -D_{past} # at + the engine + carefully (looked at the
engine carefully)

(b) $Tn + V_{oc} + NP + Man$

    $-D_{past} +$ give a present $+$ John $+$ ceremoniously

    $\Rightarrow$ give $+ -D_{past} \#$ John $+$ a present $+$ ceremoniously

                    (gave John a present ceremoniously)

(c) $Tn + V_{mid} + NP$

    $-D_{past} +$ own $+$ a car $\Rightarrow$ own $+ -D_{past} \#$ a car

                               (owned a car)

You should practice with samples of your own, including in them the options available in procedures (3), (4), and (6).

Several points should be noted from these sample derivations. By means of a transformational procedure, the manner adverbial can be moved to the front of the VP for stylistic reasons. Also, the apparent surface ambiguity of *looked over the engine* can be resolved by referring to the terminal string. In the sense of "scrutinize closely," the string would be $-D_{past} + V_t +$ particle $+$ NP; whereas if *over* meant "above," the string would be $-D_{past} + V_i +$ Loc. It is because of this surface ambiguity that the particle is often moved to the position immediately following the NP object. Finally, the procedure involving V_{oc} is not sufficiently detailed to cover all the ins and outs of this complex form, but since the purpose of this presentation is introductory, there is really no need at this point to do more than show in a general way how it operates.

We come finally to the last operation, the procedure stemming from the selection of VC:

$$(9) \quad VC \rightarrow \left\{ \begin{array}{l} V_s + Adj \\[2ex] V_{ap} + \text{to be} + \begin{pmatrix} NP \\ Adj \\ Loc \end{pmatrix} \\[3ex] V_{ac} + Adj \text{ (Man)} \\[2ex] \textit{become} + \begin{Bmatrix} NP \\ Adj \end{Bmatrix} \\[2ex] \textit{stay}/\textit{remain} + \begin{pmatrix} NP \\ Adj \\ Loc \end{pmatrix} \end{array} \right\}$$

To clarify somewhat the large number of choices and the selections and options open to each, we need to refer to the following partial listing of the rather limited lexicons of the principal categories:

V_s (sensory verbs) $\rightarrow$ seem, taste, smell . . .

V_{ap} (verbs of appearance) $\rightarrow$ seem, appear, happen . . .

V_{ac} (action verbs) $\rightarrow$ grow, turn . . .

The ellipsis marks after the word list indicate that the lexicon is open and that other words can be added to it. Note that *seem* can be either a V_s or a V_{ap}; this is indicative of a larger truth: any given word can fit into several categories. For example, in "he ate greedily," *eat* is a V_i, whereas in "he ate the meat," it is a V_t. You should bear this in mind; the elements of English are surprisingly flexible, which is something dictionary labels don't always indicate.

The basic features of the copulative verb category are summarized here, with reference to the ninth rewrite statement.

(a) Sensory verbs

$\quad$ -D_{past} + feel + strange $\Rightarrow$ feel + -D_{past} # strange

$\qquad\qquad\qquad\qquad\qquad\qquad\qquad\qquad$ (felt strange)

$\quad$ -D_{past} + taste + terrible $\Rightarrow$ taste + -D_{past} # terrible

$\qquad\qquad\qquad\qquad\qquad\qquad\qquad\qquad$ (tasted terrible)

(b) Verbs of appearance

$\quad$ with NP:

$\quad$ -D_{past} + happen + to be + a hat $\Rightarrow$ happen + -D_{past} #

$\qquad\qquad\qquad$ to be + a hat (happened to be a hat)

$\quad$ with Adj:

$\quad$ -D_{past} + happen + to be + funny $\Rightarrow$ happen + -D_{past} #

$\qquad\qquad\qquad$ to be + funny (happened to be funny)

$\quad$ with Loc:

$\quad$ -D_{past} + happen + to be + there $\Rightarrow$ happen + -D_{past} #

$\qquad\qquad\qquad$ to be + there (happened to be there)

(c) Action verbs

-D_{past} + grow + old + gracefully ⇒ grow + -D_{past} #
old + gracefully (grew old gracefully)

-D_{past} + turn + green + slowly ⇒ turn + -D_{past} #
green + slowly (turned green slowly)

(d) *Become*

with NP:

-D_{past} + become + a lady ⇒ become + -D_{past} # a lady
(became a lady)

with Adj:

-D_{past} + become + foolish ⇒ become + -D_{past} #
foolish (became foolish)

(e) *Stay/remain*

with NP:

-D_{past} + stay + friends ⇒ stay + -D_{past} # friends
(stayed friends)

with Adj:

-D_{past} + remain + good ⇒ remain + -D_{past} # good
(remained good)

with Loc:

-D_{past} + stay + home ⇒ stay + -D_{past} # home
(stayed home)

Notice that except for the action verbs, the manner adverbial option cannot be taken. Again, as with procedures (7) and (8), you should work out further instances on your own, gradually increasing their complexity by taking the options offered in previous steps.

Summary

This completes our survey of the verb phrase, using the technique of generative grammar, moving from the generalized deep structure concept of VP down to the surface structure. You should note certain basic points, particularly that these nine operations summarize a remarkably complex sequence of relationships, culminating in procedures (7), (8), and (9). Procedure (3), with its rewriting of Aux into its linear order, reveals a feature of the VP which native speakers of English tend to take for granted, and which school grammar paradigms obscure. With practice in following each step in the VP operation and studying the discussion questions and exercises which follow, you should become familiar with the whole pattern. Familiarity is crucial in the next chapter, and in the chapters to come.

Résumé of procedures for generating the verb phrase:

(1) $S \rightarrow NP + VP$

(2) $VP \rightarrow Aux + MV$

(3) $Aux \rightarrow Tn$ (M) (have + -D_{part}) (be + -ing)

(4) $Tn \rightarrow \begin{Bmatrix} \text{-}Z_{pres} \\ \text{-}D_{past} \end{Bmatrix}$

(5) $MV \rightarrow \begin{Bmatrix} V \\ be + \begin{Bmatrix} NP \\ Adj \\ Loc \end{Bmatrix} \end{Bmatrix}$ (Adv)

(6) $Adv \rightarrow$ (Loc) (Tm)

(7) $V \rightarrow \begin{Bmatrix} V_i \text{ (Man)} \\ VT \\ VC \end{Bmatrix}$

(8) $VT \rightarrow \begin{Bmatrix} \begin{Bmatrix} V_t \\ V_{oc} \end{Bmatrix} + NP \text{ (Man)} \\ V_{mid} + NP \end{Bmatrix}$

(9) $VC \rightarrow \begin{Bmatrix} V_s + Adj \\ V_{ap} + to\ be + \begin{Bmatrix} NP \\ Adj \\ Loc \end{Bmatrix} \\ V_{ae} + Adj \text{ (Man)} \\ become + \begin{Bmatrix} NP \\ Adj \end{Bmatrix} \\ stay/remain + \begin{Bmatrix} NP \\ Adj \\ Loc \end{Bmatrix} \end{Bmatrix}$

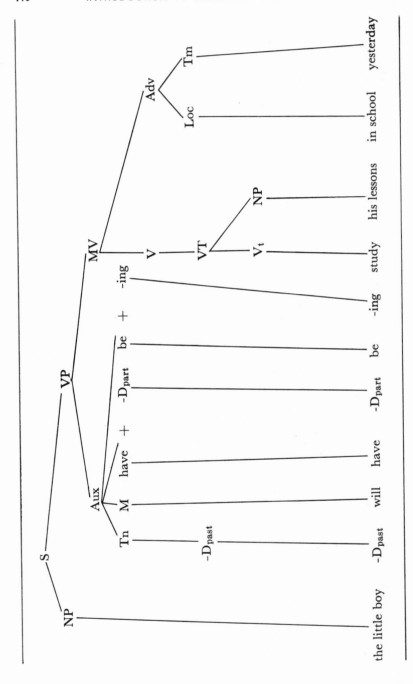

The following is a sample derivation of a kernel sentence from deep structure to surface structure, using the procedural steps for generating the verb phrase. In parentheses are the procedures followed in generating the sentence.

S

(1) $NP + VP$

(2) $NP + Aux + MV$

(3) $NP + Tn + M + have + \text{-}D_{part} + be + \text{-}ing + MV$

(4) $NP + \text{-}D_{past} + M + have + \text{-}D_{part} + be + \text{-}ing + MV$

(5) $NP + \text{-}D_{past} + M + have + \text{-}D_{part} + be + \text{-}ing + V + Adv$

(6) $NP + \text{-}D_{past} + M + have + \text{-}D_{part} + be + \text{-}ing + V + Loc + Tm$

(7) $NP + \text{-}D_{past} + M + have + \text{-}D_{part} + be + \text{-}ing + VT + Loc + Tm$

(8) $NP + \text{-}D_{past} + M + have + \text{-}D_{part} + be + \text{-}ing + V_t + NP + Loc + Tm$

(Lexicon) *the little boy* $+ \text{-}D_{past} + will + have + \text{-}D_{part} + be + \text{-}ing + study + his\ lesson + in\ school + yesterday*

(Affix T) the little boy $+ will + \text{-}D_{past} \# have + be + \text{-}D_{part} \# study + \text{-}ing \#$ his lesson $+$ in school $+$ yesterday

The above steps can be illustrated in the generative diagram shown on page 110.

QUESTIONS AND EXERCISES—THE VERB PHRASE

1. Attempts to improve the operations of a generative grammar usually end up by demonstrating the advantages of the original system. Occasionally, however, attempts to improve the

procedures do result in a breakthrough. With reference to our set of procedures here, I am not happy with the concept V_{oc} nor with the whole of procedure (9), the VC. Yet, I am equally unhappy with attempts, to date, to improve them. Study these and other portions of our grammar above, and even though you cannot offer improvements, point out the weaknesses you find.

2. I will also admit that this grammar, though adequate for our purposes, is incomplete. Find certain points where this is so. Consider in particular the **pre-verbs,** sometimes called **adverbials of frequency** (*always, often, sometimes, seldom, never*). Where would you introduce them into our grammar?

3. Another problem in any generative grammar is contextual ungrammaticality: *the boy was frequent*; *the stone spoke a piece.* What refinements are needed to avoid such terminal strings?

4. Our generative grammar does not cover the semantic concepts available and necessary in the selection of certain forms. This is particularly true of Aux. Study all of the possible occurrences of the elements included in procedure (3), in a wide variety of contexts, and attempt an explanation of their meaning. Consider also the modals, in both tenses, to determine the meanings here. This is admittedly difficult, but try anyhow.[18]

5. Review these VP procedures with another language. What differences become apparent? At what point is the difference greatest?

6. Discuss—and attempt to formulate—the morphophonemic procedures which will account for all occurrences of *be* + Tn, with reference to the NP subject.

7. You will notice that all of the procedures for generating the VP carefully isolate *be*, *have*, and the modals from the company of the verbs. What characteristics do they have or lack which necessitate this careful separation? How is *have*, the element in the

---

[18] ". . . When English is learned natively the meanings of [these] modals are learned so extremely early—necessarily before the child is ready for kindergarten— that as an adult one has left them buried deep in the subconscious where they are inaccessible to rational scrutiny by anyone but a ruthless professional analyst of languages; and when they are seen laid out and dissected . . ., we are bound to feel that we are witnessing the anatomizing of our own flesh and blood." Martin Joos, *The English Verb: Form and Meanings* (Madison, Wisc., 1964), p. 147.

phase portion of Aux, different from *have*, "to possess"? Do any of the other forms here have separate existences as full-fledged verbs?

8. Though I would not ask you to develop a generative grammar of the noun phrase, consider the possibility, and indicate what differences it would have as compared with our slot-and-filler approach.

BIBLIOGRAPHY

There are several excellent general studies of English phonology available. Among those using the IPA system similar to that adopted in this chapter are, in no particular order:

Thomas, Charles K. *An Introduction to the Phonetics of American English.* 2d ed. New York: The Ronald Press Company, 1958.

Kenyon, John S. *American Pronunciation.* 10th ed. Ann Arbor, Mich.: George Wahr Publishing Company, 1951.

Bronstein, Arthur J. *The Pronunciation of American English.* New York: Appleton-Century-Crofts, 1960.

Interesting because of its presentation of British pronunciation, in contrast to these American English texts, is A. C. Gimson, *An Introduction to the Pronunciation of English* (New York: St. Martin's Press, 1962). The best presentation of the Trager–Smith system is in W. Nelson Francis, *The Structure of American English* (New York: The Ronald Press Company, 1958), chaps. 2 and 3.

The bibliography for Chapter 3 should be consulted for general works pertaining to descriptive and generative-transformational grammar. In contradistinction to the discussion in the present chapter, for a generative approach to the noun phrase, see Robert B. Lees, *The Grammar of English Nominalizations*, Publication 12 (Bloomington: Indiana University Research Center in Anthropology, Folklore, and Linguistics, 1960); and for a slot-and-filler approach to the verb phrase, with a little bit of the transformational, see Martin Joos, *The English Verb: Form and Meanings* (Madison: University of Wisconsin Press, 1964). An ancillary study to the latter is W. Freeman Twaddell, *The English Verb Auxiliaries* (2d ed.; Providence, R. I.: Brown University Press, 1963). Another study relating to a specific area of the auxiliary is Madeline Ehrman, *The Meaning of the Modals in Present-Day English* (The Hague: Mouton & Co., 1966). And finally, two general studies of the verb phrase: Alphonse Juilland and James Macris, *The English Verb System* ('s-Gravenhage: Mouton & Co., 1962); and Robert L. Allen, *The Verb System of Present-Day American English* (The Hague: Mouton & Co., 1966), the latter containing an impressive amount of detail.

5

Sentence Patterns

TRANSFORMATIONS AND THE KERNEL SENTENCE

In the preceding chapter, using whichever grammatical theory seemed most useful for the occasion, we examined the two phrasal patterns which make up the sentence. For the purposes of this analysis, we reviewed the concept of the **kernel sentence,** the result of generative procedures followed out to completion.[1] The kernel sentence, however, is an uncomplicated simple declarative statement, and though its straightforwardness is probably commendable, we still need sentences which will do more for us than this.

The procedures by which we can alter or rearrange kernel sentences are called **transformations.** By means of these procedures, the surface structure of the kernel sentence is rearranged in strict accordance with the formulas; but the alteration is only on the surface. The deep structure remains unaffected by the surface rearrangement. In a sense, you were unconsciously making transformations when you were asked in grade school to change a given sentence into a question, a negative statement, or a command. You made the changes with very

[1] A good many descriptive grammarians have accepted the concept of the kernel sentence, and have thereby made use of the transform as a more economical explanation of more complicated structures than is possible under either IC or tagmemic analysis. It is therefore ironic that the term "transformational grammar" has come to be applied only to those principles emanating from generative theory.

114

little difficulty, relying upon what you had learned unconsciously by the time you were six or thereabouts; but underlying every change you made was the original simple declarative sentence, unaffected in its deep structure by the alteration. What is unfortunate is that you were probably never made consciously aware of the similarity between the various kinds of change patterns; moreover, you also were not informed about many additional kinds of pattern-arrangements available to you. True, you already "knew" and used them where applicable, but it's better to know them consciously as well.

One point to remember about transformational procedures is that virtually all of them are optional. The contextual situation may require them, but they aren't needed to make the utterance grammatical. For our purposes here, only two are grammatically mandatory. One of them is the "flip-flop" transformation, which we introduced into our discussion of the VP auxiliary in the last chapter; the other will be introduced shortly. The rule of thumb is to perform all of the optional operations desired first, *then* the compulsory "flip-flop" (more formally, the *affix*) transformation. It is entirely possible that the optional transformation(s) will render unnecessary (indeed, impossible) any mandatory procedure.

The Passive Transformation

The easiest way to understand transformations is by studying them directly, and the best one for introductory purposes is that which transforms the kernel sentence into a **passive structure.** Passive voice, as everyone knows, is that structural state in which the action of the verb is directed at the subject of the sentence. There is apparently only this stylistic purpose behind the passive pattern. Because it is often stylistically ponderous—and because the "actor" is sometimes omitted in the course of the operation, giving an impression of irresponsibility—many rhetoricians object to the pattern. But despite this, it is used, and frequently, as I have used it here.

The formulaic statement for the passive voice structure is simple enough, yet it sets up certain limitations on the process:

$$NP^1 + Aux + V_t + NP^2 \Rightarrow NP^2 + Aux + be + \text{-}D_{part} + V_t \ (by \ NP^1)$$

In case you weren't reading the footnotes in Chapter 4, the double arrow indicates a transformation, and may be read "is transformed into." The formula clearly requires a *transitive* verb. Likewise, it indicates that the key to the structure, $be + $ -D_{part}, follows the whole of Aux; we need not therefore write out the various components of Aux. Also required are two NP's, one functioning as subject, the other as object. The parentheses enclosing *by NP*[1] indicate that these elements in the transformation are optional and may be omitted.

We can now test this formula on an actual kernel sentence. Take as an example, *John saw the dog.* The terminal string of the kernel sentence would read:

(1) John $+$ -D_{past} $+$ see $+$ the dog

After performing the passive transformation, we would have:

(2) the dog $+$ -D_{past} $+$ be $+$ -D_{part} $+$ see $+$ by John

in which the two NP's are reversed according to the formula, and $be + $ -D_{part} is placed after Aux, in this instance, only -D_{past}. We can now perform the mandatory affix transformation:

(3) the dog $+$ be $+$ -D_{past} $\#$ see $+$ -D_{part} $\#$ by John

Finally, we complete our steps by performing the necessary morphophonemic procedures:

(4) The dog was seen by John.

The same procedures apply in a somewhat more complicated kernel string. For example, *John is reading the book*:

(1) John $+$ -Z_{pres} $+$ be $+$ -ing $+$ read $+$ the book
                                                        (terminal string)

(2) the book $+$ -Z_{pres} $+$ be $+$ -ing $+$ be $+$ -D_{part}
                                        $+$ read $+$ by John (passive T)

(3) The book $+$ be $+$ -Z_{pres} $\#$ be $+$ -ing $\#$ read
                                        $+$ -D_{part} $\#$ by John (affix T)

(4) The book is being read by John.

However formidable, and momentarily confusing, the doubling-up of *be* might seem, it all works out in the end.[2]

We have said that the kernel sentence is readily recoverable under the finished transformation. This might seem to be contradicted by the observation that the element *by NP*[1] is an optional part of the transformation. If the speaker elects to omit it, as in *The theft was reported this morning*, how then can the listener or reader possibly recover the NP[1] portion of the kernel sentence? The answer is that it was either unknown or unimportant in the first place. Therefore, the kernel sentence read:

SOMEONE + reported the theft this morning.

NP[1] is what is called a **PRO-form,** written in capitals to indicate its unknown or unimportant condition. When a PRO-form occurs in the kernel string, some sort of transformational procedure must be applied which will ultimately delete it. In this case, the passive transformation, with its optionally deleted *by NP*[1], will suffice.

The Yes/No Interrogative Transformation

Despite the frequency of its use, the passive transformation is neither very complicated nor very significant as a sentence pattern. We can go on to the more significant ones. Such a one is the **interrogative,** or question, transformation. Actually, there are two different kinds of interrogative patterns in English. The first one which we will take up is called the **yes/no interrogative,** so designated because it *can* elicit a yes or no response. We emphasize *can*, because there are sometimes instances when the answerer feels compelled to volunteer information other than a simple yes or no. For instance, in response to "Have you stopped beating your wife?", only a confirmed and acknowledged—though possibly repentant—wife-beater could answer *yes* or *no*. Anyone

---

[2] It should be remembered that this exposition on the passive voice is primarily intended to introduce the concept of the transformation. Recent scholarship seems to lead to the conclusion that the passive construction might be more complex than hitherto suspected; see Jan Svartvik, *On Voice in the English Verb* (The Hague: Mouton & Co., 1966).

else would need to deny the question's major premise. The question, however, remains in the yes/no interrogative pattern; it *can* elicit a yes or no answer.

The first portion of the yes/no interrogative transformation reads as follows:

$$NP + Tn + \begin{bmatrix} M \\ \text{have} \\ \text{be} \end{bmatrix} + X \Rightarrow Tn + \begin{bmatrix} M \\ \text{have} \\ \text{be} \end{bmatrix} + NP + X$$

The brackets around a column of elements indicate that any single element follows the pattern of the same element on the other side of the double arrow. Also, the X simply means anything following the specified elements in the formula. In effect, this transformation indicates that Tn plus a modal, *have*, or *be* is removed from its normal position and placed before the NP subject.

We can observe this process with the kernel sentence *She will go*. The terminal string would read:

(1) She + -Z_{pres} + will + go

in which *will* is a modal, and X is represented by *go*. Applying the yes/no interrogative transformation, we get:

(2) -Z_{pres} + will + she + go

We now must perform a mandatory instance of the affix transformation:

(3) will + -Z_{pres} # she + go

which, after the morphophonemic procedures, becomes:

(4) Will she go?

The same procedures apply when *have* or *be* follows Tn:

(1) she + -Z_{pres} + have + -D_{part} + go
she + -Z_{pres} + be + -ing + go

(2) -Z_{pres} + have + she + -D_{part} + go
-Z_{pres} + be + she + -ing + go

(3) have + -Z_{pres} # she + go + -D_{part} #
be + -Z_{pres} # she + go + -ing #

(4) Has she gone?

Is she going?

Note that in these examples X is represented by $-D_{part} + go$ and *-ing + go*, respectively.

But this is only part of the yes/no interrogative transformation. Suppose that in the kernel terminal string we do not have a modal, *have*, or *be* following Tn. The procedure in this case is:

$$NP + Tn + V \Rightarrow Tn + NP + V$$

where V is the *verbal*, the only other element which can follow Tn. To illustrate with the kernel sentence *She studies*, the terminal string would be:

(1) she + $-Z_{pres}$ + study

Applying the yes/no interrogative transformation, we get:

(2) $-Z_{pres}$ + she + study

Unfortunately, we seem to be at an impasse. There is no V-form following $-Z_{pres}$; hence we cannot apply the affix transformation. In this instance we say that $-Z_{pres}$ is a **floating affix,** symbolized in the following manner:

(2a) $\#-Z_{pres} \#$ she + study

As it happens, there is a floating affix transformation:

$$\# \text{ af } \# \Rightarrow \# \text{ do } + \text{ af } \#$$

which states that to relieve a floating affix from its plight, we simply insert *do* before it. Applying this to our transformation, we get:

(3) $\#$ do + $-Z_{pres}$ $\#$ she + study

or, morphophonemically,

(4) Does she study?

Notice that *do* carries with it no meaning of its own. It is simply that form in modern English which a floating affix attaches itself to, no more. Nonetheless, it is in this respect an important element, to be applied whenever there occurs a floating affix.

Substantial Interrogative Transformations

The other form of interrogative transform is that which re-quires a substantial answer. This structure assumes that a portion of it is unknown, and the response elicited is normally the supplying of the unknown. The unknowns can be any of the parts of speech, a full phrase, or the whole clause. The fact that something is unknown indicates the use of the PRO-form in the kernel terminal string, an inference substantiated by the transformation used to elicit the response for an unknown *noun*:

$$X + \begin{bmatrix} \text{SOMEONE} \\ \text{SOMETHING} \end{bmatrix} + Y \Rightarrow \begin{bmatrix} \text{who} \\ \text{what} \end{bmatrix} + X + Y$$

The formula states that the interrogative function words replacing the PRO-forms are placed ahead of whatever comes before or after them. One important stipulation must be made, however: before this procedure can be followed, one must first perform the yes/no interrogative transformation on the kernel terminal string.

This can be illustrated with the following string:

(1) SOMEONE + -D_{past} + see + the man

(2) -D_{past} + SOMEONE + see + the man (yes/no T)

(3) who + -D_{past} + see + the man (substantial T)

(4) who + see + -D_{past} ＃ the man (affix T)

After the necessary morphophonemic procedures are completed, we have, *Who saw the man?*

Step (2), the preliminary yes/no interrogative transformation, seems to be unnecessary, for in step (3) the affix is right back where it started. This preliminary step is important, however, when, for instance, the unknown noun functions as the object of the kernel sentence:

(1) you + -D_{past} + see + SOMETHING

(2) -D_{past} + you + see + SOMETHING (yes/no T)

(3) what + -D_{past} + you + see (substantial T)

(4) what ＃ do + -D_{past} ＃ you + see (floating affix T)

After the required morphophonemic procedures, we would have, *What did you see?*[3]

This procedure with the unknown noun sometimes works with an unknown verb, when the kernel string contains the sequences Tn + *have* or Tn + *be*. But this is too great a limitation, and a new procedure must be devised which is all-inclusive, in any instance of PRO_v, the unknown verb:

$$X + PRO_v \; (+ \; NP) + Y \Rightarrow what + X + do \; (to + NP) + Y$$

This transformation requires a change in the NP object, if one is present. As with all substantial interrogative transformations, it assumes the completion of the yes/no interrogative transformation first. To take a simple example:

(1) she + $-D_{past}$ + PRO_v (terminal string)

(2) $-D_{past}$ + she + PRO_v (yes/no T)

(3) what + $-D_{past}$ + she + do (substantial T)

(4) what $\#$ do + $-D_{past}$ $\#$ she + do (floating affix T)

(5) What did she do?

Again, with a somewhat more complex kernel terminal string, this one involving a NP object:

(1) you + $-Z_{pres}$ + have + $-D_{part}$ + PRO_v + your desk

(2) $-Z_{pres}$ + have + you + $-D_{part}$ + PRO_v + your desk

(3) what + $-Z_{pres}$ + have + you + $-D_{part}$ + do + to
+ your desk

(4) what + have + $-Z_{pres}$ $\#$ you + do + $-D_{part}$ $\#$ to
+ your desk (affix T)

(5) What have you done to your desk?

Notice that the affix or floating affix transformation is used where applicable. We might add that a subcategory of this transform would insert *with* or *for* rather than *to* before the NP object in

---

[3] We should note that in some circles, when SOMEONE functions as an object, *who* is rewritten as *whom*. But this practice is by no means universal, except in English classrooms.

certain contexts: *What have you done with your mittens?* or *What have you done for the old people in this state?*

These are likewise variations for unknown adjectives and adverbials. For an unknown adjective, the formula is:

$$X + PRO_{adj} + NP + Y \Rightarrow \begin{Bmatrix} \text{what} \\ \text{which} \end{Bmatrix} + NP + X + Y$$

The rationale for the choice between *what* and *which* is contextual; *what* implies an unknown quality, whereas *which* implies a choice of qualities. Sometimes *which* appears to stand for an undetermined demonstrative, as well, and ordinarily PRO_{adj} includes within it the whole limiter structure.

The following example shows the working of this transformation:

(1) you $+ -D_{past} +$ take $+ PRO_{adj} +$ hat (terminal string)

(2) $-D_{past} +$ you $+$ take $+ PRO_{adj} +$ hat (yes/no T)

(3) what $+$ hat $+ -D_{past} +$ you $+$ take (substantial T)

(4) what $+$ hat $\#$ do $+ -D_{past} \#$ you $+$ take (floating affix T)

(5) What hat did you take?

If the context allowed, it would also have been possible to derive *Which hat did you take?* from the same procedures. Notice, too, that if the unknown is the $N + -Z_{gen}$ filler for the determiner, a similar set of procedures would permit the unknown to be replaced by *whose*.

The transformation for unknown adverbials depends upon the kind of adverbial. Thus we have a variety of formulae:

$$X + PRO_{loc} + Y \Rightarrow \text{where} + X + Y$$

$$X + PRO_{tm} + Y \Rightarrow \text{when} + X + Y$$

$$X + PRO_{man} + Y \Rightarrow \text{how} + X + Y$$

These cover the kinds of adverbials which we have included in previous discussions. There are other varieties, which you can supply if need be. As an example of the substantial interrogative transformation involving an unknown adverbial:

(1) John + -Z_{pres} + will + return + PRO_{tm} (terminal string)

(2) -Z_{pres} + will + John + return + PRO_{tm} (yes/no T)

(3) when + -Z_{pres} + will + John + return (substantial T)

(4) when + will + -Z_{pres} # John + return (affix T)

(5) When will John return?

The formulae for other adverbial types work in just the same way. It would be well for you to practice with them, and with all of the transformations in this chapter, both to improve your facility with them and to understand the over-riding similarities among them, which should become more apparent as we go along. They should become familiar concepts to you, not just formulae to be learned for an *ad hoc* examination, then forgotten.

Negation

From these interrogative patterns we can turn to a less extensive examination of some others. First is the **negative** structure, the general purpose of which is to deny the truth of the whole kernel sentence. Like the yes/no interrogative structure, the negative transformation is expressed in two formulas, the first of which involves the optional elements in Aux:

$$NP + Tn + \begin{bmatrix} M \\ have \\ be \end{bmatrix} + X \Rightarrow NP + Tn + \begin{bmatrix} M \\ have \\ be \end{bmatrix} + not + X$$

As an example:

(1) she + -Z_{pres} + will + go (terminal string)

(2) she + -Z_{pres} + will + not + go (negative T)

(3) she + will + -Z_{pres} # not + go (affix T)

(4) She won't go.

and similarly when the Aux contains Tn + *have* or Tn + *be*. As with the yes/no transformation, only the first elements in a complex Aux string are directly involved:

(1) she + -Z_{pres} + will + have + -D_{part} + be + -ing + go

(2) she + -Z_{pres} + will + not + have + -D_{part} + be
    + -ing + go

(3) she + will + -Z_{pres} # not + have + be + -D_{part}
    # go + -ing #

(4) She won't have been going.

In this example, *have* + -D_{part} + *be* + *-ing* + *go* is entirely subsumed under X.

The second part of the negative transformation involves instances when a modal, *have*, or *be* is not part of Aux:

NP + Tn + V ⇒ NP + Tn + not + V

Take for our example here:

(1) she + -D_{past} + walk + to the store (terminal string)

(2) she + -D_{past} + not + walk + to the store (negative T)

Like the yes/no transformation at the same point, we find ourselves left with a floating affix, and again, as in the former instance, we apply the floating affix transformation, the insertion of *do*:

(3) she # do + -D_{past} # not + walk + to the store

ending up with:

(4) She didn't walk to the store.

What is important is to note how this parallels the yes/no transformation. First, there's the omnibus formula involving Tn plus a modal, *have*, or *be*; then the formula covering the absence of the latter, in which a floating affix is attached to an otherwise meaningless *do*.

Transformational Combinations

Possibly you have already assumed that these transformations can be combined. There's no limit to the possible combinations, save the compatibility of the concepts underlying the transformations. One of the commonest is the **negative-interrogative** combination. The following example shows how the two transformations work in combination:

(1) she + -Z_{pres} + will + go (terminal string)

(2) -Z_{pres} + will + she + go (yes/no T)

(3) -Z_{pres} + will + not + she + go (negative T)

(4) will + -Z_{pres} $\#$ not + she + go (affix T)

(5) Won't she go?

I suppose that there is really no difference in the ordering of the transformations, but it seems best to perform first those which rearrange the string, like the yes/no interrogative transformation, followed by those which insert new elements, like the negative. Note that if the order of (2) and (3) were reversed, the chances are that *not* would be thought of as part of X when -Z_{pres} + *will* is moved to the head of the string for the yes/no interrogative transformation. The result would be *Will she not go?*, which, though grammatical, sounds too artificial, too much the relic of a bygone age. The contraction -*n't* is now so common that it automatically attaches itself to Aux and moves with it.

It's difficult to articulate the precise meaning underlying this combination. In the above instance, it would seem that the speaker hopes for an affirmative response, but fears the inevitability of a negative one. But this fragile explanation is often shattered by an intonational shift. For example, if we shifted the stress in our last sample transformation to read "Won't *she* go?" we give the impression that *she*, of all people, should have been willing to travel, or whatever, and if *she's* unwilling, the plan must be a dismal failure. Likewise, in "Won't she *go*?" we seem to be expressing an attitude of incredulity at the whole turn of events. But these are all subjective definitions which point up the inability of writing to indicate such nuances or to explain them, for the precise structural meaning will probably remain on the threshold of articulation. All this aside, there are several other kinds of negative-interrogative transformations, and to them and other combinations we will turn our attention in the exercises.

The Emphatic Transformation

Yet another commonly employed transformation parallels the yes/no interrogative and negative transformations. This is the **emphatic** transformation. A kind of emphasis is often used to stress the assertion of individual words in an utterance. The normal intonation pattern of /²³¹↘/ is sometimes stretched a bit to make more emphatic a particular word or clear up a possible misunderstanding.

For example, the sentence *The old lady walked to the store*, with normal sentence intonation, makes a plain, straightforward assertion, assumed to be true. When individual words are stressed, however, the speaker communicates certain undertones as well:

(1) The *old* lady walked to the store.   (not the young one)

(2) The old *lady* walked to the store.   (not the old man)

(3) The old lady *walked* to the store.   (she didn't ride)

(4) The old lady walked *to* the store. (but she got a ride home)

(5) The old lady walked to the *store*.   (not to the post office)

In written expression, emphasis is indicated by italics, as above, or by capitals or underlining.[4]

The effect of the emphatic transformation, however, is to stress and affirm the truth *of the entire statement*. The first part of the emphatic transformation is:

$$NP + Tn + \begin{bmatrix} M \\ have \\ be \end{bmatrix} + X \Rightarrow NP + Tn + \begin{bmatrix} M \\ have \\ be \end{bmatrix} + ! + X$$

In this formula, the sign ! indicates that the morphophonemic unit preceding it must be stressed. Thus:

(1) She + -Z_{pres} + have + -D_{part} + leave (terminal string)

(2) She + -Z_{pres} + have + ! + -D_{part} + leave (emphatic T)

(3) She + have + -Z_{pres} # ! + leave + -D_{part} # (affix T)

(4) She *has* left.

---

[4] Sometimes the definite article is emphasized, usually with facetious effect, as in "This is *the* university," indicating that the speaker believes that he and his selected associates occupy a rarified position of uniqueness.

The morphophonemic elements making up *has* are stressed, and the whole statement is affirmed as effectively as a fist pounding on a table. The second part of the formula also parallels earlier transformations:

$$Np + Tn + V \Rightarrow NP + Tn + ! + V$$

Selecting an example, we have:

(1) She + -D$_{past}$ + walk + to the store

(2) She + -D$_{past}$ + ! + walk + to the store

Again we find ourselves faced with a floating affix, requiring the services of *do*:

(3) She # do + -D$_{past}$ # ! + walk + to the store

(floating affix T)

(4) She *did* walk to the store.

Unlike the five instances of emphasis in the similar sentence above, this definitely affirms the truth of the entire statement. The use of *do* here as a means of securing the floating affix is probably the reason why school grammars label any structure with *do* "emphatic," even diagrammatic rearrangements of interrogative structures. Not only is this misleading, but it demonstrates that the school grammarians failed to see the implications or the patterns in the use of *do*.

The Imperative Transformation

Another frequently used transformation, the **imperative,** differs markedly in its operation in that instead of redistributing the elements of the kernel terminal string, or making insertions amongst them, it actually makes deletions. These deletions, however, are made under rigidly prescribed situations, because the kernel sentence underlying the transformation must be readily recoverable.

The situation is clearly established in the operation of the imperative transformation:

$$\text{you} + \text{-Z}_{pres} + \text{will} + X \Rightarrow X$$

Under this procedure, the NP subject must consist only of *you*, and the Aux must contain $-Z_{pres} + will$. These elements only are deleted, and being readily recoverable as the only deletion in the basic imperative structure, the kernel sentence is still clearly evident. The school grammarians perceived this dimly when they devised the concept of the "understood *you*."

The actual operation of this transformation is simplicity itself:

You $+ -Z_{pres} + $ will $+$ close the door $\Rightarrow$ Close the door!

The meaning of this structure is that of an order, a command, or a request. This transformation as illustrated here simply makes a straightforward command. However, there are social and cultural ramifications involved here, often based on the relationship between the speaker and the one addressed. Someone in a surly mood might delete only $-Z_{pres} + will$:

You, close the door!

If there's doubt as to the one addressed, *you* may be made to identify with him:

John, close the door.

The above structure contains the embedded sentence, *You are John*. Politer company softens the force of the imperative by inserting *please* in the place of the deletion:

Please close the door.

Finally, the military often makes its desires known by combining the imperative transformation with the emphatic, making no deletions at all:

You *will* attend the meeting.

This may be spoken quietly, but its force is completely effective.

DELETIONS

The deletion is an often-used transformational device, but it rarely is used to alter or introduce structural meaning, as in the imperative transformation. More often it is used for stylistic effect, primarily to remove repetition. The very nature of generating kernel sentences is such that they contain redundancies which are not necessary for effective communication, such as:

> This book is my book.

The simplest way to remove the needless repetition is to delete one or the other instance of *book*:

> This is my book.

or,

> This book is mine.

Notice that the latter instance requires the substitution of the absolute form of the genitive personal pronoun. In speaking, when one can use gesture to advantage, the deletion can be even more drastic:

> This [pointing] is mine.

Yet, in each of these instances of deletion, the kernel sentence is fully recoverable behind the transformation.

Compounds

Another kind of redundancy deletion is the result of **compounding**—the coupling together of parallel or like kernel sentences for economy of expression. The juxtaposition of:

> Jack went up the hill. ⎫
> Jill went up the hill. ⎭

would be tedious, to say the least. It is far better to delete the repeated elements and combine the two portions which are not repeated:

> Jack and Jill went up the hill.

This self-evident combining and deletion occurs frequently— except, I'm sorry to say, in some freshman themes.

Compounding also occurs when the kernel sentences are parallel, but contain few or no repeated elements. Thus:

> I climbed the stairs. ⎫
> I went to bed.   ⎭

can be compounded, provided that the action of the second follows the first logically, with the single deletion of the repeated *I*:

> I climbed the stairs and went to bed.

But there need be no deletion at all, provided that the sentences are structurally parallel and can be seen to interrelate according to the demands of the five **conjunctions** *and, but, for, or, nor. And* is a general conjunction, implying either a simple relation between the sentences or a logical sequence of events. *But* implies that the second sentence is an exception to the first. *Or* states a choice or alternative, whereas *nor* denies the truth or force of both sentences. *Nor* is especially tricky: the first sentence in the compound has usually undergone the negative transformation, and the second must undergo the yes/no interrogative transformation:

> She didn't arrive last night, nor did she come this morning.

Similar to the conjunctions, but somewhat more sophisticated in establishing the relationship of the compounding, are the **correlatives**: *however, moreover, nevertheless,* etc. These resemble closely the relational meaning of the conjunctions, but are used either to convey a subtler nuance or for stylistic variation.

SUBORDINATION AND EMBEDDING

Another means of combining kernel sentences is **subordination.** Whereas coordination implies that the conjoined sentences are contextually equivalent and structurally parallel, subordination—which commonly involves sentence units—makes no such claims. The point is that one of the two sentences is made structurally dependent upon the other. Contrary to popular view, the subordinated, or dependent clause is not necessarily less important contextually. The decision to subordinate is made on the basis of the sentence structure itself, or of structural relationships between the two sentences. It is not done by somehow choosing the less important for subordination.

Often the subordinated sentence has a PRO-form in its terminal string, making the need to subordinate it fairly obvious. For instance, we might have:

Life wasn't the same. ⎫
She went away + PRO$_{tm}$ ⎭

These would be combined into the subordination structure, *When she went away, life wasn't the same.* Although much study still needs to be given to these structures, it would seem that the subordinated sentence undergoes the substantial interrogative transformation, *without* the prior operation of the yes/no transformation. The context and wording of the main clause (often called the **matrix**) determine the choice of word replacing the PRO-form. In the above example, had the matrix read, *Life hasn't been the same,* the PRO-form would probably have been replaced by *since.* Finally, were the two sentences viewed in isolation, no one would readily make a connection between them. It is up to the speaker (or writer) himself to note the relationship and make the connection evident.

Another means of working out subordinations is through the process of **embedding,** briefly alluded to in the discussion of imperative transformations.[5] Embedding basically involves the transformationist's assumption that within the deep structure of any NP there is the possibility of embedding one or more sentences which ultimately make up the modificational elements of the NP in its final surface state. The following might help to clarify this point:

the barn (the barn is red) (the barn belongs to Farmer Brown)
⇒ the red barn which belongs to Farmer Brown

Both of these embedded sentences enclosed in parentheses involve modification, which in our slot-and-filler discussion of the NP was handled somewhat differently. Here, the surface structure undergoes deletion of repeated elements, transposition of the adjective, and replacement of one repeated element with a relative pronoun.[6]

[5] And also in the previous chapter, when we discussed the transformational grammarian's view of the NP as opposed to the descriptivist's.

[6] The second embedded sentence would not be necessary to give us the surface result "Farmer Brown's red barn." In generative grammar, N + -Z$_{gen}$ is one of the

Even NP PRO-forms can have embedded sentences. For example:

I know SOMETHING (John did it) ⇒ I know that John did it.

In informal usage, *that* is not required. Sometimes the embedding involves two or more PRO-forms:

I know SOMETHING (SOMEONE did it) ⇒ I know who did it.

Here, the embedded sentence replaces the PRO-form in the matrix.

Using the procedures developed by orthodox generative-transformationists, we can generate structures in which the embedding process at first glance looks extremely complicated. Our phrase structure procedures can generate the following kernel terminal string (remembering that it differs somewhat from our slot-and-filler approach to the NP):[7]

(1) SOMETHING (SOMEONE (SOMEONE reads a poem) needs certain skills (SOMEONE uses certain skills (skills create a poem))) is obvious.

Within the matrix, *SOMETHING is obvious*, is one basic embedded sentence, within which are three minor ones. The first transformation involves the noun phrases: thoroughgoing transformational theory would have a procedure to change *SOMEONE reads a poem* into a NP and *skills create a poem* into a postpositional adjective phrase. The accomplishment of these steps gives us:

(2) SOMETHING (*the reader of a poem* needs certain skills (SOMEONE uses certain skills *in the creation of a poem*)) is obvious.

---

possible ways of rewriting the determiner, just as it is one of the possible fillers of the determiner slot in tagmemics, and thus the generated NP would read "Farmer Brown's barn (the barn is red)."

[7] For purposes of embedding, the first rewrite procedure for the NP would be NP → N(S). The optional embedded S is recursive. Successive rewritings of N (or nominal) would add categories such as indefinite pronouns, proper nouns, personal pronouns, count and mass nouns, and PRO-forms, plus the whole determiner apparatus.

The changes are noted in italics. Remember that these operations, which are doubtless strange to you, involve basic differences between the generating of the NP and slot-and-filler techniques. In the former, modification and the creation of certain nouns (*reader* is an **agentive noun**) are transformational operations.[8] If you prefer, you can continue to work with our slot-and-filler approach, in which case you would begin with step (2) as your terminal string.

We now have one embedded sentence within another. The passive transformation will remove the PRO-form in the former:

> (3) SOMETHING (the reader of a poem needs certain skills (*certain skills are used* in the creation of a poem)) is obvious.

Deletion of a repeated element, replacing it with a relative pronoun, will remove the interior embedded sentence:

> (4) SOMETHING (the reader of a poem needs certain skills *which* are used in the creation of a poem) is obvious.

The embedded sentence can now replace the PRO-form, with the addition of a subordinator:

> (5) *That* the reader of a poem needs certain skills which are used in the creation of a poem is obvious.

One final rearrangement is necessary simply to remove the heavy awkwardness and to add stylistic informality:

> (6) *It is obvious* that the reader of a poem needs certain skills which are used in the creation of a poem.

Analyzing another complexly embedded sentence may help you to see how the surface structure is progressively transformed from a sequence resembling the choppy style of a primer into the smoother prose style of one at home with his language.

> (1) We ought to conclude SOMETHING (the reader should rest content (the reader creates an experience (the experience is vaguely like another experience (the poet has another experience)))).

---

[8] It is possible that at the *stem* level of slot-and-filler analysis, *reader* would be considered the result of the nominalizing operation, verb + {-er}.

(2) We ought to conclude SOMETHING (the reader should rest content *with creating* an experience vaguely like another experience *of the poet*).

(3) We ought to conclude *that* the reader should rest content with creating an experience vaguely like *that* of the poet.

(4) We ought *not* to conclude that the reader should rest content with creating an experience vaguely like that of the poet.

(5) [*But*] we ought not [*therefore*] to conclude that the reader should rest content with creating an experience vaguely like that of the poet.

The first step is the terminal string with four embedded sentences, each successive one within the one preceding it. If we wish, we could amend this step to show the working of the agentive noun transform:

... SOMETHING (SOMEONE (SOMEONE reads) should ...)

But we've covered this ground already, and it seems to complicate this example unnecessarily. Step (2) shows the simultaneous operation of three transformations: a postpositional modifier, deletion of repetition, and a paraphrastic genitive. Step (3) replaces the PRO-form, subordinating the embedded sentence. Step (4) employs the negative transformation, and step (5) inserts transitional elements, meaningless out of context, which placed the sentence into the organized essay from which it was ripped for this occasion.[9]

A CAUTIONARY CONCLUSION

I hope that this whole discussion has led you to develop new attitudes about the nature of language and the workings of the English language in particular. Previously, we have noted how the linear sequence of the NP is rigidly ordered, and by generating the VP we saw how one theory describes the successive states which ultimately form completely grammatical utterances. Now we can see certain orderly forces at work in the rearrangement of surface elements to achieve other than declarative structural

---

[9] I am unable to locate the source of these two examples. They were selected arbitrarily in class by a student when I was demonstrating these procedures, taking them at random from a handy volume of critical essays.

meaning and combining them for relational and stylistic effect. These should show that man's most human invention is not a slapdash affair, but a consistent system capable of virtually limitless possibilities, responding to the desires of its users up to the limits of human experience itself.

But I want to end with two cautionary notes. First of all, I would again remind you that the generative-transformational system described here does not itself purport to be an actual picture of the processes by which each grammatical utterance is actually made. At best, it is only a plausible description of what is actually a very complicated mental process, broken down into grammatical concepts. This is all that its proponents claim—and this is what their opponents should take into account. We know very little about the actual mental processes involved in language, but we *do* know that everywhere is the attempt to articulate a mental image of some sort. To say that we begin each new sentence by consciously positing S → NP + VP is obviously silly.

Second, you should not delude yourself into thinking that you now have picked up basically all there is to know about the workings of Modern English. This would be a false comfort. Our description here is incomplete—a complete grammar is frankly impossible. Further, there may well be portions here which are unwieldy or even misleading, portions which must be changed in the light of new discoveries. Finally, there will probably be new concepts abroad which will render our discussion obsolete, "academic," as it were. Chomsky has successively revised his theory, and there are newer theories in the process of formulation, of which the so-called stratificational grammar of Professor Lamb is just one. Constantly, new concepts are advanced, discussed, debated, praised, and sometimes damned.

We opened our discussion on this note, and we close it in the same way. Nothing in language study is a closed issue. We should be encouraged, rather than disheartened by this fact. My hope is that this discussion will be the starting point for your own work with language study and your continuing, developing interest in *your* language.

Résumé of the transformational procedures covered in this chapter:

Affix:

$$af + v \Rightarrow v + af \; \#$$

Floating affix:

$$\# \, af \, \# \Rightarrow \# \, do + af \, \#$$

Passive:

$$NP^1 + Aux + V_t + NP^2 \Rightarrow NP^2 + Aux + be + \text{-}D_{part}$$
$$+ V_t \; (by \; NP^1)$$

Yes/no interrogative:

$$NP + Tn + \begin{bmatrix} M \\ have \\ be \end{bmatrix} + X \Rightarrow Tn + \begin{bmatrix} M \\ have \\ be \end{bmatrix} + NP + X$$

$$NP + Tn + V \Rightarrow Tn + NP + V$$

Substantial interrogative:

$$X + \begin{bmatrix} SOMEONE \\ SOMETHING \end{bmatrix} + Y \Rightarrow \begin{bmatrix} who \\ what \end{bmatrix} + X + Y$$

$$X + PRO_v \, (+ NP) + Y \Rightarrow what + X + do \; (to + NP) + Y$$

$$X + PRO_{adj} + NP + Y \Rightarrow \begin{bmatrix} what \\ which \end{bmatrix} + NP + X + Y$$

$$X + \begin{bmatrix} PRO_{loc} \\ PRO_{tm} \\ PRO_{man} \end{bmatrix} + Y \Rightarrow \begin{bmatrix} where \\ when \\ how \end{bmatrix} + X + Y$$

Note: apply the yes/no interrogative transformation prior to the substantial interrogative transformation.

Negative:

$$NP + Tn + \begin{bmatrix} M \\ have \\ be \end{bmatrix} + X \Rightarrow NP + Tn + \begin{bmatrix} M \\ have \\ be \end{bmatrix} + not + X$$

$$NP + Tn + V \Rightarrow NP + Tn + not + V$$

Emphasis:

$$NP + Tn + \begin{bmatrix} M \\ have \\ be \end{bmatrix} + X \Rightarrow NP + Tn + \begin{bmatrix} M \\ have \\ be \end{bmatrix} + ! + X$$

$$NP + Tn + V \Rightarrow NP + Tn + ! + V$$

Imperative:

$$you + -Z_{pres} + will + X \Rightarrow X$$

QUESTIONS AND EXERCISES

1. We have said that our discussion of transformations is incomplete. Try your hand at working up procedural transformations for the following:

　a. Substantial interrogative where the unknown noun is the object of a preposition.

　b. Interrogatives involving tag-endings (the addition of *don't they* or the like to the string).

　c. Negative interrogative involving tag-endings or rising pitch intonation.

2. We stated that the transformations can be combined, provided that their structural meanings are compatible. You cannot, for instance, combine interrogative and imperative— giving a command and eliciting a response do not jibe. However, try several compatible combinations, with special attention to any additional structural meaning they might have. Do the combinations work out according to our formulas, or must some alterations be noted in the process? Are the alterations minor, or do they portend something of greater significance?

3. In the manner given at the end of our discussion in this chapter, take any given prose sequence and analyze it according to its kernel terminal string. What structural instances do you find impossible of analysis? What implications might a continuous analysis of this sort have for an investigation of style?

4. Try to develop a transformational procedure which will transform a kernel string into an utterance paralleling "he is older than I." What problems does this particular structure present?

5. In like manner, attempt to develop transformational procedures for participial phrases and absolute constructions, patterned after the following:

  a. Having cleared the harbor, the freighter headed for open water.
  b. Speeding round the corner, the car nearly struck a child.
  c. Decks cleared for action, the frigate bore down on the enemy.
  d. The army having been warned, the scout returned to the post.
  e. Things being as they are, the dance ought to be postponed.

What problems are involved in formulating these procedures? Are these constructions more common in speech or in writing? Why is this so? Would this analysis be helpful in correcting "dangling" participial constructions ("Eating our lunch, the steamboat came round the bend.")?

6. Review the basic premises of generative-transformational theory. How might you deal with such utterances as *the more, the merrier; if I were you;* and *good-by?*

7. Review the basic tenets of descriptive theory, which is often held at odds with the transformational. Do you see any way in which the theories might intermesh—might be complementary, as it were?

8. What differences in grammatical theory are illustrated by Reed–Kellogg, immediate constituent, and generative diagramming of each of the following related sentences:

  a. He looked over the wiring system yesterday.
  b. He looked the wiring system over yesterday.
  c. Yesterday he looked over the wiring system.
  d. Yesterday he looked the wiring system over.

9. Discuss the implications of the present state of flux in the study of language. Why do you suppose so many people find this unsettling?

BIBLIOGRAPHY

Reference is again made to the bibliographical notes at the end of Chapter 3 for the basic bibliography for transformational procedures. In addition, a good introduction to the subject, though slightly dated, is Harold A. Gleason, Jr., "Transformations," chapter 12 of *An Introduction to Descriptive Linguistics* (rev. ed.), previously cited. A somewhat more advanced, specialized discussion for the student who has a highly developed sense of self-confidence is Edward S. Klima, "Negation in English," in Fodor and Katz (eds.), *The Structure of Language*, previously cited, pp. 246–323. This article is emblematic of the range and difficulty of transformational studies.

There are two recent college textbooks which deal primarily with transformational analysis. Baxter Hathaway, *A Transformational Syntax: The Grammar of Modern American English* (New York: The Ronald Press Company, 1967), presents a synthesis of several systems, though the basis is mostly transformational, or "process" grammar, as the author calls it, and more descriptive than formulaic. Andreas Koutsoudas, *Writing Transformational Grammars: An Introduction* (New York: McGraw-Hill Book Company, 1966), is basically concerned with the formulation of new grammatical descriptions and transformational processes, as the title suggests, and contains a good deal of material derived from several foreign languages. Either book would be an excellent means of further supplementing this chapter, depending upon the student's own interests.

This is as good a place as any to mention those high school texts currently available utilizing descriptive or generative-transformational techniques. The earliest single text, intended for junior high students, is Paul Roberts, *Patterns of English* (New York: Harcourt, Brace & World, 1956), which uses standard descriptive grammar techniques. An attempt to bridge the gap between descriptive grammar and transformational grammar is the same author's *English Sentences* (New York: Harcourt, Brace & World, 1962). Both of these texts are closely surveyed by James Sledd in his review article "Syntactic Strictures," *The English Leaflet*, 61 (1961–1962); reprinted in Allen (ed.), *Readings in Applied English Linguistics*, pp. 414–22. A series for grades 7–12 which incorporates the *attitudes* toward language of descriptive linguists, rather than a precise, rigorous description, is *The New English*, by Postman, Damon, Morine, and Morine, published by Holt, Rinehart and Winston, Inc.

Single texts exemplifying generative-transformational grammar are Paul Roberts, *English Syntax* (New York: Harcourt, Brace and World, 1964), intended for senior high schools, but successfully used in college-level courses; and Syrell Rogovin, *Modern English Sentence Structure* (New York: Random House, Inc., 1964), intended for use in junior high schools. Both are organized along the lines of programmed instruction. A recent entry into the field is Allen, Newsome, Wetmore, Throckmorton, and Borgh, *New Dimensions in English* (Wichita, Kan.: McCormick-Mathers Publishing Company, Inc., 1966). A recent and notable series for grades 3–9 is the *Roberts English Series* (Harcourt, Brace & World), which incorporates spelling, composition, literature, and semantics, as well as linguistics, into a sequential program.

These represent an interest in the area, but the standard best-selling series, such as you probably learned from, continue to stick to school grammar attitudes—as exemplified by the first discussion question given at the end of Chapter 2.

6

Problems in Applied Linguistics

Our discussions so far have emphasized the basic problems of grammatical analysis. Although this in itself comprises the work of several lifetimes, those specialists who are involved in the actual routine of "English" classroom instruction find themselves constantly faced with problems which are only indirectly related to grammatical theory. Because of a long-standing blurring of the line between the purely grammatical and what might be called the para-grammatical, some areas which are related only distantly to linguistics proper have tended to consume a major part of the total time spent in what should be an objectively pursued study.

One of these areas comes under the heading of *usage*; another encompasses the problems involved in writing, particularly spelling. These areas are among those which comprise the field of **applied linguistics.**[1] By analyzing them in the light of the

[1] Among the other areas in this field are the teaching of English as a second language, and its related area, teaching standard English to nonstandard speakers; foreign language instruction; and reading and literacy. Those areas which we have selected for discussion in our chapter seem to be of paramount importance to the classroom English teacher. Those interested in the other areas are referred to the relevant entries in the following bibliographies: Frank Rice and Allene Guss, *Information Sources in Linguistics* (Washington: Center for Applied Linguistics, 1965); and Harold B. Allen, *Linguistics and English Linguistics* (New York: Appleton-Century-Crofts, 1966).

linguistic discoveries we have discussed, we can make an effort to clear up many of the problems of the past, despite the fact that these areas have only an indirect connection with linguistics. It is entirely possible that such a discussion will demonstrate to people that a prolonged preoccupation with "good English," with spelling, with the "written language," and with kindred classroom pursuits is generally time needlessly wasted. To our discussion is added a brief commentary on *style*, which might engender some interest in this relatively unexplored field.

WRITING AND SPELLING

The Impact of Writing

We live in an age of written communication. Writing and printing are so much a part of our civilization that we find it impossible to conceive of a nonliterate society. We rely so heavily upon books, pamphlets, directives, memoranda, signs, and letters that we have come to believe that we would be helpless without them. Consequently, we have come to assign to writing the major position in a mythical hierarchy of language. Furthermore, many educated people have become so emotionally attached to literature as an aggregate of "beautiful thoughts" that they are offended by relatively objective attempts (as in the preceding chapters) to analyze language in other than "traditional" ways. This, they say, does violence to the language of Shakespeare *et al.*; and they fight, often successfully, any attempt to widen the impact of linguistic study. This large group includes, shameful to say, a large number of English teachers.

The Origin of Writing

Because of this tendency to glorify the written word, it would be well for us to begin with a discussion of the origin of writing, enlarging upon the comments in Chapter 1. Language itself—as we have defined it—had its beginning so far back in the misty recesses of time that it eludes any attempts to seek it out. The origin of writing, however, is somewhat more accessible historic-ally. Despite the attempts of many well-intentioned people to equate writing with literature, the unfortunate fact remains that writing did not develop in response to the needs of the poet or author. On the contrary, it was developed in response to the needs of what is probably the very antithesis of literature—dirty, money-grubbing old commerce. The ancient businessman was able to keep firmly in his mind the traditions, mythology, epic literature, and royal genealogy of his society, but he needed a way to keep straight certain day-by-day problems of his business—namely, how many jars of olive oil he exported last year. In other words, a preliterate society easily and automatically develops such mnemonic devices as the forms of poetry for the oral transmission of its cultural traditions. It is in the area of commercial expansion, with a corresponding expansion in the operations of government, that the need arises for keeping physical records.

The history of the development of writing is interesting, as is the story of the deciphering of ancient writing. However, we have not the space here to recount the latter at all,[2] and we can only briefly touch on the former, making mention of the five stages in the development of writing down to the present. Our major purpose here is to remove some of the folklore behind writing, and then go on to something which gives most of us no end of trouble—spelling.

The Development of Writing

The earliest stage in the development of writing was probably the **picture,** which was so rudimentary a representation that it can scarcely be considered writing at all. Out of either boastfulness or a compulsion to be methodical, the hunter coming home from the field would draw in some accessible place a picture of his quarry and devise some kind of representation for multiple kills— either more than one picture or a more sophisticated system of tick marks. In like manner, the olive oil trader of a later age would keep pictorial summaries on clay tablets, which were then sunbaked dry and stored for future reference. Some of these pictures could get pretty elaborate, as when tribes would record

[2] Readable general accounts of paleography are P. E. Cleator, *Lost Languages,* and chapter 6 of Holger Pedersen, *Linguistic Science in the Nineteenth Century,* both previously cited.

alliance agreements, or even when a hunter would record the game supply of various districts.

We should pause for a moment to consider the passing reference to recording multiples. Necessity quickly led to the development of special tick marks to record tens, hundreds, and thousands, especially when the embryo scribe found that there was neither time nor room to inscribe everything in terms of single units. Such a system of multiple notations led to its ultimate ossification in Roman numerals. Our present system of Arabic numerals came out of a different development, one relying upon considerable interest in mathematical theory. At any rate, the representation of numerical concepts probably had an earlier development than what we call writing.

The trouble with pictures is that they depend upon the artistic ability of the drawer for their ease of deciphering. Further, there are so many abstract concepts which do not lend themselves easily to depiction that the picture could only be of limited usefulness as an objective means of nonverbal communication. These two problems were resolved by the development of the **ideograph,** an arbitrary sign which all users agree upon as the representation of any verbal concept. Thus, the ideograph, which was probably first developed out of a need to make pictures hastily and efficiently, made possible the expansion of writing to include more than just objects which could be observed and drawn.

Some writing systems have gone no further than the ideographic stage. But all of them have required a further development in order to become completely useful. This third development is the **morphemic ideograph,** an arbitrary sign which represents a grammatical meaning, as, for instance, number, tense, person, and the like. This is the current state of the Chinese writing system—thousands of characters which represent lexical units, plus a number which represent units of grammatical meaning. Certain signs which we have used in our discussions might be called ideographic, as, for instance, $\{-D_{past}\}$; and in our writing conventions, our numbers, represented as 1, 2, 3 . . . , are ideographs, as are such frequently used signs as & and %.

The Chinese system mentioned above has another characteristic—every lexical unit, and thus every character, is one syllable in length. This fact probably accounts for the freezing of the Chinese writing system into its present form, although some reports coming out of Red China indicate that the ruling hierarchy is trying to introduce an alphabetical system by administrative fiat. One important point to note, however, is that the grammatical system of the language itself is of no account in the development of the ideographic writing system. Thus, because the so-called Chinese language actually consists of five or more "dialects," which are actually mutually unintelligible languages, it often happens that a native of Peiping, speaking Mandarin Chinese, can write to an acquaintance in Canton who speaks only Cantonese, and the letter can be read, even though neither could understand the other if he spoke. With a little effort, anyone can learn to read Chinese characters, though he should not therefore delude himself into believing that he "knows" Chinese.

One problem of an ideographic system is that there are thousands of characters that must be learned for even minimal reading competence. Thus, for languages which had regularly recurring patterns of syllable clusters, of which English is *not* one, there arose the development of the **syllabary.** In this system, each sign was made to represent each recurring syllable cluster, which usually consisted of a single vowel or a consonant-plus-vowel combination. Where these cluster combinations are regular, as in Japanese, these systems work well, and doubtless the systems developed from the observation that certain ideographs represented ideas or concepts which were also regularly recurring syllables. Thus, to take a hypothetical instance from English, the ideograph for *eye* might be used for the first person pronoun, and later for the first syllable in *idea.*

However, this system wouldn't work at all for those languages which do not have a small, regularly recurring syllabic inventory. This, plus the inexorable fact of language change, led to the development of the **alphabet,** the final and, to our way of thinking at least, most significant step in the story of writing systems. In theory, an alphabet should be a sequence of signs which represent each significant sound of the language on a one-to-one basis. In practice, each alphabet falls short of this ideal.

There can be no doubt that the alphabet is directly related to the syllabary. At one time, to cite another hypothetical instance, the signs XY might be established to represent the two-syllable sequence /ba-sa/, each sign representing a single syllable. In time, the language had changed to the point where the sequence was pronounced /bas/, but the scribes continued to record XY, until it was noticed that this and like instances occurred, whereupon X came to signal /b/ and Y, /s/. Thus gradually, over a long period of time, the alphabet was developed out of the syllabary. This also helps to explain the reason why early alphabets, like the Egyptian hieroglyphics and the Hebrew, consisted only of consonant signs—the placement and value of the vowels in the sequence have to be guessed at from the context. Another late development was the concept of word division; in early writing systems, the letters were allruntogetherlikethis.

It also seems clear that the present alphabetical systems of the world all developed from a single source, probably from the system used by the ancient Phoenicians. Table 6–1 will help to clarify the historical relationships as our alphabet developed. From this table, it seems clear that the ancient Greeks borrowed the system from the Semitic, changing the representations to suit themselves, in the process developing vowel signs. The Greek system was then borrowed by the Etruscans, and our present Latin alphabet came in part from the Etruscan system, and partly from the Classical Greek.[3]

---

[3] The Old Semitic alphabet seems to have been based upon a rough pictorial representation of things whose initial sound the representation signaled: for instance, *'alef* "ox"; *bēth* "house"; *kaf* "palm of the hand"; *tāw* "mark, cross". The Greeks adapted it to their uses; having no "rough breathing" sound, they took *'alef* over as *alpha*, representing its initial vowel sound. The Hebrew scribes later adopted the occasional use of *vowel points*.

With reference to the chart, notice the evidence for the "backward" (to our way of thinking) linear sequence of the alphabet signs in early Greek and Etruscan—from right to left. Early Greek inscriptions often ran both ways, the artisan simply working back and forth, reversing the letters as he worked back. This is efficient working procedure, but tough on the reader. Standard left-to-right ordering was established during the classical period and adopted subsequently by all who borrowed from the Greeks.

Old Semitic		Oldest Greek Alphabet		Classical Greek				
Character	Name in Hebrew (phonetic value)	Character	Name	Character	Name	Etruscan	Early Latin	Roman
𐤀	'alef (')	𐤀	alpha (a)	A		A	A A A	A
𐤁	bēth (b)	𐤁	bāta (b)	B	bēta		B B	B
𐤂	gimel (g)	Γ	gamma (g)	Γ		>	< C	C
𐤃	dāleth (d)	Δ	delta (d)	Δ			D	D
𐤄	hē (h)	Ⴄ	epsilon (e)	E		Ⴄ	Ɛ E	E
𐤅	wāw (w)	Y Ⅎ	vau, digamma (v, w)			Ⅎ	Ⅎ F	F
								G (from C)
I	zayin (z)	I	dzāta (dz)	Z	zēta (z)	⨍		H
𐤇	ḥēth (ḥ)	𐤇	hāta (h)	H	ēta (ē)	𐤇	H	H
⊕	ṭēth (ṭ)	⊗	thāta (th)	Θ	thēta	⊙		
𐤆	yōd (y)	⌐	iāta (i)	I	iōta	/	/	I, J
𐤊	kaf (k)	𐤊	kappa (k)	K		𐤊	K Ⴌ	K
𐤋	lāmed (l)	𐤋	lambda (l)	Λ		J	L	L
𐤌	mēm (m)	𐤌	mū (m)	M	mȳ	𐤌	Ⳇ M	M
𐤍	nūn (n)	𐤍	nū (n)	N	nȳ	𐤍	Ⲛ	N
≠	sāmoch (s)	I	ksē (khs)	Ξ	ksī, xī			
O	'ayim (')	O	ō (o)	O	omicron		◊ O Ω	O
𐤐	pē (p)	𐤐	pē (p)	Π	pī	Ⴈ	Ɽ P	P
𐤑	ṣādē (ṣ)	𐤌	sampī (s)			Ⳇ		
𐤒	ḳof (ḳ)	𐤒	koppa (k)			Q	Ɂ Ɋ	Q
𐤓	rēš (r)	Ⴘ	rhā (r)	P	rhō	Ⴘ	Ɽ R	R
W	šīn (š)	Ϟ	sigma (s)	Σ		Ϟ	Ϟ S	S
+	tāw (t)	T	tau (t)	T		+	T	T
				Υ	ūpsilon (y)	V	V	U, V, W
				Φ	phī (ph)	φ		
				X	chī (kh)	↓		X
				Ψ	psī (ps)			
				Ω	omēga (ō)			
								Y (from ūpsilon) Z (from zēta)

Table 6–1. Development of the Roman Alphabet.

The Alphabet and Spelling

We have already said that no alphabetical system currently in use is perfect. That used for English is certainly no exception. Our alphabet consists of twenty-six letters, yet there are over forty phonemes (depending on the dialect spoken). Further, this already inadequate system is wasteful: three letters, *c*, *k*, and *s*, are used to represent two phonemes /k, s/; and we really don't need *x* and *q*. The deficiency must be supplied by digraphs, like *th*. Further, there are partial adaptations from other languages, like the twelve different spellings for the single phoneme /š/, as in ti*ss*ue, *sh*ow, *s*ure, to enumerate just three. Finally, there are the patent absurdities which can mislead the unwary, like en*ough*, b*ough*, thr*ough*, thor*ough*.

There are several reasons for this state of affairs, one of which stems from the invention of the printing press (1455) and the wide dissemination of books following its establishment in England (1476). Despite the great service the press performed both to learning and to literacy, the fact remains that it has been a commercial venture since its beginning, and the primary consideration of the printer or publisher, then as now, was whether or not a work would sell. Therefore, the early printers, Caxton and his successors, were quicker to print older writers like Chaucer, for whom there was a great demand, than to take a chance on some untested contemporary. This conservative practice led to the introduction in England of a conservative orthography, the core of which has been with us ever since.

This is not to suggest that our spelling practices are identical with Chaucer's. In point of fact, the printers did not establish a standard orthography until about 1700. In the meantime, they were, within limits, pretty free with their spelling. In order to keep the right-hand margin even—justifying the page, they called it—they would frequently alter the spelling of words to squeeze or expand a line. Some spellings became standard through pure idiosyncrasy. Flemish printers, for instance, introduced the practice of the initial *gh* in *ghost*. In sum, the tendency has been for printing to inaugurate a distinctively conservative trend, and spelling changes since 1700 have been so few as to be virtually nonexistent.

Another factor is pedantry. Nothing except a misplaced pride of learning can account for such spellings as *doubt* and *debt*, established for no other reason than that their Latin cognates included a *b* which had since disappeared. But despite the pedantry and the development of standard orthography in printing, a good many highly educated Englishmen, and later, Americans, continued to spell pretty much as they pleased in their own informal writing, leaving it to the typesetter to standardize their orthography in writing for publication.

It took another phenomenon to make "correct spelling" a virtue, and this was the wide spread of free public education, with the concurrent introduction of the speller, notably Webster's, and the development of spelling games. From this sequence of developments, there arose the notion that the most readily accessible measure of a man's intelligence was whether or not he could spell every word correctly. Thus, what began as a convenience to the printers has since become a positive virtue, a notion that persists undiminished down to our own time. A somewhat more problematical theory holds that our rigid insistence upon orthographical purity is an aristocratic tendency, a means of separating the socially acceptable from the Great Unwashed, a further example of *conspicuous consumption*.[4] Whatever the reason, the fact is that, like it or not, we are obliged to spend a good deal of time learning a spelling system which has the appearance of being highly erratic.

The System of English Spelling

Fortunately, this erratic appearance is only on the surface. Any kind of investigation will demonstrate that underlying our spelling system is, in fact, a real *system*, just as the word implies. And, as Professor Robert A. Hall, Jr., has demonstrated, this system can be incorporated into any school classroom in the early elementary years.[5]

[4] As you might have guessed, this thesis was advanced by Thorstein Veblen in *Theory of the Leisure Class*. See Robert A. Hall, Jr., "Thorstein Veblen and Linguistic Theory," *American Speech*, XXXV (1960), 124–30.

[5] See Hall's pamphlet *Sound and Spelling in English* (Philadelphia: Chilton Books, 1961), part of which is incorporated into chapters 45, 73, and 74 of *Introductory*

First of all, the consonant letters, with some trifling exceptions, seem to accord fairly well with the consonant phonemes. The unusual divergences, like *ph* for /f/, are all learned with a fair amount of ease. The problem comes with the vowel letters, of which there are admittedly too few to make any significant one-to-one correlation with the vowel phonemes. Yet here there is system. We can recognize the regular letters and letter combinations which invariably correspond to specific sounds, as /ɪ/ spelled *i* or /i/ spelled *ee*. We can also recognize the "irregular regularities," as when /i/ is spelled *ie* or *ea*, the reasons for which can easily be found in any good etymological dictionary. The vast majority of English spellings fall into these two categories. Only a very few are genuinely irregular and must be learned individually: w*o*m*e*n, s*ie*ve, dou*b*t, and the like.

In short, the letters of the English alphabet fall into a regular distributional pattern which can itself be learned, eliminating the necessity of memorizing the spelling of each word by rote, except in the rare instance where the spelling falls outside of the pattern. Thus, the late George Bernard Shaw was talking learnéd nonsense when he insisted that *ghoti* should be pronounced /fɪš/: *gh* as in *enough*, *o* as in *women*, and *ti* as in *action*. The distributional pattern of English won't allow this pronunciation for this cluster of letters. The *gh* combination occurs only in a final position as /f/, *o* as /ɪ/ occurs only in *women*, so far as I can tell, and *ti* as /š/ occurs only as the initial cluster in the combination *-tion*. Ask any casual passerby what *ghoti* spells, and unless he is in on Shaw's joke, he will invariably reply /góti/. Under the circumstances, this is the only possible response for this particular group of letters.

The Spelling System Applied

The results from such a study clearly indicate that there is a sensible approach to reading and spelling. First, the regular spelling patterns should be introduced early, saving the irregular

---

Linguistics, previously cited. I am greatly indebted to Hall's study, of which the discussion following is only the barest summary.

ones for later on in the elementary grades (except for some necessary irregularities which are essential even to elementary reading, such as *was*). And second, teachers should learn to recognize that some spelling errors are worse than others. Some misspellings result from an attempt on the child's part to super-impose regularity upon irregularity, while others are indicative of the child's complete inability to correlate letter and sound. Unfortunately, both kinds of errors receive equal punishment, and in neither instance does much good result from the correction.

Obviously, this represents a departure from the two most widely used methods of teaching reading and spelling. The so-called *look–say* method is now justly criticized because it doesn't attempt to correlate letters and letter combinations with sounds, and because it encourages the child to guess or to rely on pictures. On the other hand, the so-called *phonics* approach is deficient in that it does not really recognize the category of the "irregular regular" spellings. Thus, when by analogy a child spells *leave* "leve," he is told only that the correct spelling is "irregular" and must be memorized, usually by writing it twenty-five times. In short, the phonics approach assumes too much irregularity, requiring unnecessary rote learning.

It would appear, therefore, that despite its recognizable deficiencies, our spelling system isn't so bad after all. Certainly, spelling reform isn't the answer. Even discounting the astronomical expense—for every book would have to be reprinted—and the chaotic confusion resulting from having to work initially with two spelling systems at once, there remains the fact that the inescapable certainty of language change would make a new reform necessary. For better or worse, we are stuck with the spelling system we have, and rather than complain about it, we would do better to learn to use it efficiently.

QUESTIONS AND EXERCISES—WRITING AND SPELLING

1. In any decent desk dictionary, under *alphabet*, you should find charts showing the Hebraic and Cyrillic alphabets, the latter

being that used in Russia, Bulgaria, and the Serbian portion of Yugoslavia. Some dictionaries also print the Arabic alphabet. Study them carefully, and show the nature of their relationship to the alphabets in the chart on page 146.

2. *Before* you look into Hall's pamphlet, classify the vowel letters and letter combinations into the three categories given above, using any extended prose passages as your working text. Check your results against Hall's.

3. This is primarily for those contemplating careers in elementary education:

>   a. Check any spelling text used in the early elementary grades, classifying the words to be learned into our three categories. How well does the book follow the suggestion that spelling patterns be introduced working from regular to irregular? The same analysis might also prove interesting for an upper-grade text, preferably one from the same series.
>   b. In like manner, check the word lists printed in the teacher's edition of an early elementary reader. What percentage of the words follow the regular spelling patterns?

4. In any desk dictionary, check the pronunciation key against the phoneme lists in Chapter 4. How closely is the dictionary key predicated on spelling? What are the advantages and disadvantages of basing the key on spelling, rather than using phonemic symbols?

5. From time to time, advocates of spelling reform come forward with proposals for changing English spelling. Usually, their proposed reform is based on the standard alphabet with the addition of diacritical markings. How valid are the following reasons which have been advanced to justify these reform movements?

>   a. Conventional spelling is retarding the acceptance of English as a universal language.
>   b. Standard English orthography is only eight per cent phonetic.
>   c. Because Russian is spelled phonetically, the Russian school-children are three years ahead of their compeers in America.
>   d. A phonetic system will eliminate mispronunciations which are commonly caused by illogical spelling.

e. Because inability to read is the major cause of school dropouts, reformed spelling would help to stop this tragic situation.

USAGE

The Problem of Usage

Probably no single by-product of linguistic science has caused so much consternation in the English-speaking world as what has come to be called the **doctrine of usage.** This is especially curious when one discovers that there is nothing particularly new or startling about it. The concept that *the details of a language are what the speakers of that language make them* is a corollary of the principles developed in the mid-nineteenth century by the philologists. Yet, when American linguists advanced the doctrine of usage, almost in an offhand way, as one of the axioms of their studies, the opposition from the public was surprising in its fury and intensity, and it has continued virtually unabated ever since. Just when the uproar seems to die down, something comes along to whip it up all over again. The most recent episode of this sort which comes to mind followed the publication, in 1961, of *Webster's Third New International Dictionary.*

It is not our purpose here to summarize this debate. This has been done many times before. Nor are we going to cover individual items of divided usage, for there are plenty of excellent usage handbooks on the market. Rather, we shall try here to focus upon the whole concept of usage as it relates to language theory, thereby crystallizing it for the discriminating student of English.

Plainly stated, usage involves a choice between two forms or pronunciations which both appear to do the same thing, objectively considered. Obviously, the procedure would be to follow the lead of one's peer group, and this is generally what people do. Unfortunately, the problem is intensified by social pronouncements about the "best English," by which the usage lawmaker usually means "my English." There is really no problem with usages which plainly divide vertically by classes, as *he don't* for *he doesn't,* or *I is* for *I am.* One of the difficulties comes when usage is divided horizontally over regions, as with *hadn't ought to* vs. *ought not to,* each regional champion claiming that the other is wrong. Another source of trouble is divided standard usage, such as *will* vs. *shall* or *like* vs. *as,* when a "rule" is invented by appealing to logic, a rule which does nothing except increase one's sense of linguistic insecurity. The whole trouble comes from an insistence upon complete rigidity, a failure to recognize that language has both vertical and horizontal relativity.

The Source of the Misunderstanding

It is clear to anyone who has followed the problem that much of the trouble is based on a misunderstanding of the nature of writing. Hopefully, this has been clarified in Chapter 1 and in the preceding section. But even so, it is obvious that the critics of the usage doctrine, and, by an illogical extension, of linguistics itself, identify language with writing. This is not surprising in itself, since so many of these critics are very sensitive writers. Writing, by its very nature, is the fixing of the writer's thoughts in relatively permanent form. Speech, on the other hand, is momentary, fragmentary, even "sloppy." No wonder then that those who are most concerned about expression would tend to deify writing.

Besides distorting the position of writing, this attitude fails to recognize an essential difference between spoken and written usage. First of all, some usages are limited to speaking only, and never occur in writing. It is impossible to conceive of a written context for *it's me,* for instance, and anyone who utters *it is I* will stop any conversation cold. Likewise, those who habitually say *ain't,* especially in the context *ain't I,* including at least one distinguished professor of English, would never write it. Second, because written expression can be polished, revised, and reshaped before it is presented for public scrutiny, it regularly has both formal organization and conscious attention to complete sentence structure, which informal speaking lacks. On the other hand, informal speaking doesn't require these simply because there are suitable substitutes for them, such as the presence of the speaker, his intonation patterns, and his use of gestures. Finally, writing has tended to reflect the ideal of language, rather than its actuality. Formal writing lacks contractions, for instance, which are normal to speaking, and very seldom does writing of any kind reflect the regional usages of the writer.[6] Upon reflection, one can see that the view which holds to the superiority of writing over speaking is simply naive.

Usage Reality

Recognition of this false dichotomy, then, should be the primary responsibility of the student of language. To hold dogmatic opinions about usage is worse than foolish—it is useless. Everyone, and particularly teachers and parents, must realize that each individual uses language which is appropriate to the occasion. Anyone who ignores the occasion—who, for instance, does not use the slang of his in-group when in that company—does so at his own peril. In like manner, college students who take summer jobs with factory workers or construction crews find that while they are on the job their speech reflects certain usages of their co-workers which are not part of the classroom dialogue or the banter of the fraternity house. If the student wants to gain the acceptance and goodwill of his temporary co-workers, he must adopt their language standards in their company.

Strange to say, the college student's speech is never permanently affected by this contact, however prolonged. He is, in fact, able to change to his regular usage patterns easily and quite unconsciously, as soon as he punches out at the end of his shift. And this is a common occurrence in our own lives. Many times in the course of a day each of us shifts his usage patterns unconsciously according to the situation. In my contacts with students, I am successively lecturer, discussion leader, critic, advisor, tutor, and counselor, in no particular order, and each of these capacities requires a perceptible change in usage patterns.

---

[6] A single exception would be the possible use of dialectal vocabulary items, where the usage is a regional standard.

Add to this, interchanges with my departmental colleagues, those from other departments, book salesmen, tradespeople, repairmen, and the like, and it is easy to see that there is no such thing as complete consistency where usage is concerned.

Two cautionary items should be mentioned here, particularly for the benefit of the teacher. First, you must recognize the usage patterns characteristic of the local dialect. It is sheer folly even to attempt to impose the pronunciation patterns of Upper New York State, for instance, on schoolchildren in San Antonio. In this connection, I can remember being told by my seventh-grade teacher never to use *et* as the past tense of *eat*, a usage which neither I nor my fellow students had ever heard of before. But the form tickled us, and soon we found ourselves using it, humorously, of course, in many situations—a development which must have pained the teacher greatly.[7]

Second, when teachers find themselves in a district where the prevailing usage is, by middle-class norms, substandard, it is a commendable practice to attempt to raise the usage levels of their charges. But this must be accompanied by sufficient motivation, or it will be time wasted, and the teacher must take care to point out that all usage is appropriate within its contexts. Otherwise, what the teacher is trying to do will either seem unreal, or instill a feeling of linguistic inferiority. In either case, the instruction will do more harm than good. In this respect, the teacher should carefully select which items to stress. Too many prohibitions can be both discouraging and disheartening.[8]

---

[7] Our teacher was, of course, simply following the book. So impressed are we all by the fact of publication that we often govern our lives by the maxim, "I saw it in print, so it must be true." It never occurred to the teacher to verify the usage prohibition or to determine whether such a stricture was necessary. All of us need to remember that the printed word, including usage rules, is written, edited, and set up by mortal men—feeble, fallible, and prone to error.

[8] It doesn't take much to convince the student who receives no educational encouragement at home that the classroom is completely divorced from reality. Just imagine the impact of the Dick and Jane readers on the children of the ghetto! But even the well-motivated students will find many usage prescriptions to be unreal, and though they will go along with them in school, they will ignore them outside. The eavesdropping teacher will think that he has failed—but he really hasn't. He's just wasted some classroom time. Too much time wasted on unreality, however, and he will have failed.

Summary

We can summarize our discussion of the doctrine of usage with the following precepts:

1. There are no hard and fast rules about usage. One's usage is always relative as to place, time, situation, and social condition.

2. One should bear in mind the distinction of John S. Kenyon between cultural *levels* of usage, which are social, and functional *varieties*, which are situational, within the framework of one's cultural level.[9] There is justification in trying to raise the cultural level of a student's language habits, at least by precept and example, but one can do virtually nothing about functional varieties—and it sometimes takes a sharp teacher to be able to distinguish the difference between the two.

3. Always remember that one's speech is a deeply personal thing. Arbitrarily insisting, even with the best of intentions, that something is "wrong" with someone's speech will raise either hackles or a barrier. With the shy and insecure, it can lead to complete alienation, which is the worst possible result.

4. We have had these popular notions of "right" and "wrong" in language for a long time, and they won't disappear for quite a long time, either. Consequently, people have become linguistically insecure. They look to the teachers of English for guidance, and when the teachers honestly admit that they don't have the answers either, the general public, in shock and surprise, accuses them of abrogating their responsibility. If you accept the tenets of the usage doctrine, you will have to resign yourself to repeating them over and over, and you will come to accept the fact that your statements will frequently fall on deaf ears.

The answer is that your own ear is the final arbiter in all instances and situations (acknowledging an assist from your own personal prejudices). Reliance upon mythical "authorities" can only lead to contradiction and confusion. However much we give

---

[9] See his "Cultural Levels and Functional Varieties of English," *College English*, X (1948–1949), 31–36; reprinted in Allen (ed.), *Readings in Applied Linguistics*, pp. 294–301, and Rycenga and Schwartz (eds.), *Perspectives on Language*, pp. 229–36.

lip service to usage absolutes, in practice we actually follow the usage doctrine all the way.

QUESTIONS AND EXERCISES—USAGE

1. Some time ago, Robert C. Pooley formulated the following set of standards for teachers,[10] with an additional list of usage items which they were *not* to bother with:

> The standard we can rightfully set for ourselves, our colleagues in other departments, and our students, for public and private use, contains at present [1960] these particulars:
>
> 1. The elimination of all baby-talk and "cute" expressions
> 2. The correct uses in speech and writing of *I, me, he, him, she, her, they, them.* (Exception, *it's me.*)
> 3. The correct uses of *is, are, was, were* with respect to number and tense.
> 4. Correct past tenses of common irregular verbs such as *saw, gave, took, brought, bought, stuck.*
> 5. Correct use of past participles of the same verbs and similar verbs after auxiliaries.
> 6. Elimination of the double negative: we don't have no apples, etc.
> 7. Elimination of analogical forms: *ain't, hisn, hern, ourn, theirselves,* etc.
> 8. Correct use of possessive pronouns: *my, mine, his, hers, theirs, ours.*
> 9. Mastery of the distinction between *its,* possessive pronoun, and *it's, it is.*
> 10. Placement of *have* or its phonetic reduction to *v* between *I* and a past participle.
> 11. Elimination of *them* as a demonstrative pronoun.
> 12. Elimination of *this here* and *that there.*
> 13. Mastery of use of *a* and *an* as articles.
> 14. Correct use of personal pronouns in compound constructions: as subject (Mary and I), as object (Mary and me), as object of preposition (to Mary and me).

[10] In "Dare Schools Set a Standard in English Usage?" *English Journal*, XLIX (1960), 176–81; reprinted in Allen, pp. 324–29. Reprinted with the permission of the National Council of Teachers of English and Robert C. Pooley.

15. The use of *we* before an appositional noun when subject; *us* when object.
16. Correct number agreement with the phrases *there is, there are, there was, there were.*
17. Elimination of *he don't, she don't, it don't.*
18. Elimination of *learn* for *teach*, *leave* for *let.*
19. Elimination of pleonastic subjects: *my brother he*; *my mother she*; *that fellow he.*
20. Proper agreement in number with antecedent pronouns *one* and *anyone, everyone, each, no one.* With *everybody* and *none* some tolerance of number seems acceptable now.
21. The use of *who* and *whom* as reference to persons. (But note, *Who did he give it to?* is tolerated in all but very formal situations. In the latter, *To whom did he give it* is preferable.)
22. Accurate use of *said* in reporting the words of a speaker in the past.
23. Correction of *lay down* to *lie down.*
24. The distinction between *good* as adjective, and *well* as adverb, e.g., He spoke *well.*
25. Elimination of *can't hardly, all the farther* (for *as far as*) and Where is he (she, it) *at?*

This list of twenty-five kinds of corrections to make constitutes a very specific standard of current English usage for today and the next few years. Some elements in it may require modification within ten years; some possibly earlier. Conspicuous by their absence are these items which were on the usage lists by which many of us were taught and which survive today in the less enlightened textbooks.

1. Any distinction between *shall* and *will.*
2. Any reference to the split infinitive.
3. Elimination of *like* as a conjunction.
4. Objection to the phrase "different than."
5. Objection to He is one of those boys who *is.*
6. Objection to the reason . . . is because . . . .
7. Objection to *myself* as a polite substitute for *I* as in "I understand you will meet Mrs. Jones and myself at the station."
8. Insistence upon the possessive case standing before a gerund.

These items and many others like them will still remain cautionary matters left to the teacher's discretion. In evaluating the writing of a superior student I would certainly call these distinctions to his attention and point out to him the value of observing them. But this is a very different matter from setting a basic usage standard to be maintained. I think it is fair to say that the items I have listed in the basic table lie outside the tolerable limits of acceptable, current, informal usage; those I have omitted from the base table are tolerated at least, and in some instances are in very general use.

Study these lists carefully. Which items should be removed from the first list as lost causes? Which are more problems of writing than of speaking, and *vice versa*? Do you agree in every instance with Pooley's comment in the last paragraph of the quotation, especially with the statement that the items in the first list "lie outside the tolerable limits of acceptable, current, informal usage"? Do you have strong feelings about any of the items in the second, shorter list?

2. Nothing so incenses self-appointed usage guardians as any utterance of *ain't*. An interesting insight into this problem can be gleaned from a perusal of the exchange of letters over this word in *College English*, XXVI (1964–1965), 91–110, 298–303, 402–5, resulting from the entry on *ain't* in *Webster's Third New International*. Study this dictionary entry. Does it actually sanction the use of this word? Why do you suppose that the entry aroused so much criticism?

3. Consult the usage section of any high school or college English handbook. Which items do you think are unrealistically presented? What authority does the author cite in making his pronouncements? Do you notice any evidence that the doctrine of usage, as presented above, has had any effect on the author or his publisher?

STYLE

Toward a Definition of Style

Saying anything intelligent about **style,** of all the areas of applied linguistics, is extremely difficult. Many studies in this area have the misfortune of appearing so obvious that they scarcely seem worth writing. Further, we really know so little about the whole subject. It's even impossible to reach agreement on a definition. Should one attempt a structural analysis of a literary passage, he is apt to incur the righteous wrath of those who feel that any analysis is inappropriate to the subject. Worse, he is also apt to have his own rhetorical infelicities pointed out to him in all their nakedness, especially if he has done similar service to others in the course of his study.

With these inhibiting factors in mind, I propose to do no more here than sketch the subject rapidly, hoping that I can suggest some aspects of this field which might serve as points for further study. To this end, a good starting point would be to at least hazard a definition.

A working definition of style would be the *distinctive manner in which one handles one's language, with due consideration given to its appropriateness for the occasion.* Thus, with its attention to the situation, style bears a close relationship with usage. Note, too, the modern tendency to enlarge the application of style to include the whole man—the common expression, "Jones is a good man. I like his style." On the other hand, style should be kept distinct from **rhetoric,** which is the study (or the practice) of *effective* use of language. Very often the distinction is blurred, and I often feel that studies purporting to be of rhetoric are more truly studies of stylistic practice. Besides, "rhetoric" is at the moment a vogue word in professional circles.

The Levels of Style

There is a strong inclination to limit style to written expression, but this is far too narrow a concept of the word. Martin Joos has recently written an analysis of five levels—or perhaps better, functional varieties—of style which ties together spoken and written language and also shows the relationship between style and usage.[11] These levels, with their characteristics are:

11 *The Five Clocks,* Publication 22, Indiana University Research Center in Anthropology, Folklore, and Linguistics (April, 1962). Reprinted, 1967, by Harcourt, Brace & World, Inc.

1. *Intimate,* limited to very close relationships, as within the family, characterized by virtually a private jargon of the group.
2. *Casual,* widened to include a social or occupational in-group with which one is identified, characterized by language practices to mystify and hence exclude the outsider—ellipsis (or sentence deletion) and slang.
3. *Consultative,* used between relative strangers, in which the speaker constantly supplies conversational background, while the addressee participates to the extent that he continuously interjects nods or affirmative syllables to show that he's listening.
4. *Formal,* a planned presentation, as a lecture, in which the speaker holds the floor detached from those addressed— always a group—who listen respectfully and passively.
5. *Frozen,* the style of literature.

These five styles, while admittedly subjective—Joos's study is remarkable for its extreme informality—at least show the relationship between spoken and written style and the relationship of style to usage. Notice how slang, the ephemeral language of the in-group, fits in here. It serves to identify the individual, its very ephemeral nature a protection against outsiders. Any teacher who declares war against it is simply tilting at windmills. This serves to demonstrate the inappropriateness of slang outside of the group itself—nothing dates a person like his use of his own teen-age slang.

Yet the subjectivity of this list severely limits it as an effective basis for the study of style. The key to Joos's analysis is his *consultative* level, but this is a level hedged with special distinctions. We must admit the frequent use of this style—the speaker constantly filling in background while the listener interjects "yes . . . yes . . . of course . . . uh-huh . . ." every five or ten seconds. Rarely, however, does it appear that this style is used for very long. Either the two participants become casual, or one takes charge, addressing the other "like a public meeting." The nature of the telephone automatically makes most conversation consultative simply because of the lack of propinquity. The conversers take turns holding forth, while the other utters the syllables which mean only, "I'm still here; I haven't hung up."

Stylistic Analysis of Literature

The very vagueness, too, of the category of frozen style puts us right back where we began. We recognize the existence—broadly considered—of the other categories, and we would not deny the individual development in each of highly personal, distinctive modes of expression. But these are virtually automatic. For the teacher, however, or the writer for that matter, there is the need of an effective and useful means of stylistic analysis whereby the distinctive traits of a writer can be revealed for analysis and that which seems ineffective or inappropriate can likewise be examined. We sense, for instance, that there is a wide difference between the writing of Faulkner and Hemingway—we can distinguish between them with little trouble. I'll even wager that, similar though they are, you could easily distinguish between the styles of Faulkner and Henry James, were parallel passages set before you.[12] But this is still subjective; without resorting to absolute behaviorism, isn't there some way in which stylistic traits can be open to analysis and intelligent comment?

I believe that this is a distinct possibility, and if I fail to give analytical details, it is primarily because our discussion in preceding chapters hasn't investigated these means in sufficient depth, though I also feel that I am rushing into deep water. However, I believe that there do exist several distinct possibilities for stylistic analysis.

1. Extended passages can be analyzed transformationally in terms of the surface rearrangements of a writer's sentences. Analysis would reveal recurring transformational patterns which the author constantly uses—and also those which are relatively rare.

2. Structure is only part of style. The writer's use of words would also be important. We would need to analyze the etymologies of key words—are they Latinate or Germanic, learned or common? Less amenable to analysis is the author's choice of a word over another. This involves problems of connotation, which is the province of semantics.

---

[12] Along this line, a popular game of literary solitaire is to guess the identity of the author of a *New Yorker* short story without peeking at the name at the end.

3. For pedagogical purposes, stylistic analysis is intended not for purposes of imitation, but for help in the development of style. Here we become concerned with the effectiveness of a passage—a subjective judgment, and part of the province of rhetoric—but once one has identified ineffective writing, he can analyze the surface transformations. Such analysis can reveal possible alternatives, gaps in sentence embedding, and instances of ambiguity.

4. There is no reason why poetry cannot be similarly analyzed, save for incurring the poet's displeasure. Such analysis can be useful in demonstrating poetic diction, ambiguity (considered admirable in poetry), and poetic density. This clearly comes within the range of criticism, and could make an objective basis for what must ultimately be a deeply personal subjective reaction.

Perhaps these offerings are obvious; perhaps they are ultimately unimportant. Certainly they must not be abused by becoming ends in themselves. I feel that their best use is pedagogical, a possible means of interrelating the discrete subjects that make up "English." Certainly the subject of style offers a more promising opportunity for the classroom than dwelling on spelling lessons or usage workbooks. Here, at least, is a fresh field. Perhaps its newness can generate a genuinely enthusiastic response.

QUESTIONS AND EXERCISES—STYLE

1. Based on the preceding discussion, what impediments do you think stand in the way of applying the discoveries and techniques of linguistics to an analysis of style? Are these impediments primarily internal or external—that is, are they built into the problem, or are they imposed from outside? Can they be overcome sufficiently to make stylistic analysis viable?

2. This will have to be optional: attempt a stylistic analysis— its depth is purely relative to your inclination or ability—of a passage from a major prose writer of the past century or so. Possibilities might include Carlyle, Pater, Ruskin; James, Howells, Crane, Lewis, Hemingway, Faulkner; Lincoln, Woodrow Wilson, Franklin Roosevelt, Churchill, John F. Kennedy.

Granted the impossibility of complete analysis, can you make any generalizations on what makes the author's style distinctive?

3. The following student theme is admittedly stylistically inept. Analyze it for the linguistic ineptness, and—if you like— offer amendments or improvements.

"People who play cards at home never know when it snows." This old Chinese proverb has deep and truthful meaning. It means simply that people who sit home all the time and play cards and care only about themselves never know what's going on in the outside world today or even if it's snowing out.

I think this is relevant to people today. So many of us are tied up in our own affairs we don't know about other people's problems or even the nation's problems.

You have to concern yourself with the problems of today in order to be the type of person our country needs. Only small-minded pessimists stay at home and keep to themselves.

I think this proverb also leads to bring out the point of don't always sit at home and do the same things, but spread your wings a little and experience part of the world around you. Become broadminded.

How can you carry on any conversations of any intelligence without a little knowledge of the things around you?

You won't always be able to sit back and watch the world because each day it's getting to involve you more and more. Stop playing your hand and take time out to look at your opponents.

This proverb tells us that people who sit at home don't know what's going on and have a limited view of life. Don't play cards so long and often that you don't even know if it's snowing out.

4. The following poems all present interesting problems of criticism which might be helped by making reference to stylistic analysis. What recurring grammatical patterns give evidence of the poet's style? What grammatical conventions are stretched or broken for the greater needs of the poet, and why did the poet ignore or circumvent the dictates of standard grammatical practice? In which passages does grammatical analysis aid in interpretation?

Gerard Manley Hopkins

SPRING AND FALL: to a young child[13]

Márgarét, are you gríeving
Over Goldengrove unleaving?
Léaves, líke the things of man, you
With your fresh thoughts care for, can you?
Áh! ás the heart grows older
It will come to such sights colder
By and by, nor spare a sigh
Though worlds of wanwood leafmeal lie;
And yet you wíll weep and know why.
Now no matter, child, the name:
Sórrow's spríngs áre the same.
Nor mouth had, no nor mind, expressed
What heart heard of, ghost guessed:
It is the blight man was born for,
It is Margaret you mourn for.

HURRAHING IN HARVEST[14]

Summer ends now; now, barbarous in beauty, the stooks arise
  Around; up above, what wind-walks! what lovely behaviour
  Of silk-sack clouds! has wilder, wilful-wavier
Meal-drift moulded ever and melted across skies?
I walk, I lift up, I lift up heart, eyes,
  Down all that glory in the heavens to glean our Saviour;
  And, éyes, héart, what looks, what lips yet gave you a
Rapturous love's greeting of realer, of rounder replies?

And the azurous hung hills are his world-wielding shoulder
  Majestic—as a stallion stalwart, very-violet-sweet!—
These things, these things were here and but the beholder
  Wanting; which two when they once meet,
The heart rears wings bold and bolder
  And hurls for him, O half hurls earth for him off under his feet.

---

[13] Robert Bridges and W. H. Gardner (eds.), *Poems of Gerard Manley Hopkins* (3d ed.; New York: Oxford University Press, 1948).
[14] *Ibid.*

Emily Dickinson[15]

The Robin's my Criterion for Tune—
Because I grow—where Robins do—
But, were I Cuckoo born—
I'd swear by him—
The ode familiar—rules the Noon—
The Buttercup's, my Whim for Bloom—
Because, we're Orchard sprung—
But, were I Britain born,
I'd Daisies spurn—
None but the Nut—October fit—
Because, through dropping it,
The Seasons flit—I'm taught—
Without the Snow's Tableau
Winter, were lie—to me—
Because I see—New Englandly—
The Queen, discerns like me—
Provincially—

What Soft—Cherubic Creatures—
These Gentlewomen are—
One would as soon assault a Plush—
Or violate a Star—

Such Dimity Convictions—
A Horror so refined
Of freckled Human Nature—
Of Deity—ashamed—

---

[15] Reprinted by permission of the publishers and the Trustees of Amherst College from Thomas H. Johnson (ed.), *The Poems of Emily Dickinson* (Cambridge, Mass.: The Belknap Press of Harvard University Press). Copyright 1951, 1955 by the President and Fellows of Harvard College. "The Robin's my Criterion for Tune" copyright 1929, © 1957 by Mary L. Hampson, reprinted also by permission of Little, Brown and Company.

It's such a common—Glory—
A Fisherman's—Degree—
Redemption—Brittle Lady—
Be so—ashamed of Thee—

I heard a Fly buzz—when I died—
The Stillness in the Room
Was like the Stillness in the Air—
Between the Heaves of Storm—

The Eyes around—had wrung them dry—
And Breaths were gathering firm
For that last Onset—when the King
Be witnessed—in the Room—

I willed my Keepsakes—signed away
What portion of me be
Assignable—and then it was
There interposed a Fly—

With Blue—uncertain stumbling Buzz—
Between the light—and me—
And then the Windows failed—and then
I could not see to see—

BIBLIOGRAPHY

A good basic introduction to the history of writing can be found in David Diringer, *Writing* (New York: Frederick A. Praeger, 1962), Volume 25 of the *Ancient People and Places* series. More advanced studies are the same author's *The Alphabet: A Key to the History of Mankind* (2d rev. ed.; New York: Philosophical Library, 1948); and Ignace J. Gelb, *A Study of Writing* (Chicago: University of Chicago Press, 1952). Hall's studies of English spelling have already been mentioned. His suggestions for teaching spelling have been incorporated into the *Roberts English Series*.

The basic study on the background of usage prescriptions is Sterling A. Leonard, *The Doctrine of Correctness in English Usage 1700–1800* (Madison: University of Wisconsin Press, 1929), recently reprinted by Russell and Russell. Two classic studies of actual usage are A. H. Marckwardt and Fred Walcott, *Facts About Current American Usage* (New York: Appleton-Century-Crofts, 1938); and Charles C. Fries, *American English Grammar* (New York: Appleton-Century-Crofts, 1940). The only objective usage handbook is Margaret M. Bryant, *Current American Usage* (New York: Funk and Wagnall's, 1962); the others, ranging from the classic Fowler, through Bergen Evans, to the recent Wilson Follett, reflect the reactions and prejudices of the editors— though many purists would be surprised if they read Fowler on *ain't* (s.v. *be*) and the split infinitive. A representative collection of the reviews and reactions greeting the publication of the new Webster's is found in James Sledd and Wilma R. Ebbitt (eds.), *Dictionaries and* That *Dictionary* (Chicago: Scott, Foresman and Company, 1962). Robert C. Pooley, *Teaching English Usage* (New York: Appleton-Century-Crofts, 1946), though dated, still contains good advice for the teacher. A descriptive grammar of English which was written according to basic principles of the usage concept is J. N. Hook and E. G. Mathews, *Modern American Grammar and Usage* (New York: The Ronald Press Company, 1956).

An early contribution to the field of stylistics is Thomas A. Sebeok (ed.), *Style in Language* (New York: Technology Press and John Wiley & Sons, Inc., 1960). It is a collection of papers read at a round-table conference—uneven, inconclusive, yet remarkably suggestive of new possibilities. In addition to the Joos monograph, two interesting recent studies of prose style are Walker Gibson, *Tough, Sweet and Stuffy: An Essay on Modern American Prose Styles* (Bloomington: Indiana University Press, 1966); and Huntington Brown, *Prose Styles: Five Primary Types* (Minneapolis: University of Minnesota Press, 1966).

7

Language in
Shakespeare's Day

THE BACKGROUND OF EARLY MODERN ENGLISH

The Fact of Language Change

In Chapter 1, we noted that change is one of the principal attributes of language. No one denies this fact in history, but there are some who apparently assume that all linguistic change ended at some indefinite date in the past and consider any recent variation from their personal standard to be a ·corruption. It is important, therefore, for the student of English to be aware of the change which has taken place during the 1500-year existence of the English language. Once he discovers that the whole character of the language has changed within this period of time, that the changes are by and large consistent, and that the whole of this change is entirely natural, he should at least be more tolerant of those variations and innovations which creep into contemporary conversation and writing.

The Historical Periods of English

Looking at the English language as a whole, it is possible for us to distinguish four periods in its history. These periods, with their dates, are:

1. Old English (500–1100)
2. Middle English (1100–1450)
3. Early Modern English (1450–1700)
4. Modern English (1700–   )

Old English, sometimes called *Anglo-Saxon*, stretches from the first settlement of Germanic tribes in the British Isles to the consolidation of the Norman position there following the Conquest, with the temporary imposition of Norman French as the language of privilege.[1] **Middle English** covers the period of the Norman dynasty, ending at the time when English suzerainty over France was largely a sentimental memory. For several reasons, the greatest being the social and cultural precedence of Norman French, this period should be considered transitional, bridging the completely Germanic Old English period and the much modified Modern English period. Because change has of course continued since 1450, it is convenient to consider separately the periods of the English Renaissance and the more immediately modern. Otherwise we would find ourselves having to cope with a complex 500-year period.

The dates and period designations must be accepted with caution. Though the periods themselves are valid enough, the dates are only approximate. People didn't wake up on New Year's Day, 1100, and begin speaking Middle English. The dates serve to indicate the approximate time when there had been sufficient significant change from the general character of the language at the "height" of the preceding period. In addition, the designations of the periods are those as seen from *our* point of view. Throughout their history, speakers of English have always automatically considered themselves to be speaking *Modern* English. At any point in the history of English the language adequately served the needs of its speakers. Because historical surveys tend to emphasize differences, we are apt to forget that what now seems odd was once normal.

---

[1] Most Old English documents, literary and otherwise, save for a few charters and wills, date from after 900 A.D. This includes those written long before then. The extant manuscripts are copies of originals long since lost.

Early Modern English

All of this is by the way of introducing an intensive survey of **Early Modern English,** focusing specifically on Shakespeare. It will be our practice in this chapter and the next to survey the history of English in *reverse* chronological order. The advantage of this method is that we will start from the *known*—assuming that you've absorbed the preceding chapters—venturing progressively into the unknown, rather than beginning with Old English, which is for all practical purposes a foreign language. This method has its disadvantages; it precludes, for example, any thorough study of phonological changes. But the sum total of disadvantages does not overshadow the principal advantage: it is, I believe, the best way to introduce the subject to those who are unfamiliar with it.

Another advantage of this method is that it permits us to concentrate for a time on the Early Modern English period. This period often gets misplaced in orthodox histories, which give greater attention to the language attitudes of the period, rather than the grammatical practices. This is particularly unfortunate, because it re-enforces the widespread opinion that the English of Shakespeare's day is only a quaint variation of our own. Thus, the student reading the literature of what is without too much exaggeration called the Golden Age of English Letters loses some of the force and impact of such writers as Spenser, Shakespeare, Jonson, Donne, Herbert, and Milton. To the student of literature, the poetry and drama of the English Renaissance is not difficult reading; but to the *average* student, whose teachers may not be fully aware of language change over the past four hundred years, the differences are great enough to make the literature almost incomprehensible. The responsible student and teacher should therefore become familiar with the linguistic differences between Shakespeare's day and our own, and understand their importance. They should also realize that modernized spelling of most Elizabethan and seventeenth-century texts serves to obscure a small but significant difference in pronunciation.

The subject of our study will be Shakespeare's *Henry IV, Part I.* There are several reasons for this choice. The date of the work (1596–1597) places it at about the "height" of the Early Modern period. It represents Shakespeare himself at his mature best. There is a good mixture of both heightened scenes and those depicting London lowlife. It is rarely taught below college level, which forces the prospective teacher studying this text to work up anew his materials for *Macbeth, Merchant of Venice, Julius Caesar*, or whatever—and in the process, perhaps discover new qualities in them. The play presents no major textual problems.[2] Finally, it happens to be a favorite of mine, which ought to be reason enough for using it.

Although it wouldn't be impossible to follow the exercises in this chapter with another play, it would certainly be difficult. All the references, unless otherwise noted, are to *Henry IV, Part I*. To emphasize the distance of 370 years, all of the quotations will be in Shakespeare's spelling—or more correctly, that of his printers. Unfortunately, there is no inexpensive old-spelling edition in print. The most readily available such edition is Volume 21 of the Variorum Shakespeare (ed. Samuel B. Hemingway, 1936; supplement edited by G. Blakemore Evans, 1956), which is both expensive and hard to use. Facsimiles of both the 1598 Quarto (eds. Sir Walter W. Greg and Charlton Hinman, 1966) and the 1623 Folio (ed. Charlton Hinman, 1968) should be in any college library. The best modern-spelling text is probably the New Arden Shakespeare edition (ed. A. Rolf Humphreys, 1960); and the best inexpensive paperback text is that in the Laurel

---

[2] The play was very popular, and there were six quarto editions published prior to the first folio edition of 1623 (F). Of these, only the first quarto of 1598 (Q1) has any basic textual authority; the succeeding editions were each set from the preceding with a progressive accretion of corrupt readings. There is in existence a single quarto sheet from an earlier quarto published in the same year as the first (Q0), but it contains only the second half of I, iii, and scenes i and ii of Act II, for which it is the textual authority. Anyhow, the play was published with relative care: there were no "bad" quartos, and none of the editorial problems of *Hamlet* or *King Lear*.

Speaking of texts, teachers of English at any level should be warned that textbook editors often take unwarranted liberties with the works they are supposed to be editing. Sometimes they bowdlerise naughty passages (understandably, perhaps), and sometimes they rewrite passages presumed too difficult for students, which is much more serious. Worst of all is the habit of abridgement; many an anthology has several lines of a Shakespearean play silently excised, and one "edition" of *Romeo and Juliet* consists only of one-fourth of the original play—the rest is summarized for the student in editorial prose between the passages which were allowed to stand. A teacher examining a new anthology for possible adoption would do well to spot-check the contents against standard or definitive editions of the works.

Shakespeare series, based on the edition by C. J. Sisson (1953). But any text will do, so long as the line numbers follow those of the time-honored Globe edition of 1891.[3]

Our presentation will be inductive; that is to say, you will be asked to accumulate most of the data and draw most of the conclusions yourself. Possibly the work will be divided among your classmates, and you will be called on to give reports; or perhaps you will be asked to turn in a written project. At any rate, the work which you will do will stick with you better than if you simply read an account of Shakespeare's grammatical practices; and it will also give practice for doing analyses of this sort on your own later on. For the moment, however, we will postpone induction to give you the background and an overview of Shakespeare's pronunciation. After that, you're on your own.

THE PRONUNCIATION OF ENGLISH IN SHAKESPEARE'S DAY

Pronunciation at the End of the Middle English Period

Up to the time of the death of Chaucer (1400), the English letters representing vowel sounds had what might be called "continental equivalencies." That is, the letters represented very much the same sounds as they did, and for the most part still do, in the major languages of Western Europe. The following table illustrates these equivalencies in the tense vowels of Middle English (ME):

a represented /a/ as in *father*		
e	/e/	*prey*
i	/i/	*police*
u	/u/	*lute*

[3] It is strange that neither the New Variorum nor the New Arden texts use the Globe line numberings. This is immaterial for the verse scenes; the numbering would be the same regardless. However, in the longer prose scenes, especially II, iv, variations in page and type sizes can cause a difference of one hundred lines. As a check against the text you are using, the Globe edition numbering of II, iv, has 600 lines. (It should have been 601, but somehow the Globe numbering slipped a line.)

Incidentally, some modern editors are in the process of scrapping the Globe numberings entirely, and are numbering the lines consecutively throughout the play, without reference to artificial act and scene divisions.

The letter *o* is somewhat problematical, for it varied in its representation from /a/ to /ɔ/ to /o/. A shortage of letters caused some problems with the lax sounds /æ/, /ɪ/, /ɛ/, and /ʊ/, but the medieval scribes generally solved this by doubling the succeeding consonant letters. However, the lax vowels did not change appreciably throughout the history of English, though some tense or near-tense vowel sounds did change, under certain circumstances, to /ɛ/ and /ʊ/ during the Early Modern English period. All this aside, we can, with a little ingenuity, determine what Old English (OE) and ME must have sounded like, after making allowances for orthographical variations and dialect differences, even though we have only written records to go by.

The Great Vowel Shift

However, sometime between 1400 and 1450 began that linguistic event in England called "The Great Vowel Shift." No one really can do more than conjecture how it came about, but its results are patently evident. To summarize briefly, each tensed vowel gradually was raised, displacing the significant sound above it, the most close vowels, /i/ and /u/, diphthongalizing as off-glides of /a/. The following diagram illustrates this shifting:

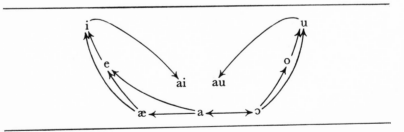

What is important to remember is that while the vowel sounds were shifting, the spellings generally remained the same and hence became representative of the new sound. Any tendency toward an analogous shift in spelling was offset by the invention of printing and the resultant wide distribution of earlier texts. The lax vowels, generally speaking, remained much as they were, save for the tendency of /ʊ/ to center as /ə/.

Some examples of this change will suffice to show its general effect:

ME *bath* /baθ/ > Modern English (NE) *bath* /bæθ/

ME *oxe* /ɔ́ksə/ > NE *ox* /aks/

ME *old* /ɔːld/ > NE *old* /oːld/ (often diphthongalized, /owld/)

ME *hous* /huːs/ > NE *house* /haus/

ME *depe* /déːpə/ > NE *deep* /dip/

ME *mys* /miːs/ > NE *mice* /mais/

Because of the forces of contingent consonants and of analogy, this shift was not always consistent. Where one might expect ME /o/ > NE /u/, it more often became /ʊ/; for example, ME *fot* /foːt/ > NE *foot* /fʊt/. Sometimes the forces of analogy pushed this shift one step further to /ə/: ME *blod* /bloːd / > Early Modern English (ENE) *bloud* /blʊd/ > NE *blood* /bləd/. A large number of words pronounced with /æ/ passed through /e/ to /i/, and the development of those sounds which ended up as /e/ at first glance seems remarkably confused.

Much of this shifting had already taken place by Shakespeare's day (c. 1600). However, certain sounds were still in a transitional phase, differing in enough significant details to warrant more attention today than his pronunciation usually receives from critics of Elizabethan literature.[4] It is interesting to note that while students studying Chaucer accept with cheerful resignation the necessity of mastering his "quaint" pronunciation, those studying Shakespeare assume that he and his contemporaries spoke today's English, thereby often missing such significant features of his art as rimes, rhythm, and word play, misled by the modern spelling texts of his plays, not to mention the diction of contemporary actors.

---

[4] When we speak of "Shakespeare's pronunciation," we mean the standard speech of London of about 1600. We do not know how much of his native Warwickshire dialect he maintained after moving to the capital, nor do we really know how much the speech of the stage differed—if at all—from the London standard. We can be sure, however, that Shakespeare wrote with the speech patterns of his London audience firmly in mind.

Because the alphabet is not sufficient to indicate all of the variations in vowel sounds, and also because The Great Vowel Shift was not quite complete in his day, we must reconstruct Shakespeare's pronunciation from a variety of helps and sources:

1. The writings of orthoepists—those who taught "correct pronunciation."
2. Orthography, particularly when compared with attempts to represent dialect and foreign language sound equivalents. This is especially helpful when there is reasonable evidence that spellings may be analogical variants.
3. Rimes.
4. Meter and rhythm, especially for discovering stress patterns.
5. In Shakespeare's case, known homonymic puns.

Each of these, however, can be misleading if relied upon exclusively. Elizabethan orthoepists often reflected their own personal prejudices in determining correct pronunciation. Dialect has often been a matter more of stage convention than of reality. Rimes can be purely conventional or based only on spelling—*love/move* is an eye rime still found in our hymnals. And sometimes meter can reflect greater shifts of emphasis than a modern reader of Donne, for example, would suspect. But taken together, they permit us to formulate as accurate a reconstruction of Shakespeare's speech as we can hope for, short of phonograph transcriptions.

Tables 7–1 and 7–2 show, in somewhat simplified form, the early seventeenth-century equivalents of modern-day pronunciation, with their usual spellings, and some of the more significant exceptions. It should be noted that we are using a broad transcription, which does not, for example, reflect such subtleties as the fronting or retracting of the low vowels.

By Shakespeare's time, a good many of the vowels had already undergone their shifting. Others, particularly the lax vowels, were never involved in the shift. These have come down to us much as Shakespeare pronounced them, as indicated in Table 7–1. Some vowels, however, had not yet completed their shifting. Their pronunciational differences from our own sounds are noted in Table 7–2.

NE Sound	Typical ENE Spelling	Exceptions in ENE
/i/ *sweet*	h*e*, h*ee*, sl*ee*p, th*ee*u*e*s, thi*e*fe, gri*e*fe, th*e*se	NE /i/ before -r (*here, deer*) usually ENE /ɛ/; NE /i/ spelled *ea* (*hear, speak*) pronounced /ɛː/
/ɪ/ *it*	d*i*d, w*i*ll, *i*s; b*y*, m*y* (unstressed)	*give* sometimes /giːv/ in rimes
/ɛ/ *bed*	t*e*l, l*e*t, th*e*m	*get, yet* informally pronounced with /ɪ/
/æ/ *that*	f*a*t, l*a*ugh, b*a*ck*e*	
/a/ *want*	f*a*ther, w*a*ter	pretentious NE use of /a/ for /æ/ in *ask, dance*, etc., unknown in ENE; /a/ spelled *o* (*hot, not*) retracted to /ɔ/ in ENE; NE /a/ before -r was ENE /ɔ/ (*dark, far*)
/ə/ *but* (unstressed)	any vowel letter in unstressed position	*tongue* pronounced with /ɔ/; *one, none, once* sometimes with /o/
/ɔ/ *off*	n*o*t, f*ou*ght, s*aw*ce, d*au*ghter, c*a*ld, f*a*lne	
/o/ *go*	s*o*, g*oe*, n*o*se, r*o*be, r*oa*be, g*oa*t, *oa*th, kn*ow*, s*ou*le, g*o*ld, c*o*lt	NE /o/ before -r usually /ɔ/ or (unstressed) /ə/: *for*
/ʊ/ *pull*	l*oo*ke, p*u*t	
/u/ *moon*	pr*oo*fe, m*oo*u*e*s, n*e*w*e*s, r*u*le, b*eau*ty	*duke, new, beauty* pronounced with on-gliding diphthong: /diuk, niu, biúti/

Table 7–1.

NE Pronunciation	ENE Pronunciation	Comment
/e/ *name*	/ɛː/ or /æː/	spelled s*a*me, br*a*ve, f*ai*th, pl*a*y
/i/ *feast*	/ɛː/ or possibly /e/	spelled *ea*: t*ea*ch, sn*ea*k, sp*ea*ke; the most unstable of all the vowels
/ə/ *cull* (stressed position)	/ʊ/	spelled bl*oo*d, bl*ou*d, d*o*th
/ai/ *why*	/əi/	unstressed *my, by*, etc., pronounced with /ɪ/
/au/ *house*	/əu/	
/oi/ *join*	/əi/	
/ər/ *bird*	/ɜː/ (same tongue position as /ər/ but without retroflection)	sometimes /ar/ in *person, clerk, heard*

Table 7–2.

Under certain conditions, Shakespeare's vowel sounds tended to lengthen, especially when final, as in *we*, or when preceding a voiced consonant, as in *weed*, almost exactly as today. However, the lengthened tense vowels today tend to diphthongalize, especially /e/ and /o/, which have respectively a fronting and a retracting off-glide—/ei, ow/. In Shakespeare's day, these vowels preserved their "pure" quality even when lengthened. When attempting to duplicate Shakespeare's pronunciation, you should try not to diphthongalize them. Note the difference in length in the /o/ sounds of *obey* and *load*. When pronouncing the latter lengthened sound in the Elizabethan fashion, try to avoid the tendency to increase the lip-rounding which causes the retracting off-glide.

Consonant Sounds in Early Modern English

Generally speaking, the consonant sounds of Shakespeare's day very closely approximate our own. However, we should note some of the following differences. The intervocalic *-r-* was probably a tongue tap, as in the current representations of British *very* as "veddy." The postvocalic *-r* was only very slightly articulated, and is now completely silent in Standard British English. The final *-ing* was pronounced /-in/—that "slovenly habit" of "dropping the final *g*" seems to have been standard then. Among the lesser points, initial *h-* was often dropped in highly informal speech, and *th* in such words as *author, Anthony, throne* was pronounced /t/ (an acquaintance with ME spelling practices is useful here). Finally, the endings *-tion* and *-sion* were pronounced /-tìən, -sìən/, especially for rhythmic purposes; and /č/ in such words as *nature* and *virtue* was pronounced /t/.

Sample Transcriptions

Proficiency in being able to duplicate Elizabethan speech is largely a matter of practice, though it would also be helpful if some inexpensive original spelling texts of Shakespeare's plays were available. There are two recordings by the late Professor Helge Kökeritz, in which he gives readings of Shakespeare's plays and poems, based upon his reconstruction of Shakespeare's speech. The first, *Shakespeare's Pronunciation*, was made to accompany his book of the same title.[5] The second recording is *A Thousand Years of English Pronunciation*, with selections ranging from *Beowulf* to Alexander Pope.[6] If these records are available to you, they would be very helpful in catching the spirit of Elizabethan speech, as well as any twentieth-century man can do.

Included here for your information and practice are Falstaff's discourse on honor (V, i, 128–43), broadly transcribed in reconstructed informal Elizabethan pronunciation, and Prince Hal's more formal soliloquy (I, ii, 218–40), in which he outlines his reasons for keeping low company. The parentheses enclose sounds which the actor might have omitted in rapid speech; the single parenthesis precedes the postvocalic -*r* to indicate its very slight articulation. The symbol for vowel lengthening /:/ is placed after vowels which we do not ordinarily lengthen in that position today. These lengthened vowels should be tense, but not diphthongalized. Finally, the double bar ‖ is used to set off the phrasal patterns in the prose selection, indicating a brief pause. Underneath the transcriptions are the lines in the original spelling and punctuation of Q1, except for the old long *s* and spelling out in full one or two abbreviations.

From *Henry IV, Part I*, V, i:

tɪz nɔt-diu jɪt ‖ əi wʊd   bi loːð   tə pɛː (h)ɪm
Tis not due yet, I   would be loath to pay him

bəfɔ(r (h)ɪz dɛː ‖ wət   nid   əi bi sə fɔ(rwɜːd wɪð
before his   day, what   need I   be so forwarde with

---

[5] (New Haven, Conn., 1953). On pp. 343–68 of this book are close phonetic transcriptions of several passages from Shakespeare—none, unfortunately, from *Henry IV, Part I*. Several of these transcriptions are included on the record.

[6] Including Hotspur's explanation to the King for not turning over to him his prisoners (I, iii, 29–69), and Falstaff acting the part of the King in the impromptu play (II, iv, 354–82).

hɪm ðət kɔlz nɔt ɔn mi ‖   wɛl   tɪz no mǽtə(r ‖
him that cals not on mee? Well, tis no matter,   130

ɔ́nə(r prɪks   mi ɔn ‖ jɛː   bət həu ɪf ɔ́nə(r
honor prickes me on; yea, but how if honor

prɪk   mi ɔf wɛn   əi kʊm   ɔn ‖   həu ðɛn ‖   kən
pricke me off when I   come on?   how then can

ɔ́nə(r sɛt tu ə lɛːg ‖ noː ‖ ɜː ən ɔ(rm ‖   noː ‖ ɜː tæːk
honor set to a leg? no,   or an arme? no,   or take

əwéː ðə grif   əv ə wʊnd ‖   noː ‖ ɔ́nə(r (h)æθ no
away the griefe of a wound? no,   honor hath no

skɪl ɪn sɜ́ːjərì   ðɛn ‖   noː ‖ (h)wət ɪz ɔ́nə(r ‖ ə
skil in surgerie then? no,   what   is honor? a   135

wɜːd ‖ (h)wət ɪz ɪn ðət   wɜːd ɔ́nə(r ‖ (h)wət ɪz ðət
word, what   is in that word honor? what   is that

ɔ́nə(r ‖   ǽː(r ‖ ə trɪm rékənìn ‖   hu   hæθ ɪt
honour? aire,   a trim reckoning. Who hath it?

hi ðət dəid ə wénzdi ‖   dʊθ i fiːl   ɪt ‖ noː ‖
he that died a Wednesday, doth he feele it? no,

dʊθ i   hɛː(r ɪt ‖ noː ‖ tɪz ɪnsénsəbəl ðɛn ‖ jɛː   tə
doth he heare it? no,   tis insensible then? yea, to

ðə ded ‖ bət wəl nɔt lɪv   wɪθ-ðə   lívɪn ‖   noː ‖
the dead, but wil not liue with the liuing; no,   140

(h)wəi ‖ dətrǽktiən wəl nɔt súfə(r ɪt ‖ ðɛ́ː(rfɔ(r əil
why?   detraction will not suffer it, therefore ile

noːn əv ɪt ‖ ɔ́nə(r ɪz ə mɛː(r skútiən   ən(d) soː
none of it; honor is a meere skutchion, and   so

ɛn(d)z mɪ kǽtɛkìzəm ‖
ends   my Catechisme.

From the same, I, ii:

əi noː   ju   ɔːl ən(d) wɪl ə (h)wəil əphóːld
I know you all, and   wil a while   vphold

ðɪ ə́njòːkt (h)iúmə(r əv jur ə́idəlnès
The vnyokt humour   of your idlenes,

jɪt héːrɪn wɪl əi ímətèːt ðə sʊn
Yet herein wil I   imitate the sunne.   220

hu dʊθ pə̀(rmít ðə bɛːs kəntéːjiəs kləudz
Who doth permit   the base contagious clouds

tə smúðə(r əp (h)ɪz biúti   frəm ðə wɜːld
To smother vp his   beautie from the world,

ðət (h)wɛn (h)i plɛːz əgéːn tə biː (h)ɪmsélf
That when   he   please againe to be himselfe,

biːn wɔ́ntəd hiː mɛː biː mɔ(r wʊ́ndɜːd æt
Being wanted he may be   more wondred at

bɪ bréːkɪn θruː   ðə fəul ən(d) úgli mɪs(ts)
By breaking through the foule and   ougly mists   225

əv vǽːpə(rz ðæt dɪd siːm tə strǽŋgə̀l (h)ɪm
Of vapours   that did seeme to strangle him.

ɪf ɔːl ðə jɛː(r wə(r plǽːɪn hɔ́lədèːz
If all the yeere were playing holly-dayes,

tə spɔ(rt wʊd   biː əz tídjəs   æz tə wɜːk
To sport would be as tedious   as to worke;

bət (h)wɛn ðɛː séldəm kʊm ðɛː wɪšt fə(r kʊm
But when   they seldome come, they wisht for come,

ən(d) nɔ́θɪn pléːzəθ bət rɛː(r ǽksədə̀nts
And   nothing pleaseth but rare accidents: 230

so (h)wɛn ðɪs lus bɪhéːvjə(r əi θro ɔf
So when   this loose behauiour I throw off,

ən(d) pɛː ðə dɛt əi névə(r prɔ́məsèd
And   pay the debt I neuer   promised,

bɪ həu məč bétə(r ðən mɪ wɜːd əi æm
By how much better then my word I am,

bɪ soː məč-šæl əi fɔ́lsəfəi mɛnz hops
By so much shall I falsifie mens hopes,

ən(d) ləik brəit   métəl   ɔn ə súlən   grəund
And   like bright mettal on a sullein ground,   235

mɪ rèfə(rmé:tjən glítrɪn   ɔ:r mɪ fɔlt
My reformation   glittring ore my fault,

šəl šiu   mɔ(r gúdli   ən(d) ətrǽkt mɔ(r əiz
Shal shew more goodly, and   attract more eyes

ðən   ðæt (h)wɪč hæθ no fəil tə sɛt ɪt ɔf
Then that which hath no foile to set it off.

əil so: əfénd tə mæ:k əféns   ə skɪl
Ile so offend, to make offence a skill,

rɛdímɪn   təim (h)wɛn mɛn θɪŋk   lɛ:st əi wɪl
Redeeming time when   men thinke least I wil.   240

Some of these transcriptions are problematical. For instance, at V, i, 142, *skutchion* may have been /skúčìən/, and at I, ii, 221, *contagious* may have been /kənté:ĵəs/. *By* at I, ii, 225, 233, 234, could be /bəi/ and the first *my* in 236 could be /məi/. *Being* in I, ii, 224, is transcribed /bi:n/ to make it monosyllabic; however, we cannot assume that Shakespeare's verse speeches were absolutely regular iambic pentameter. If you interpret *holly-dayes* (I, ii, 227) as "holy days," rather than "holidays," the transcription would be /hóli dè:z/ or /hɔ́li dè:z/. No doubt there will be other areas for argument; but give or take a few quibbles, this is about as close as we can come to the speech of London in Shakespeare's day.

QUESTIONS AND EXERCISES

Pronunciation

1. The following passage—the famous quarreling scene between Hotspur and Glendower (III, i, 13–71)—is copied verbatim from the first quarto text (1598), with the exception of the "long *s*" letter. Read it through carefully, then answer the questions at the end of the passage.

Glen.　　　　　At my natiuity
The front of heauen was full of fiery shapes
Of burning cressets, and at my birth　　　　　15
The frame and huge foundation of the earth
Shaked like a coward.

Hot. Why so it woulde haue done at the same season if
your mothers cat had but kittend, though your selfe had
neuer beene borne.　　　　　20

Glen. I say the earth did shake when I was borne.

Hot. And I say the earth was not of my mind,
If you suppose as fearing you it shooke.

Glen. The heauens were all on fire, the earth did tremble.

Hot. Oh then the earth shooke to see the heauens on fire,　25
And not in feare of your natiuity,
Diseased nature oftentimes breakes forth,
In strange eruptions, oft the teeming earth
Is with a kind of collicke pincht and vext,
By the imprisoning of vnruly wind　　　　　30
Within her wombe, which for enlargement striuing
Shakes the old Beldame earth, and topples down
Steeples and mossegrown towers. At your birth
Our Grandam earth, hauing this distemprature
In passion shooke.

Glen.　　　　　Coosen of many men　　　　　35
I do not beare these crossings, giue me leaue
To tell you once againe that at my birth
The front of heauen was full of fiery shapes,
The goates ran from the mountaines, and the heards
Were strangely clamorous to the frighted fields.　　　40
These signes haue markt me extraordinary,
And all the courses of my life do shew
I am not in the roule of commen men:
Where is he liuing clipt in with the sea,
That chides the bancks of England, Scotland, Wales,　　45
Which cals me pupil or hath read to me?
And bring him out that is but womans sonne
Can trace me in the tedious waies of Arte,
And hold me pace in deepe experiments.

Hot. I thinke theres no man speakes better Welsh:　　50
Ile to dinner.

Mor. Peace coosen Percy, you wil make him mad.

Glen. I can cal spirits from the vasty deepe.

Hot. Why so can I, or so can any man,

But wil they come when you do cal for them [?]   55

Glen. Why I can teach you coosen to command

the Deuil.

Hot. And I can teach thee coose to shame the deuil,

By telling truth. Tel truth and shame the deuil:

If thou haue power to raise him bring him hither,   60

And ile be sworne I haue power to shame him hence:

Oh while you liue tel truth and shame the deuil.

Mor. Come, come, no more of this vnprofitable chat.

Glen. Three times hath Henry Bullenbrooke made head

Against my power, thrice from the bankes of Wye,   65

And sandy bottomd Seuerne haue I sent him

Booteles home, and weather beaten backe.

Hot. Home without bootes, and in foule weather too,

How scapes he agues in the deuils name?

Glen. Come here is the map, shal we diuide our right?   70

According to our three fold order tane.

———

a. What seems to be the pattern of the letters *u* and *v*?

b. How are contractions and possessives handled?

c. What spelling pattern is used to distinguish between syllabic
and nonsyllabic past tense and past participle regular endings?
Is this same pattern carried out with the noun plural and
possessive and verb present tense ending?

d. Note the spelling of *beene* (20), *shooke* (23), *feare* (26), *wombe*
(31), *deepe* (49). What evidence can you adduce to show that
the final *-e* here and in other instances in this passage was
extraneous and not pronounced? How do you account for
the spelling?

e. What does the spelling of the following words indicate was
the probable pronunciation?

(1) coosen (35), coose (58)

(2) heards (39)

(3) roule (43)

(4) shew (42)

2. Study the following words taken from the first quarto text of *Henry IV, Part I*. What does the spelling indicate was the probable pronunciation?

 a. eare (ere), ieast (jest)[7]
 b. Buckrom
 c. Poules (Paul's), Dowglas
 d. diuell (devil), then (than), bin (been)
 e. birlady
 f. lane (lean), sware (swear), banes (banns), clame (claim)
 g. yeeres
 h. tast (taste)
 i. retrait (retreat)
 j. toung (tongue)
 k. musitions (musicians), vngratious
 l. Sathan (Satan), swathling cloaths, fadome (fathom)

3. Why do the following first quarto spellings warn against relying too heavily upon orthography as an indication of pronunciation?

 a. clearkes (clerks)
 b. Falstalffe
 c. waight (wait), maisters
 d. beoff (beef), enfeoft
 e. rag of muffins, two of clocke

4. At III, iii, 66–67, all the quartos and folios read, "the *tight* of a haire was never lost in my house before." All modern editors emend the crux-word as "tithe." What do you think is the most likely solution?—does this spelling reflect the pronunciation of *tithe*, is it a compositor's misprint, or is Samuel Hemingway on the right track in stating that it's "possibly a typical Quickly-Malapropism"?

5. Because much of the play is in verse, we can make some use of scansion and rime in determining pronunciation.

[7] Printing conventions of this period used the letter *i* for both *i* and *j*, in both upper and lower case. In a few instances, this may account for a pronunciation shift from /ɪ/ or /i/ to /j/ when the current alphabetical convention was adopted.

    a. What does the scansion of I, i, 96, indicate was the probable syllabication of the word *Worcester*? What is the probable syllabication of this word at I, iii, 15? How do you account for this difference?

    b. What does the scansion of I, iii, 147 and 150, indicate was the pronunciation respectively of *proclamation* and *expedition*? Spot-check other verse passages for similar metrical evidence. Do you find any which are exceptions to those noted here?

    c. What is the evidence offered by the end rime at IV, ii, 85–86, for the pronunciation of the rimed words? Do any of the other end rimes in the play offer us special evidence of pronunciation?

    d. What does the scansion of V, ii, 97, indicate was the pronunciation of the motto of the Percys? Is this evidence necessarily negated at II, iii, 74?

6. The following quotations contain instances of puns and word play, all of which except (c) are lost in modern pronunciation. Explain the bit of word play in each instance, and the evidence it offers as to the ENE pronunciation of the words involved.

    a. *Falst.* Yea, and so vs'd it that were it not here apparant that thou art heire apparant.

                              (I, ii, 64–65)

    b. *Hot.* . . . this proud king, who studies day and night
       To answere all the debt he owes to you,
       Euen with the bloudie paiment of your deaths.

                             (I, iii, 184–86)

    Fal. I would twere bed time Hal, and all well.
    Prin. Why, thou owest God a death.
    Falst. Tis not due yet, I would be loath to pay him before his day. . . .

                           (V, i, 125–28)

    c. *Gad.* . . . And yet (zoundes) I lie, for they pray continually to their Saint the Common-wealth, or rather not pray to her, but pray on her, for they ride vp and downe on her, and make her their bootes.

Cham.   What, the Common-wealth their bootes? will shee
hold out water in foule way?

(II, i, 87–93)

d. *Hot.*   What horse, Roane? a cropeare is it not?
Ser.   It is my Lord.
Hot.   That roane shall be my throne.

(II, iii, 72–73)

e. *Poy.*   Come your reason, Iacke, your reason.
Falst.   What, vppon compulsion: Zoundes, and I were at the
strappado, or all the rackes in the worlde, I would not tell
you on compulsion. Giue you a reason on compulsion? if
reasons were as plentifull as blackberries, I would giue no
man a reason vppon compulsion, I.

(II, iv, 260–66)

f. *Bar.*   My Lord do you see these meteors? do you behold these
exhalations?   *Prin.*   I do.
Bar.   What thinke you they portend?
Prin.   Hot liuers, and cold purses.
Bar.   Choler, my Lord, if rightly taken.
Prin.   No if rightly taken[,] halter.

(II, iv, 351–57)

g. *Falst.*   Doest thou heare Hal? neuer call a true piece of golde
a counterfet, thou art essentially made without seeming so.
Prin.   And thou a naturall coward without instinct.
Falst.   I deny your Maior, if you wil deny the Sheriffe[,] so,
if not, let him enter.

(II, iv, 539–45)

h. *Falst.*   Tut neuer feare mee, I am as vigilant as a Cat to steale
Creame.
Prin.   I thinke to steale Creame indeed, for thy theft hath
alreadie made thee butter . . . .

(IV, ii, 64–67)

i. *Falst.*   Well if Percy be aliue, ile pierce him . . . .

(V, iii, 59)

j. Death hath not strooke so fat a Deere to day,
   Though many dearer in this bloudy fray . . . .

(V, iv, 107–108)

7. The following is from *William Shakespeare: A Biography*, by A. L. Rouse (New York, Harper and Row, 1963), pp. 54–55. It contains a highly subjective description of Shakespeare's speech. What misconceptions and errors of fact do you find in the passage, and how did the author err in arriving at these conclusions?

How then did Shakespeare speak?

We can tell from his highly idiosyncratic spellings, and it is not surprising that he spoke as a Warwickshire man would, with that country flavour—as Tennyson spoke with a Lincolnshire inflexion, and Wordsworth with a North Country burr. In Elizabethan times disparities of speech were much wider, local dialects stronger, the patterns richer and more diversified. . . .

Characteristic of old Warwickshire was the deeper "u," which we saw reflected in the corporation accounts in the spelling "goones" for "guns." Shakespeare said "woonder," where we say "wonder," and so with that sound consistently: "woone" for "won," or "one." The word "smother" is spelt "smoother." Several of the vowel-sounds are deeper, as in Warwickshire or Staffordshire dialect today: one said "smoake" not modern, rather too refined, "smoke," and, more heavily, "sturre" for "stir." On the other hand there was the light Midlands "u," an inversion of southern usage: it seems from his spelling that Shakespeare said "kuckoo," as proper Midlands folk still do. Other vowel-sounds were deeper, especially the long "a": Shakespeare said auncient and daunger, inchaunt and awnser.

Another feature was the stronger enunciation of consonants indicated in Shakespeare's spellings, shedde, kisse, mistresse, chidde, comming, musique, starre, farre, jarre—the "r" being rolled. The terminal "y" had more value as we see in spellings like legacie, perjurie, solitarie. One excellent vowel-sound has been lost from modern standard English, though one still hears it among old-fashioned provincial people in words like "fruit," pronounced by them "friwt," as the Elizabethans did. This vowel-sound appeared in words like "truant" and "fuel," spelt by Shakespeare "trewant" and "fewell." Then there is the "er" sound that was pronounced broadly "ar" in that age: we still preserve it in words like "serjeant" and "clerk." Altogether, the language as Shakespeare spoke it had a much stronger and warmer sound. With a broader range and more emphatic enunciation, it was better suited to dramatic declamation: compared to our modern speech, having more character, at once more masculine and more truly poetic. It would be good to hear a Shakespeare play once more as the Elizabethans heard it.

8. On the basis of our understanding of the pronunciation of Elizabethan English, and of the approximate correspondencies of the spelling, read and analyze the following poem by John Donne. What does the pronounciation do to the rhythmic patterns and the rimes? Can you discover underlying meanings or punnings on key words which might aid in interpretation?

A FEAVER

Oh doe not die, for I shall hate
    All women so, when thou art gone,
That thee I shall not celebrate,
    When I remember, thou wast one.

But yet thou canst not die, I know,
    To leave this world behinde, is death,
But when thou from this world wilt goe,
    The whole world vapors with thy breath.

Or, if, when thou, the worlds soule, goest,
    It stay, tis but thy carkasse then,
The fairest woman, but thy ghost,
    But corrupt wormes, the worthyest men.

O wrangling schooles, that search what fire
    Shall burne this world, had none the wit
Unto this knowledge to aspire,
    That this her feaver might be it?

And yet she cannot wast by this,
    Nor long beare this torturing wrong,
For such corruption needfull is
    To fuell such a feaver long.

These burning fits but meteors bee,
　Whose matter in thee is soone spent.
Thy beauty, 'and all parts, which are thee,
　Are unchangeable firmament.

Yet t'was of my minde, seising thee,
　Though it in thee cannot persever.
For I had rather owner bee
　Of thee one houre, than all else ever.

Morphology and Parts of Speech[8]

Nouns

1. Study the following passage carefully:

> *Host.* So hee doth you my Lord, and saide this other day you ought him a thousand *pound.*
> *Prin.* Sirrha, do I owe you a thousand *pound?*
> *Falst.* A thousand *pound* Hall? a million, thy love is worth a million, thou owest me thy love.
>
> (III, iii, 151–56)

Similar instances are at II, ii, 12–13; II, iv, 343–44; and III, iii, 94–95. How do you account for the lack of the expected plural inflection in these passages? Can you think of instances similar to this in contemporary usage?

2. Of the following passage,

> But this our purpose now is *twelve month* old,
> And bootelesse tis to tell you we wil go.
>
> (I, i, 28–29)

E. A. Abbott, in *A Shakespearian Grammar* (London, 1870), pp. 62–63, says, "*A* was frequently inserted before a numeral adjective, for the purpose of indicating that the objects enumerated are regarded collectively as *one*. We still say 'a score,' 'a fo(u)rt(een)-night.' ... The *a* is omitted in [this passage]." Do you agree with this analysis?

---

[8] Throughout the remainder of these exercises, we will continue to quote passages in the old spelling, except that the *u* and *v*, and *i* and *j*, will be normalized.

3. Note the instances of plurality in the following passages:

Upon whose dead *corpes* there was such misuse,

(I, i, 43)

Charles-waine is over the new Chimney, and yet our *horse* not packt.

(II, i, 2–3)

looke to thy servaunts, cherish thy *ghesse* . . .

(III, iii, 193–94)

What phonological reason explains the apparent lack of the inflection? Why could the third be explained as a compositor's mistake in hearing it read to him as he set type?[9] What possible differences in meaning account for the inconsistency in the inflections of the following passage:

Ver.   . . . certain *horse*
Of my coosen Vernons are not yet come up,
Your Uncle Worcesters *horses* came but to day, [*horse*, Q5, F]
And now their pride and mettall is a sleepe,
Their courage with hard labour tame and dull,
That not a horse is halfe the halfe of himselfe.
Hot. So are the *horses* of the enemie
In generall journey bated and brought low . . .

(IV, iii, 19–26)

To which, compare the following:

Prin. I have procured thee Jacke a charge of foot.
Fal. I would it had been of *horse*.

(III, iii, 209–10)

4. In general, we can say that Shakespeare's plural forms are like our own. Why would you probably *not* cite the following example as an exception to this statement?

. . . if to be fat be to be hated, then Pharaos lane *kine* are to be loved.

(II, iv, 519–20)

---

[9] This is the Q1 spelling. In the remainder of the quartos and in F, it is variously emended to *ghests*, *Ghestes*, and *Guests*.

5. As with the plural inflection, so the genitive inflections in Shakespeare follow our own usage, save for the absence of the apostrophe in writing. However, at III, ii, 119, and III, iii, 129–30, are examples of a special exception. What specific pattern do they follow, and why do you suppose that the pattern has since changed?

6. What phonological reasons can you give for the apparent absence of a genitive in each of the following:

> . . . tut, there are other Troyans that thou dreamst not of, the which for *sport sake* are content to do the profession, some grace, that would (if matters should be lookt into) for their owne *credit sake* make all whole.
>
> (II, i, 76–80; see also I, ii, 173–74, and V, i, 65)
>
> *Charles*-waine   (II, i, 2)
> the *Douglas* sonne   (I, iii, 261)
> in your *highnes* name   (I, iii, 23)

7. "These newes" (III, ii, 121) is an example of an idiomatic change from Elizabethan plural to present-day singular. Find similar instances of this sort in this or another Elizabethan work, using the evidence of demonstratives or of subject-verb agreement.

Pronouns

1. The most striking difference in pronoun usage between Shakespeare's time and our own is the use of *thou*, with its subsidiary forms *thee*, *thy*, and *thine*. Study the use of this form in the following passages, and identify the various relationships of the speaker and the person addressed with this pronoun, rather than with *you*:

> II, iii, 40–120: Hotspur and Lady Percy
> I, ii, 89–98: Falstaff to Hal
> III, ii, 4–161: King and Hal
> I, iii, 125–302: Hotspur, Worcester, and Northumberland
> I, iii, 15–21: King to Worcester
> I, iii, 113–22: King to Hotspur
> V, iii, 1–13: Douglas and Blunt (masquerading as King)

Why do you suppose the form virtually died out by 1700? What uses do we put it to today?

2. What other means do the characters have for asserting their relative superiority or inferiority? In particular, study the relationships between the carriers, Gadshill, and the Chamberlain in II, i; the frequenters of the tavern in III, iii; and the rebels in IV, i.

3. Historically, the form *ye* was the second person, nominative plural pronoun. However, only in the somewhat archaic language of the King James Bible (1611) is the form so used consistently in any extended literary document contemporary with Shakespeare. More typical of Shakespeare's usage are the following passages:

> Zoundes *ye* fat paunch, and *ye* call me cowarde by the Lord ile stab thee.
>
> (II, iv, 159–60)
>
> Hang *ye* gorbellied knaves, are *yee* undone, no *ye* fatte chuffes I woulde your store were here: on bacons on, what *yee* knaves yong men must live, you are grand jurers, are *ye*, weele jure *ye* faith.
>
> (II, ii, 93–97)

What uses does this pronominal form appear to have? Are there any instances in this play of this form in its historical pattern?

4. The opening speech in the play (I, i, 1–33) contains several instances of the "royal *we*," as do portions of I, iii, and V, i. Point out passages where this might seem ambiguous to the modern reader. Why does the King drop this usage after the first two lines of III, ii, and then pick it up after l. 170? Do we use a similar form today, perhaps in less regal circumstances?

5. At I, i, 17–18; V, i, 1–8; V, i, 79–80; and V, v, 41, are instances of the genitive form of the neuter pronoun. Note the development of this form in *Merchant of Venice*, V, i, 90; *Henry IV, Part II*, I, ii, 131–34; *King Lear*, I, iv, 235–36; and *Winter's Tale* I, ii, 151–58 (but see also III, ii, 101!). What process led to the present form? According to the *Oxford English Dictionary* (OED), when did the form *its* come into general usage in English? Was there a parallel falling away of the earlier forms at the same time, or was there some overlapping? In John Bunyan's *Pilgrim's Progress* (1678), the character Presumption, in response to Christian's offer of help, replies, "Every Fatt [i.e., vat] must stand upon

his own bottom." Why would this *not* be a likely example of a late usage of the old form?

6. The traditional view of the genitive pronouns *my/mine* and *thy/thine* in the determiner slot of the NP was identical to that for *a/an*: the /-n/ form preceded an initial vowel sound. However, of this usage Abbott says (p. 160), "The two forms . . . are both used by Shakespeare with little distinction before vowels. Though there are probably many exceptions, yet the rule appears to be that *mine* and *thine* are used where the possessive adjective is to be unemphatic, *my* and *thy* in other cases." Test this rule: compare *my uncle* (II, iii, 25; IV, iii, 54; V, ii, 28) against *mine uncle* (IV, iii, 99, 110); *my owne* (II, iv, 362 [cf. 360], 444–45) against *mine owne* (II, iii, 1; III, iii, 72; V, i, 23; V, iii, 35–36). See also III, iii, 92–93.

7. There are nine instances in this play of reflexive pronoun forms used substantively, of which the following may be taken as representative:

> *Your selfe* and I will not bee there
>
> (I, ii, 183)
>
> *my selfe* did heare it.
>
> (I, iii, 157)
>
> It pleasd your majesty to turne your lookes
> Of favor from *my selfe*, and all our house . . .
>
> (V, i, 30–31)
>
> I have two boies
> Seeke Percy and *thy selfe* about the field . . .
>
> (V, iv, 31–32)

How might the spelling of these forms indicate the way they were taken by the Elizabethans? What is the traditional prescriptive view of this usage? Why do we make use of it today?—what psychological effect does it have? Did it appear to have the same effect in Shakespeare's day?

8. On the other hand, most of the following passages contain personal pronouns where we would expect to find reflexive forms:

> Thou art so fat-witted with . . . unbuttoning *thee* after supper
>
> (I, ii, 2–3)

She bids you on the wanton rushes lay *you* downe

(III, i, 214)

thou bearest *thee* like a king

(V, iv, 36)

and nowe I remember *me*

(II, iv, 467–68)

but the sacke that thou hast drunke *me*, would have bought *me*
    lights as good cheape

(III, iii, 49–51)

See how this river comes *me* cranking in,
And cuts *me* from the best of all my land

(III, i, 98–99)

he that kils *mee* some sixe or seven douzen of Scots

(II, iv, 114–15)

Sweare *me* Kate like a ladie

(III, i, 257)

Explain each of these usages. What would probably be the
present-day form in each of these passages?

9. Note the following usages of the relative pronoun:

The prisoners
Which he in this adventure hath surprizd . . .

(I, i, 92–93)

Where is he living clipt in with the sea,
That chides the bancks of England, Scotland, Wales,
Which cals me pupil or hath read to me?

(III, i, 44–46)

Why Harry do I tell thee of my foes,
Which art my nearest and dearest enemy?

(III, ii, 122–23)

How does this differ from the use of *that*, as it occurs in the second
example? Note the instances of *who/whom*, especially at I, iii,
39–41, 103–6; I, ii, 220–21. What seems to be the state of the
usage of *who* as opposed to *which*?

Adjectives and adverbs

1. It has become a kind of game to find in Shakespeare
adjectival constructions similar to the famous "This was the most

unkindest cut of all" (*Julius Caesar*, III, ii, 187). Note the following constructions:

> the *soveraignest* thing on earth
>
> (I, iii, 57)
>
> the *most comparative rascalliest* sweet yong Prince
>
> (I, ii, 90–91)
>
> It lends a lustre and *more great* opinion
>
> (IV, i, 77)
>
> a *most sweet* wench
>
> (I, ii, 45)
>
> a *most sweet* robe of durance
>
> (I, ii, 48–49)

Granted that these would probably not pass usage-muster today, and also that Shakespeare is usually excused on the grounds that the rules hadn't been formulated then, what stylistic and rhetorical considerations led Shakespeare to prefer them over other possible alternatives? Consider the example from *Julius Caesar*, too; most teachers have to deal with it sooner or later.

2. Note the unusual form in the Archbishop of York's comment, "And many *mo* corivals and deare men" (IV, iv, 31). Look up this word in the OED. What connotative difference does it have over *more*? In the King's comment:

> Not an eye
> But is *a weary* of thy common sight,
>
> (III, ii, 87–88)

what is the derivation of the prefix *a*(-)? Compare, "*A* horsebacke (ye cuckoe) but *a foote* hee will not budge a foote" (II, iv, 387–88). What common present-day words share this derivation?

3. Examine the following special instances of an adjective form:

> it is *like* wee shall have good trading that way
>
> (II, iv, 400–01)
>
> thou art *like*
> Never to hold it up againe
>
> (V, iv, 39–40)

What has been the subsequent development of this form? Is there a specific pattern here, or must this form be treated as simply another "idiomatic expression"?

4. The following may be taken as representative of adverbs which vary substantially from current usage:

art not thou *horrible* afearde?

(II, iv, 402; cf. 405–06)

he is *grievous* sicke.

(IV, i, 16)

ten times more *dishonourable* ragged then an olde fazd ancient

(IV, ii, 33–34)

me thinkes they are *exceeding* poore and bare

(IV, ii, 74–75)

What conclusions can you draw from these about Shakespeare's adverbial formations? What trends have developed since? Are any of these prompted by possible reasons of style or special effect?

Verbs and verb formations

1. From the King's speech contrasting himself and Richard II (III, ii, 29–91) reconstruct the Aux structure of Shakespeare's time. What portion of the current Aux was conspicuously absent? What means did Shakespeare have of supplying a reasonable substitute?

2. What differences in meaning do you find between the following Aux patterns and the same pattern today? What patterns do we now use to convey the former meaning?

a. Else hee *had bin* damnd for coosening the divell.

(I, ii, 135)

hadst thou fought at Holmedon thus
I never *had triumpht* upon a Scot.

(V, iii, 14–15)

twas time to counterfet, or that hot termagant Scot *had paide* me scot and lot too.

(V, iv, 113–15)

b. I *had rather be* a kitten and cry mew,
Then one of these same miter ballet mongers

(III, i, 129–30)

I *had rather live*
With cheese and garlike in a Windmil far
(III, i, 161–62)
I *had rather heare* lady my brache howle in Irish.
(III, i, 240)

c. You *must needes learne* Lord to amend this fault
(III, i, 180)
Why, you are so fat, sir John, that you *must needes be* out of all compasse:
(III, iii, 24–25)
Which oft the eare of greatnes *needs must heare*
(III, ii, 24)

How would you accommodate these patterns into your reconstruction of the Aux of this period?

3. Study the following structures. At first glance, they would appear to be examples of the passive transformation, but this is not so.

He *is walkt* up to the top of the hill
(II, ii, 8)
Worcester *is stolne* away to night, thy fathers beard *is turned* white with the newes,
(II, iv, 393–94)
is Gilliams with the packet *gone*?
(II, iii, 68)

for the houre *is come*
To end the one of us,
(V, iv, 68–69)
they *are come* to search the house,
(II, iv, 536–37)
The King himselfe in person *is set forth*,
(IV, i, 91)
am I not *falne* away vilely since this last action?
(III, iii, 1–2)

How would you accommodate this pattern into the generative procedures of the verb phrase without doing violence to the Aux? What reason can you propose for the disappearance of this pattern since?

4. One of the notable differences in Shakespeare's verb patterns is his use of *do* other than as a form to which to attach a floating affix. What seems to be the purpose of this form? It is *not* employed for emphasis, and though it occurs most frequently in the verse passages, it is not necessarily a means of making a line scan. The following are just a few of the many instances of this in the play:

What yesternight our counsell did decree

(I, i, 32)

        the foule and ougly mists
Of vapours that did seeme to strangle him.

(I, ii, 225–26)

And then it was, when the unhappy king,
(Whose wrongs in us God pardon) did set forth
Upon his Irish expedition;
From whence he intercepted, did returne
To be depos'd, and shortly murdered.

(I, iii, 148–52)

        this sicknes doth infect
The very life bloud of our enterprise,

(IV, i, 28–29)

And you did sware that oath at Dancaster,
That you did nothing purpose gainst the state,

(V, i, 42–43)

Can you find any instances of *do* in the play which might be the forerunner of the emphasis transformation?

5. What inflection does the verb take after *thou*? Does it take the same inflection in the past tense? What purpose does the inflection serve? What are the forms of the modals and *be* after *thou*, in both the present and past tenses? Study the following variations of this inflection:

What, *stands* thou idle here? [*stand(e)st*: Qq 2–5, F]

(V, iii, 41)

if Percy be alive thou *gets* not my sword [*getst*: Qq 2–5, F]

(V, iii, 52–53)

What phonological reason can you give for these variations? Note that they occur in the same passage, set by the same compositor—

more evidence that the copy was read to the typesetter while he worked.

6. Except for the standard forms *hath* and *doth*, the third person singular, present tense indicative inflection is generally the same as our own. There are only fourteen instances in this play of the earlier inflection (e.g., at I, ii, 230; II, iv, 469; III, i, 10; IV, iii, 28; V, iv, 43; etc.). Does there seem to be any pattern to this divergence from the norm? There are two instances of *has* and four of *does*, at I, iii, 291; III, i, 172; III, iii, 31 and 64; and IV, i, 17. Does the status of the characters who say them or the manner in which they are said help you to draw any conclusion about this usage?

7. Study the following instances of singular verbs with plural subjects:

> there *lives* not three good men unhangde in England
>
> (II, iv, 143–44)
>
> His letters *beares* his mind
>
> (IV, i, 20)

Although the patterns are too dissimilar for comparison, can you advance any reasons for the lack of concord in each of these sentences?

8. There are a few instances in this play of past tense forms which are different from our own. Examples are at I, i, 47–48; II, iv, 169, 170–71, 201; III, i, 15–17; V, i, 63; II, iv, 25–26, 287; V, ii, 63. Which of these are fossil remains of older strong forms, and which are examples of analogical regularization which have not become general usage?

Note the following usage:

> . . . and saide this other day you *ought* him a thousand pound.
>
> (III, iii, 151–52)

What hint does this give as to the former meaning of the auxiliary?

9. Study the following instances of present tense usage where we would now expect to find the past tense:

> he doth it as like one of these harlotrie plaiers as ever I *see*.
>
> (II, iv, 436–37)
>
> Thats the worst tidings that I *heare* of yet. [of it: Qq 1–4]
>
> (IV, i, 127)

What is the contextual pattern here which explains this idiom?

10. In the same manner as in exercise (8) above, analyze the following examples of past participles: I, i, 2, 37; ii, 143–44; iii, 12–13, 60–61, 135, 178; II, iv, 401–02, 410; III, i, 5, 11–12, 40; IV, i, 84–85; iii, 45–46; V, iv, 48–49. Account for the following instances phonologically:

> To shew how much thou art *degenerate*.
>
> (III, ii, 128)
>
> These things indeed you have *articulate*
>
> (V, i, 72)

At V, iv, 107, the old spelling of the participle, *strooke*, is usually rendered *struck* in modern texts. (The same is true of the past tense form at I, iii, 139.) Does this spelling simply mirror a pronunciation difference, or does it indicate a difference in inflectional form?

11. There are at least twenty-five instances in this play of "understood" verbs, of which the following are typical:

> you must to the court in the morning.
>
> (II, iv, 367–68)
>
> We must all to the wars
>
> (II, iv, 594–95)
>
> with our small conjunction we should on
>
> (IV, i, 37)
>
> Sheele be a souldier to, sheele to the wars.
>
> (III, i, 195)
>
> Our hands are full of businesse, lets away
>
> (III, ii, 179)

What is the general category of the deleted verbs? What must be present before deletion is possible? Can you furnish any modern usages similar to this? One editor has remarked that this is "a practice which seems often to impart a dramatic rush to a line."[10] Do you agree? Note the following example:

> therefore ile none of it
>
> (V, i, 141–42; see also II, i, 69)

---

[10] F. Langford, in his introduction to the Swan edition (Toronto, 1962), p. xxvii.

In what way is it an exception to the other examples quoted above? How would you analyze and classify instances of this sort?

Sentence Structure

1. In Chapter Five, we found that there is a distinct parallel pattern in the *negative* and *yes/no interrogative* transformations. Shakespeare's patterns in this respect are divided; many are like our own, but a few vary significantly. How do Shakespeare's patterns in these two transformations compare with ours when a modal, *have*, or *be* follows Tn in the Aux? What happens when none of these elements follow Tn? Can you determine a consistent transformational pattern in the instances where his structure differs from ours? Is this variant pattern completely dead (see I, iii, 52; II, ii, 11–12; II, iii, 93–94)? What seems to have been the state of these two transformations, based upon the number of variant forms and those which are like our own?

2. In like manner, analyze the substantial interrogative transformations in this play. What characterizes those which are like our own patterns? Do those which differ follow a consistent pattern?—do they follow our own two-step transformational arrangements? If the yes/no transformation of Tn + V in Shakespeare's day often varied from our own, how do you account for the patterns at I, iii, 139; IV, i, 18; V, i, 137; iii, 39–40— which are identical with our own?

3. Analyze the *negative-interrogative* transformation combinations in the play. In what single respect do they differ from ours? —a minor difference, but one that makes them sound unintentionally stiff and formal.[11] The following examples show major differences from modern patterns:

Why comes he not himselfe?

(IV, i, 15)

lookes he not for supply?

(IV, iii, 3)

---

[11] This apparent stiffness likewise occurs with the tag-ending negative-interrogatives: see I, iii, 269; I, i, 75; II, iii, 72; and II, iv, 65, 573.

Though different from ours, do they still follow consistent transformational pattern sequences, specifically those uncovered in the
previous two problems?

4. In general, the *imperative* transformations in this play follow
the same pattern as ours today. What polite insertions are sometimes added to soften the order or demand? What particular
problems of analysis do the following imperative structures have?

   a. I preethe doe thou stande in some by-roome
                                   (II, iv, 31–32)
      do thou never leave calling Frances
                                   (II, iv, 34–35)
      Do thou stand for my father and examine me
                                   (II, iv, 413)
      Do thou amend thy face, and ile amend my life
                                   (III, iii, 27)

   b. Lord Douglas go you and tell him so.
                                     (V, ii, 33)
      Lord John of Lancaster go you with him.
                                     (V, iv, 2)
      Heare you cosen a word.
                                     (I, iii, 227)

   c. Worcester get thee gone
                                     (I, iii, 15)
      Bardol get thee before to Coventry
                                     (IV, ii, 1)
      come you along with me.
                                     (V, iv, 131)

   d. Go hide thee behind the Arras
                                     (II, iv, 549)
      goe call him forth.
                                     (II, iv, 576)

Can you determine any transformational patterns for these
structures?

5. Shakespeare's *negative-imperative* structures generally differ
from ours, usually because of the nature of the negative transformation. In this play, only a handful seem familiar to us: I, ii,
69–70; III, ii, 129; IV, iii, 6; V, v, 44—and the first seems

stiffly formal. Here are some examples of Shakespeare's more usual structures:

> let not us . . . bee called theeves of the daies beauty
> $$(\text{I, ii, 26–28})$$
> let not him be slandered with revolt.
> $$(\text{I, iii, 112})$$
> Weepe not sweet Queene
> $$(\text{II, iv, 431})$$
> banish not him thy Harries companie
> $$(\text{II, iv, 525–26})$$
> > and thinke not Percy
> To share with me in glory any more
> $$(\text{V, iv, 63–64})$$

Work out the transformational steps by which these and others may be patterned.

6. One of the most difficult structural patterns for the modern reader is the *subjunctive*, plentiful in Shakespeare's day, but virtually extinct today. The following are some examples of this pattern:

> a. nowe shall we knowe if Gadshill *have* set a match.
> $$(\text{I, ii, 118–19})$$
> if he *fight* longer then he sees reason
> $$(\text{I, ii, 207})$$
> if I *be tane*, ile peach for this
> $$(\text{II, ii, 47})$$
> I am a rogue if I *were* not at halfe sword
> $$(\text{II, iv, 182})$$
> but how if honor *pricke* me off when I come on?
> $$(\text{V, i, 131–32})$$
> if thou *see* me downe in the battel and *bestride* me, so, tis a poynt of friendship.
> $$(\text{V, i, 121–22})$$
> *wert* not for laughing I should pittie him.
> $$(\text{II, ii, 117})$$
> b. An it *be* not foure by the day ile be hangd
> $$(\text{II, i, 1–2})$$
> and *twere* not as good a deed as drinke to turne true-man
> $$(\text{II, ii, 22–24})$$

and I *were* nowe by this rascall I could braine him

(II, iii, 23–24)

and the indentures *be* drawn ile away

(III, i, 264)

c. I thinke this *bee* the most villainous house

(II, i, 15)

I thinke it *be* two a clocke.

(II, i, 37; II, iv, 574)

me thinkes it *were* an easie leape

(I, iii, 201)

d. I woulde to God thou and I knewe where a commodity of good names *were* to be bought

(I, ii, 92–94)

I woulde your store *were* here

(II, ii, 94)

I would my face *were* in your belly.

(III, iii, 56)

Oh I could wish this taverne *were* my drum.

(III, iii, 230)

I would *twere* bed time

(V, i, 125)

e. when he *please* againe to be himselfe

(I, ii, 223)

so he *unsay* it now.

(I, iii, 76)

Send danger from the East unto the West [,]
So honor *crosse* it, from the North to South

(I, iii, 195–96)

to drive awaie the time till Falstalffe *come*

(II, iv, 31)

You must needes learne Lord to amend this fault,
Though sometimes it *shew* greatnes

(III, i, 180–81)

I was as vertuously given as a gentleman *need* to be

(III, iii, 16–17)

Unlesse thou *yeeld* thee as my prisoner.

(V, iii, 10)

                    ere the king
Dismisse his power, he meanes to visit us

(IV, iv, 36–37)

I am afraid of this gunpowder Percy, though he *be* dead

(V, iv, 123–24)

Let us not leave till all our owne *be* won.

(V, v, 44)

f. Pray God my newes *be* worth a welcome lord

(IV, i, 87)

tis more then time that I *were* there

(IV, ii, 60–61)

Twere best he did.

(V, ii, 3)

But *be* he as he will

(V, ii, 73)

Thy ignominy *sleepe* with thee in the grave

(V, iv, 100)

What are the special uses of each of these groups of subjunctive forms? What special conditions must be present before the subjunctive is manifested? What transformational patterns are present in these examples? Do we have any vestigial remains of these patterns? Why do you suppose these patterns have died out? What do the examples in group (d) above suggest is the probable derivation of *will/would*? Note the structures at I, ii, 7ff, 107–08, 119–20; II, iv, 189–91, 204–07. Would you consider them subjunctives? Why, or why not?

7. The following exclamations exhibit certain subjunctive features:

God save thy Grace:

(I, ii, 19)

Whose wrongs in us God pardon

(I, iii, 149)

O the divel take such coosoners

(I, iii, 255)

happieman be his dole, say I

(II, ii, 80)

all the titles of good fellowship come to you.

(II, iv, 307–308)

good maners be your speed

(III, i, 190)

So please your Majestie

                                        (III, ii, 18)

Godamercy

                                        (III, iii, 57)

God forbid.

                                        (V, ii, 36)

What common pattern do these expressions share? Is this still a live transformation—that is, do we still use it to form new exclamations, as Shakespeare apparently did?

8. Though they appear to be similar to the examples in exercises 6 and 7, the following are not instances of subjunctives:

How many be there of them?

                                        (II, ii, 66)

there be foure of us here have tane a thousand pound this day morning.

                                        (II, iv, 175–76)

let men say wee be men of good governement

                                        (I, ii, 30–31)

Explain why these are not subjunctive forms, and give possible reasons for the use of *be* rather than *are*.

9. Except for structural rearrangements for word emphasis or considerations of poetic meter, the general structural patterns in this play do not vary significantly from our own. However, the following noun phrases do have an unusual placement of the adjective:

heire apparant	(I, ii, 65)
the bloud roiall	(I, ii, 156–57)
our indentures tripartite	(III, i, 80)
some things true	(III, ii, 26)
a roabe pontificall	(III, ii, 56)
militairie title capitall	(III, ii, 110)
revolted tapsters, and Ostlers, tradefalne	(IV, ii, 31–32)
pardon absolute for your selfe	(IV, iii, 50)
considerations infinite	(V, i, 102)

Is the embedding process any different from present operations? What changes would be required in changing from the embedded state to the final surface states above? Are the following structures the same as the forms above?

> on wednesday next our councel we wil hold
> (I, i, 103; also III, ii, 173)
> thy soule that thou souldest him on good friday last
> (I, ii, 127)

There are two instances of the expression "good my Lord", used as a form of address (II, iv, 601; III, iii, 109). Compare them with the structures at I, ii, 179, and IV, iv, 21. How do you suppose the inverted structure was formed?

10. Study the following structures:

> ile have a starling shalbe taught to speake
> (I, iii, 224)
> And tis no little reason bids us speed
> (I, iii, 283)
> ther's a Frankelin in the wild of Kent hath brought three hundred Markes with him in golde
> (II, i, 59–61)
> there is many a soule,
> Shall pay full dearely for this incounter
> (V, i, 83–84)

How do these differ from contemporary relative clauses? How does the subordinating process differ from our own?

Conclusion

As a review, consider the following:

1. What are the most significant differences between Shakespeare's grammatical practices and our own?

2. What specific forces have been operating in this change over these 350 years?

3. Which differences would give the average student the most trouble?

4. What language problems other than grammatical need to be overcome?

BIBLIOGRAPHY

The important texts and editions of *Henry IV, Part I* have been enumerated earlier in this chapter (pp. 172–73). For grammars of Early Modern English, see the bibliography for Chapter 8.

The pronunciation of this period is covered in Helge Kökeritz, *Shakespeare's Pronunciation* (New Haven, Conn.: Yale University Press, 1953); and E. J. Dobson, *English Pronunciation 1500–1700* (2 vols.; Oxford: The Clarendon Press, 1957). The only extensive study of Shakespeare's grammar is E. A. Abbott, *A Shakespearian Grammar* (2d. ed.; London: The Macmillan Company, 1870), which is sadly dated and often misleading. There is a real need for a study of Shakespeare's grammatical practices incorporating the relevant aspects of modern grammatical theory (and up-to-date textual criticism).

Many studies purporting to be of Shakespeare's language turn out to be highly subjective studies of his style. The best ones along this line are Otto Jespersen, *Growth and Structure of the English Language* (9th ed.; Garden City, N.Y.: Doubleday and Company, Inc., 1955), chap. 10; and Gladys D. Willcock, "Shakespeare and Elizabethan English," *Shakespeare Survey*, VII (1954), 12–24; representing respectively an early and more recent viewpoint. The most complete survey of Shakespeare's rhetorical devices is Sister Miriam Joseph, C.S.C., *Shakespeare's Use of the Arts of Language* (New York: Columbia University Press, 1947).

The work of identifying and locating many of the forms of Henry IV, Part I in this chapter has been greatly facilitated by the recent publication of the first two volumes of Marvin Spevack, *A Complete and Systematic Concordance to the Works of Shakespeare* (Hildesheim, W. Germany: Georg Alms Verlagsbuch-handlung, 1968–); especially volume II, *Drama and Character Concordance to the Folio Histories*. Projected to be completed in six volumes, this concordance was processed by computer, its base text being that prepared by G. Blackmore Evans and published by the Houghton Mifflin Company.

8

A Historical Survey of English

INTRODUCTION

Review and Prospectus

In the preceding chapter, we studied the differences and similarities between the English of today and Shakespeare's day, and we tried to find some direction to the change. In sum, we noted that there are not only differences in word meanings and usages, which is obvious to anyone who ever glanced over the glossaries appended to an Elizabethan play or poem, but significant changes over the past 350 years in pronunciation, inflections, and syntax as well. We also noted that these changes, individually not terribly disconcerting, can in the aggregate make the literature of the Tudor and Stuart periods very difficult reading for the average student.

This chapter is a continuation of the preceding one. After a brief review of the Early Modern English period, we will continue our historical survey of the English language in reverse chronological order, moving to the Middle English period and the Old English period. Our survey will also include a brief look at ME dialects, the most significant feature of that period, and at the Germanic backgrounds of English. Our primary concern is morphology and syntax. Very little will be said about phonological development; the inductive procedures we have adopted here do not permit us to pursue it with ease. Furthermore, ME pronunciation is usually surveyed in Chaucer courses; and OE phonology is definitely the province of graduate courses, where there is the opportunity to pursue the philological details leading to conclusions about probable pronunciations. With this major exception, we will follow the same basic procedure as in the preceding chapter.

Our basis for this historical study will consist of passages from several translations of *The Consolation of Philosophy*, written in 524 A.D. by the Roman statesman-philosopher Boethius, while in prison awaiting execution on a trumped-up charge of treason. This work was probably the most influential philosophical treatise of the Middle Ages, and even during the Renaissance it was continually retranslated from the original Latin. We will review passages of this work in translations from the Early Modern, Middle English, and Old English periods.[1]

The Lord's Prayer over One Thousand Years

But before we look at this unfamiliar work, we should pause for a brief overview of a much more familiar passage. Printed below are four separate English translations of the Lord's Prayer (Matt. 6:9–13), preceded by the Latin Vulgate translation on which all but the contemporary version were based.

THE LORD'S PRAYER

Pater noster qui es in cælis, sanctificetur nomen tuum, adveniat regnum tuum, fiat voluntas tua sicut in cælo et in terra; panem nostrum supersubstantiale da nobis hodie, et demitte

---

[1] There have been at least twenty English translations of this work, in part or in whole, commencing with the OE translation at the end of the ninth century. The most convenient Latin text is in the Loeb Classical Library series, No. 74, eds. H. F. Stewart and E. K. Rand (Cambridge, Mass., 1918). The best modern English translation is that by Richard Green in the Bobbs-Merrill Library of Liberal Arts series, No. 84 (Indianapolis, Ind., 1962). For an exhaustive study of the influence of Boethius during the Middle Ages and Renaissance, see H. R. Patch, *The Tradition of Boethius: A Study of His Importance in Mediaeval Culture* (New York, 1935).

nobis debita nostra sicut nos demittimus debitoribus nostris;
et ne inducas nos in temtationem, sed libera nos a malo.

LATIN VULGATE

Fæder ure þu þe eart on heofonum, si þin nama gehalgod;
to-becume þin rice; gewurþe þin willa on eorðan swa swa on
heofonum; urne gedæghwamlican hlaf syle us to dæg; and
forgyf us ure gyltas, swa swa we forgyfað urum gyltendum; and
ne gelæd þu us on costnunge, ac alys us of yfele, soþlice.

OLD ENGLISH [West Saxon, c. 1000]

Oure fadir that art in heuenes, halwid be thi name; thi
kyngdom cumme to; be thi wille don as in heuen and in erthe;
ʒif to vs this day oure breed ouer other substaunce; and forʒeue
to vs oure dettis; as we forʒeue to oure dettours; and leede vs
nat in to temptacioun, but delyuere vs fro yuel. Amen.

MIDDLE ENGLISH
[Wycliffite, c. 1385 (eds. Forshall and Madden, 1850)]

Our father which art in heauen, hallowed be thy name. Thy
kyngdome come. Thy will be done in earth, as it is in heauen.
Giue vs this day our daily bread. And forgiue vs our debts, as
we forgiue our debters. And lead vs not into temptation, but
deliuer vs from euill. For thine is the kyngdome, and the power,
and the glory, for euer.[2] Amen.

EARLY MODERN ENGLISH
[Authorized (King James) Version, 1611]

Our Father in heaven, Thy name be hallowed;
Thy kingdom come, Thy will be done, On earth as in heaven.
Give us today our daily bread.
Forgive us the wrong we have done, As we have forgiven those
who have wronged us.
And do not bring us to the test, But save us from the evil one.

MODERN ENGLISH [New English Bible, 1961]

---

[2] This line, which has become an intimate part of Protestant liturgical tradition,
is now generally conceded to be a noncanonical interpolation, a marginal note that
crept into the text through scribal error. Once in, however, it has been impossible
to erase it, for it does give the prayer a "finished" touch. Its inclusion or omission
serves to divide Catholics and Protestants almost as sharply as "debts" vs. "trespasses"
separates Presbyterians from Methodists.

Obviously, the most familiar passage is that taken from the ENE King James Version of 1611. This is the version which is still used in churches, with the possible substitution of "who" for "which" in the first line. The contemporary NE version, though perhaps more readily understandable to the very young, seems strangely awkward and unrhythmic by comparison with what we're used to. The ME version, though clothed in unfamiliar spelling, has the same basic patterns as the King James, and the variations are easily understood.

It is the Old English version which no doubt gives pause. Here is a translation[3] written about one thousand years ago in what is supposed to be *our* language, yet it is for all practical purposes a foreign language. To begin with, we have unfamiliar letters, like the digraph *æ*, and þ (called "thorn") and ð (called "eth"). When this difficulty is resolved by explaining that the digraph is used for the vowel /æ/, and the *thorn* and *eth* are used interchangeably for the same sounds today symbolized by the combination *th*, the language still seems hopelessly complex to the neophyte. Yet there are a good many words which, after study, turn out to be the obvious ancestors of similar words used today. For instance, the first clause, translated, reads, "Father our thou that art in Heaven, be thy name hallowed (lit. 'made holy')." Only *si* "be" (imperative), and possibly þe "that," are really unfamiliar. And so on, through the whole passage.

However, your ability to translate this passage depends entirely upon your derivation of the vocabulary and its ordering from your knowledge of a more modern version. You have not really noted anything about the Old English grammatical relationships as indicated by the inflections which abound even in this relatively short passage. For instance, *ure*, *urne*, and *urum*, which are all translated "our" today, represent three different inflected forms of this possessive pronoun, depending upon the case and number of the noun headword. Though this is a tiny sampling, it is an indication that Old English included many

---

[3] Actually a *gloss*, an interlinear transcription of the Latin manuscript into English, recorded word for word, like the old "ponies" of high school language courses. The necessarily slavish following of the Latin word order makes them of dubious value as records of OE sentence form.

inflections which are lost today. A glance at the ME version will show that these three forms were all rendered "our"; in less than four hundred years, this inflectional distinction was lost. Yet Middle English was somewhat more highly inflected than Early Modern and Modern English. Because almost all of the verb forms in this passage are subjunctives or imperatives, we cannot use it to learn about a number of inflectional distinctions in the ME verb which are now lost, too.

Obviously, then, this is the main point of our inquiry. Though the chronology of sound and semantic changes is interesting, the most important consideration in the history of English is the study of the gradual losses of inflections, the possible reasons for these losses, and the forms and arrangements which replaced them. Every aspect of our study, beginning with the Early Modern English version of Boethius, will be directed to this purpose.

EARLY MODERN ENGLISH (1450–1700)

The Consolation of Philosophy

The choice of parallel translations of Boethius's *Consolation of Philosophy* as the basic documents for a historical survey of English, rather than the more usual use of Bible texts, stems from the nature of the material itself. The basic source of all the translations was the original Latin text, rather than a diversified use of Vulgate Latin, or corrupt or corrected Greek texts, which is the case with the Bible. This is not to say that the translations of Boethius will be absolutely parallel; on the contrary, the ideal of complete fidelity in translation is comparatively recent. Still, we are making use of a document which had a profound effect upon the Western world for over a thousand years after its composition, and every translator took pains to be as faithful to the author's intentions as he could, even though he did not necessarily translate it word for word.

The work, as the title implies, is the attempt of a Roman statesman, imprisoned and exiled on a questionable charge, awaiting an indefinitely postponed execution, to find some sort of good in his misfortune, and by extension, to define the Western concept of "living the good life" itself. Although Boethius was an orthodox Christian (his imprisonment is thought to have resulted from a theological difference of opinion with the Germanic Arians then in political control of Rome), there is little direct reference in his work to Christianity itself. In fact, the passage which we will be mostly concerned with is in large part a paraphrase of Plato's *Gorgias*; and throughout are echoes and sometimes direct quotations from several ancient writers. Perhaps this wide, yet judicious use of classical literature and philosophy accounts for the great appeal of this work in the Middle Ages; for the Western world had, even before the East–West division of the Church (completed in 1054), lost all direct contact with the culture of ancient Greece, save from Latin commentaries and paraphrases like Boethius's.

The work is divided into five parts, or books. Each book is further subdivided into alternating metrical and prose passages of varying lengths. I have selected for our consideration all of the first prose and metric passages, and the first half of the second prose passage of Book IV. This choice was not made for the intrinsic merit of these passages. In fact, these may be among the least distinguished of all the passages in the work, consisting, as they largely do, of a Socratic dialogue between Boethius and Lady Philosophy. Rather, the selection was made because this was the longest connected portion of the work which *all* of the translators followed with reasonable faithfulness. The passages are cut short in the middle of Prose II simply because this is where the Old English translator arbitrarily made a division in his version, after which he abridged the materials drastically.

Our first translation is from the Early Modern English period, done by the anonymous I. (possibly J.) T., and published in 1609. All efforts to uncover the identity of the translator have proved fruitless.[4] His version, though uninspired, is at least competent, and so faithful is it to the original that it is the basis for the English text in the Loeb Classical Library edition. Because we have

---

[4] See the introduction to William Anderson's edition of this translation (Carbondale, Ill., 1963), especially p. 15. Because this edition was so carelessly printed and proofread, I have not used it as the basis for the text in this book.

already studied the Early Modern period extensively, this will be little more than a brief review, the translation itself acting as a base text for the other translations.

THE CONSOLATION OF PHILOSOPHY
In the Translation of I. T. (1609)

[Text: From the copy in the Newberry Library, Chicago. The spelling of *u* and *v*, and *i* and *j*, as well the old "long *s*," has been normalized.]

THE FOURTH BOOKE OF BOETIUS.
Conteining the reasons, why God permitteth evill.

THE I. PROSE.

Boetius merveileth at the impunitie and prosperitie of evill men.

When Philosophy had sung these verses with a soft & sweete voice, observing due dignitie and gravitie in her countenance and gesture, I not having altogether forgotten my inward griefe, interrupted her speach, which shee was about to continue, and sayed, O thou, who bringest us to see true light, those things,   5 which hetherto thou hast treated of, have manifestly appeared to bee Divine in their owne knowledge, and invincible by thy reasons, and thou hast said, that though the force of griefe had made me forget them of late, yet heretofore I was not altogether ignorant of them. But this is the chiefest cause of my sorrow, that,   10 since the governour of all things is so good, there can either be any evill at all, or passe unpunished. Which alone I beseech thee consider, how much admiration it deserveth. But there is another greater then this, for wickednesse bearing rule and sway, vertue is not onely without reward, but lieth also troden under   15 the wickeds feet, and is punished in stead of vice. That which things should be done in the kingdome of God, who knoweth all things, can doe all things, but will doe onely that, which is good, no man can sufficiently admire nor complaine. To which she answered, It were indeede infinitly strange, and surpassing all   20 monsters, if, as thou conceivest, in the best ordered house of so

great an housholder, the vilest vessels were made account of,
and the pretious neglected, but it is not so. For if those things
which were a little before concluded, be kept unviolated, thou
shalt by his helpe, of whose kingdome we speake, know, that the   25
good are alway powerfull, and the evill alway abject and weake,
& that vices are never without punishment, nor vertue without
reward, and that the good are alway prosperous, and the evil unfortunate, and many things of that sort, which will take away all
cause of complaint, and give thee firme and sollide strength.   30
And since by my meanes thou hast already seene the forme of
true blessednesse, and knowen where it is placed, running over
all those things, which I thinke necessary to let passe, I will shew
thee the way, which will carry thee home. And I will also fasten
wings upon thy mind, with which shee may rouse herselfe, that al   35
perturbation being driven away, thou mayest returne safely into
thy countrey by my direction, by my path, and with my wings.

The I. Verse.

How Phylosophy bringeth men to the contemplation of God.

> For I have swift and nimble wings,
>   which will ascend the lofty skies,
> With which when thy quick mind is clad,
>   it wil the loathed earth dispise
> And goe beyond the airy globe,   5
>   and watry cloudes behind it leave
> Passing the fire, which skorching heat
>   doth from the heav'ns swift course receive,
> Untill it reach the starry house,
>   and get to treade bright Phœbus waies   10
> Joyning it selfe in company
>   with aged Saturnes lightsome raies,
> And trace the circles of the starres,
>   which in the night to us appeare,
> And having stai'd there long enough   15
>   goe on beyond the farthest sphere,
> Sitting upon the highest orbe
>   partaker of the glorious light,

Where highest King his Scepter holds,
    and the worlds raines doth guide aright,   20
And in his Chariot standing firme,
    doth every thing in order set.
Unto this seat when thou art brought,
    thy countrey, which thou didst forget,
Thou then wilt challenge to thy selfe,   25
    saying this is the glorious land,
Where I was borne and in this soile
    my feet for evermore shall stand.
Whence if thou pleasest to behold
    the earthly might which thou hast left,   30
Those Tyraunts, which the people feare,
    will seeme of their true home bereft.

The II. Prose.

That good men are powerfull, and evill men weake.

Oh (quoth I.) How great things doest thou promise? And I doubt not but thou canst performe them, wherefore stay me not now, that thou hast stirred up my desire. First then (quoth she) that good men are alway powerfull, and evill men of no strength, thou mayest easily knowe, and the one is proved by the other.   5 For since that good and evill are contraries, if it be convinced, that goodnesse is potent, the weakenesse of evil will be also manifest; and contrariwise if we discerne the frailty of evill, wee must needes acknowledge the firmenes of goodnesse. But that our opinion may be more certainely embraced, I will take both waies,   10 confirming my propositions, sometime from one part, sometime from another. There bee two things, by which all humane actions are effected, will and power, of which if either be wanting, there can nothing be performed. For if there want will, no man taketh any thing in hand against his will, and if there be not power, the   15 will is in vaine. So that, if thou seest anie willing to obtaine that, which he doth not obtaine, thou canst not doubt, but that he wanted power to obtaine, what he would. It is manifest (quoth I) and can by no meanes be denied. And wilt thou doubt, that he could, whom thou seest bring to passe, what he desired? No.   20

But every man is mighty in that which he can doe, & weake in that which he cannot doe. I confesse it (quoth I.) Doest thou remember then (quoth she) that it was inferred by our former discourses, that all the intention of mans will doth hasten to happinesse, though their courses be divers? I remember (quoth I) that that 25 also was proved. Remembrest thou also that blessednesse is goodnesse it selfe, and consequently when blessednesse is sought after, goodnesse must of force be desired? I have that also fixt in my memory. Wherefore all men both good and bad, without difference of intentions endevour to obtaine goodnesse. It followeth 30 (quoth I.) But it is certaine, that men are made good by the obtayning of goodnesse. It is so. Wherfore good men obtaine what they desire. So it seemeth. And if evill men did obtaine the goodnes they desire, they could not be evill. It is true. Wherefore since they both desire goodnesse, but the one obteineth it, and the 35 other not, there is no doubt but that good men are powerfull, and the evill weake. Whosoever doubteth of this (quoth I) hee neither considereth the nature of things, nor the consequence of thy reasons. Againe (quoth shee) if there bee two, to whom the same thing is proposed according to nature, and the one of them, 40 bringeth it perfectly to passe with his naturall function; but the other cannot exercise that natural function, but after another maner, then is agreeable to nature, & doth not perform that, which he had proposed, but imitateth the other who performeth it: Which of these two wilt thou judge to bee more powerfull? 45 Though I conjecture (quoth I) at thy meaning, yet I desire to heare it more plainely. Wilt thou denie (quoth shee) that the motion of walking is agreeable to the nature of men? No (quoth I.) And makest thou any doubt, that the function of it doth naturally belong to the feet? There is no doubt of this neither (quoth I.) 50 Wherfore if one, that can go uppon his feete, doeth walke, and another, who hath not this naturall function of his feete, endevoureth to walke by creeping upon his hands: which of these two is deservedly to bee esteemed the stronger. Inferre the rest (quoth I) for no man doubteth, but that hee which can use that naturall 55 function is stronger then he which cannot. But (quoth she) the good seeke to obtaine the chiefest good, which is equally proposed

to badde and good, by the naturall function of vertues, but the
evill endevour to obtaine the same by divers concupiscensces,
which are not the natural function of obtaining goodnesse.　60
Thinkest thou otherwise? No (quoth I) for it is manifest, what
followeth. For by force of that which I have already granted, it is
necessary, that good men are powerful and evil men weake. Thou
runnest rightly (quoth she) and it is (as Physitions are wont to
hope) a token of an erected and resisting nature. Wherefore,　65
since I see thee most apt and willing to comprehend, I will therefore heape up manie reasons together.

QUESTIONS AND EXERCISES—EARLY MODERN ENGLISH

1. Because we have already covered this period in detail in the
previous chapter, review the grammatical practices of the times
by comparing your previous conclusions against the practices of
the anonymous I. T., with attention to:

   a. The inflections of nouns, verbs, adverbs, and adjectives.
   b. The use of pronouns and their forms.
   c. The components of the Aux and the VP.
   d. The transformations involved in forming:
      (1) The yes/no interrogative
      (2) The substantial interrogative
      (3) The negative
      (4) The imperative
      (5) The subjunctive
      (6) Possible combinations of the above

Do any of these vary significantly within the translation? Are
there any significant differences between the translation and the
same practices in Shakespeare?

2. What limitations does the translation have (other than
relative brevity), as compared with Shakespeare's plays, when
attempting to uncover the language practices of this period?
Would these same limitations probably hold true for the ME and
OE translations, too?

3. Taking a number of consecutive sentences at random, analyze the differences between the language of the translator and contemporary usage. Are the differences mainly generative or transformational? For the generative differences, do they occur at or near the deep structure or the surface structure level?

4. The following is a translation of Verse I of Book IV, done by Queen Elizabeth I of England in 1593. In the unique manuscript in the Public Record Office, London, this passage is in the Queen's own handwriting. What variations do you find in the grammatical practices, as opposed to Shakespeare's and I. T.'s? Which of these may be the result of the exigencies and requirements of verse? What orthographical and metrical evidence do you find of the Queen's pronunciation?

[Text: EETS, o.s. 113, ed. Caroline Pemberton (London, 1899)]

THE FOURTH BOOKE.

I. Myter

For Spedy quilles have I
   That fur above the Pole do reache,
Wiche whan my fliinge mind putz on,
   hating the erthe despice hit,
And hiar hies than erthes Globe,   5
   and Cloudes behind me See,
And pas above the fiars top,
   With swiftnis that the heavens heat
Until to Starry house hit comme
   With Φebus sorteth way,   10
And Soldiar made of shining Star
   Cold Saturne doth felowe,
   Or wher the shewing night,
The Circle Round doth make;
   and whan got ynough she hathe,   15
The owtmost Pole he leves,
   And worthy made of hiest Light
Presseth the waight of spidy skie.
   he, Lord, holdz of kings the Septar
   and Raines of world doth gide,   20
And stable rules the Spidy Cours.

Of all the noble Juge.
Hither if the way bak do bring thè,
  Wiche now forgetting thou requirest:
"This," wilt thou Say, "my country is, I knowe;   25
  hens Came I, hire wyl I stay my step."
And if of erthe hit please thè
  the darkenes left to vewe,
The grimme Lookis, that people dredeth so,
  Of banissed Tirantz shalt behold.   30

MIDDLE ENGLISH (1100–1450)

The Norman Conquest and Its Aftermath

In Chapter 7, it was mentioned that the Middle English
period should be considered a transitional stage in the development of the language. The rapid conquest and occupation of
England by the Norman French reduced English to a third-class
position, far inferior to Latin and French. And, as the language
declined abruptly in both learned opinion and social favor, so
went those who stubbornly persisted in speaking it. The native
English, who continued to be an overwhelming numerical
majority, were forced into third-class citizenship, or no citizenship
at all. The Norman invaders bound most of the English to a
position of serfdom, hitherto unknown to them, establishing the
continental feudal system which weakened England politically
until the beginning of the Tudor dynasty (1485). But despite this
foreign incursion, with arbitrary power wielded by barons under
a loose fealty to the king, with the rearing of castle strongholds
and the waging of unpopular foreign wars, the English-speaking
population persisted and ultimately triumphed; but their language
at the end bore little resemblance to its state at the time of the
invasion.

A good deal has been written about what English might have
been like had Harold won at Hastings, assuming that England's
record in successfully warding off subsequent invasions remained
intact. The truth is probably that it would vary only slightly from

its present form, perhaps showing a few more overtly Germanic characteristics. For the English language as spoken by the rank-and-file was undergoing changes at the time of the Norman Conquest not reflected in contemporary documents, for the scribes tended to maintain a conservative orthographical tradition. King Edward the Confessor (1042–1066) had grown up in France, where his father had been exiled. Further, he and his queen had introduced French favorites into the court before the Conquest and thus unconsciously succeeded in making French a necessary accomplishment for ambitious retainers. From a linguistic view-point, therefore, the Norman invasion was not the shock it is popularly thought to be.

As the political trauma of the invasion wore away, sheer weight of numbers, plus political events at home and on the continent, made the ultimate triumph of English a foregone conclusion. At the beginning, there had to be at least minimal contact between master and servant, the master ultimately being forced to learn the servant's language because, outside of London, there were so few who were able (or willing) to speak French. Then political events intervened, and when the French king rose to a position equivalent to the English monarchy, rather than sub-servient to it, each Norman nobleman was forced to choose between one kingdom or the other. If he elected to be English, his political decision would likely be followed by a linguistic allegiance as well. By the second decade of the fifteenth century, King Henry V was sending back dispatches in English from his French campaigns. Long before that, parish priests and friars were preaching to the commoners in English, reserving Latin strictly for liturgical use. After the middle of the fifteenth century, even the conservative law courts and the parliament conducted their business in English. And all the while, an important native literature had continued to grow throughout the land.

Chaucer's Translation of Boethius

It is to this literature which we now turn to learn something of the language of the time. It is something of a tribute to the impact Boethius had on medieval England that his outstanding

Middle English translator is none other than Geoffrey Chaucer himself, who was so influenced by the work that he adopted the basic philosophical position in his second most famous poem, *Troilus and Creseyde*.[5] Temporarily eschewing poetry, even for the metrical passages of the Latin original, he translated the whole of *The Consolation of Philosophy* into an accurate, literarily creditable English version which reflects, somewhat conservatively, the English of London in the last quarter of the fourteenth century, just before the Middle English transitional period came to an end.

London and the Middle English Dialects

We stress here the *dialect of London*, which by Chaucer's day was rapidly becoming the standard for the English-speaking population of the country. Contrary to a widespread opinion, Chaucer had little, if any, influence upon this development; he was a Londoner, a frequenter of the court, a minor political functionary—and it is to be expected that he would write the literary version of that dialect which came most naturally to him. The development of the London standard was influenced by the national focus upon the English court at Westminster and upon London as the business and commercial center of the country. The writings of England's foremost medieval poet had nothing to do with the adoption of the standard dialect. Fortunately, he just happened to be writing in it at the time.

But the adoption of the London standard came slowly. A century later, the printer William Caxton found it necessary to complain about the still-current proliferation of dialect usages, which he thought a hindrance to his trade, then in its infancy.[6]

---

[5] Chaucer made direct reference to the metrical passage in our selection in *The House of Fame* (ll. 972–78):

> And thoo thoughte y upon Boece,
> That writ, "A thought may flee so hye,
> Wyth fetheres of Philosophye,
> To passen everych element;
> And whan he hath so fer ywent,
> Than may be seen, behynde hys bak,
> Cloude,"—and al that y of spak.

Boece was the common medieval name for the writer.

[6] "And that comyn englysshe that is spoken in one shyre varyeth from a nother. In so moche that in my dayes happened that certayn marchauntes were in a shippe

One can therefore assume that prior to Chaucer's time the dialects over the various regions of England must have manifested wide differences. Moreover, the situation was helped very little so long as the subjugated English were kept on their own bits of land and discouraged from traveling, save in their lord's service. The dialects therefore represent an important aspect of Middle English, and we will conclude this portion of the chapter with a brief survey of them.

Our first consideration, however, is to understand the London standard of the late Middle English period and to compare it with the language of Shakespeare's day. Thus it is that we turn our attention to it, as exemplified by Chaucer's translation of Boethius.

CHAUCER'S BOECE (*c.* 1380)[7]

Incipit Liber Quartus Boecii de Consolacione Philosophie

"*Hec cum philosophia dignitate vultus.*"—Prosa I

Whanne Philosophie hadde songen softly and delitably the forseide thinges kepynge the dignyte of hir cheere and the weyghte of hir wordes, I, thanne, that ne hadde nat al outrely foryeten the wepynge and the moornynge that was set in myn herte, forbrak the entencioun of hir that entendede yit to seyn some othere   5
thinges. "O," quod I, "thou that art gyderesse of verray light, the thinges that thou hast seid me hidirto ben to me so cleer and so schewynge by the devyne lookynge of hem, and by thy resouns, that they ne mowen nat ben overcomen. And thilke thinges that thou toldest me, al be it so that I hadde whilom foryeten hem for   10

---

in tamyse for to have sayled over the see into zelande, and for lacke of wynde thei taryed atte forlond, and wente to lande for to refreshe them. And one of theym named sheffelde a mercer cam in to an hows and axed for mete [food], and specyally he axed after eggys. And the goode wyf answerde, that she coude speke no frenshe. And the merchaunt was angry, for he also coude speke no frenshe, but wolde have hadde egges, and she understode hym not. And thenne at laste a nother sayd that he wolde have eyren, then the good wyf sayd that she understod hym wel. Loo what sholde a man in thyse dayes now wryte: egges or eyren? Certaynly it is harde to playse every man by cause of dyversite and chaunge of langage." Prologue to *Eneydos* (1490).

[7] *The Works of Geoffrey Chaucer*, ed. F. N. Robinson. Reprinted by permission of the publisher, Houghton Mifflin Company.

the sowre of the wrong that hath ben don to me, yet natheles thei
ne weren not al outrely unknowen to me. But this same is namely
a ryght gret cause of my sowre: that so as the governour of
thinges is good, yif that the evelis mowen ben by any weyes, or
elles yif that evelis passen withouten punysschynge. The which   15
thing oonly, how worthy it es to ben wondrid uppon, thou con-
siderest it wel thiselve certeynly. But yit to this thing ther is yit
another thing ijoyned more to ben wondrid uppon: for felonye
is emperisse, and floureth ful of richesses, and vertu is nat al
oonly withouten meedes, but it is cast undir and fortroden undir   20
the feet of felonous folk, and it abyeth the tormentz in stede of
wikkide felouns. Of alle whiche thinges ther nys no wyght that
may merveillen ynowgh, ne compleyne that swiche thinges ben
don in the reigne of God, that alle thinges woot and alle thinges
may and ne wole nat but oonly gode thinges."   25

Thanne seide sche thus: "Certes," quod sche, "that were a
greet merveille and abaysschinge withouten ende, and wel more
horrible than alle monstres, yif it were as thou wenest; that is to
seyn, that in the ryght ordene hous of so mochel a fadir and an
ordeynour of meyne, that the vesselis that ben foule and vyl   30
schulden ben honoured and heryed, and the precious vesselis
schulden ben defouled and vyl. But it nys nat so. For yif the
thinges that I have concluded a litel herebyforn ben kept hoole
and unaraced, thou schalt wel knowe by the auctorite of God, of
the whos reigne I speke, that certes the gode folk ben alwey myghty 35
and schrewes ben alwey outcast and feble; ne the vices ben nevere-
mo withouten peyne, ne the vertus ne ben nat withouten mede;
and that blisfulnesses comen alwey to goode folk, and infortune
comith alwey to wykkide folk. And thou schalt wel knowe manye
thinges of this kynde, that schullen cesen thi pleyntis and streng- 40
then the with stedfast sadnesse. And for thou hast seyn the forme
of the verray blisfulnesse by me that have whilom yschewid it the,
and thow hast knowen in whom blisfulnesse is yset, alle thingis
ytreted that I trowe ben necessarie to putten forth, I schal schewe
the the weye that schal bryngen the ayen unto thyn hous; and I   45
schal fycchen fetheris in thi thought, by whiche it mai arisen in
heighte; so that, alle tribulacioun idon awey, thow, by my

gyding and by my path and by my sledys, shalt mowen retourne
hool and sownd into thi contree.

"Sunt etenim penne volucres michi."—METRUM I

"I have, forthi, swifte fetheris that surmounten the heighte of
the hevene. Whanne the swifte thoght hath clothid itself in tho
fetheris, it despiseth the hateful erthes, and surmounteth the
rowndnesse of the gret ayr; and it seth the clowdes behynde his
bak, and passeth the heighte of the regioun of the fir, that   5
eschaufeth by the swifte moevynge of the firmament, til that he
areyseth hym into the houses that beren the sterres, and joyneth
his weies with the sonne, Phebus, and felawschipeth the weie of
the olde colde Saturnus; and he, imaked a knyght of the clere
sterre—and thilke soule renneth by the cercle of the sterres in   10
alle the places there as the schynynge nyght is ypainted. And
whan the thought hath don there inogh, he schal forleten the laste
hevene, and he schal pressen and wenden on the bak of the swifte
firmament, and he schal be makid parfit of the worschipful lyght
of God. There halt the lord of kynges the septre of his myght and 15
atemprith the governementz of the world, and the schynynge juge
of thinges, stable in hymself, governeth the swifte wayn. And yif
thi wey ledeth the ayein so that thou be brought thider, thanne
wiltow seye that that is the contre that thou requerist, of which
thou ne haddest no mynde—'but now it remembreth me wel, here   20
was I born, her wol I fastne my degree.' But yif the liketh thanne
to looken on the derknesse of the erthe that thou hast forleten,
thanne shaltow seen that these felounous tirantz, that the
wrecchide peple dredeth now, schullen ben exiled fro thilke faire
contre."   25

"Tum ego pape ut magna."—PROSA II

Thanne seide I thus: "Owh! I wondre me that thow byhetist
me so grete thinges. Ne I ne doute nat that thou ne maist wel
performe that thow behetist; but I preie the oonly this, that thow
ne tarie nat to telle me thilke thinges that thou hast moevid."

"First," quod sche, "thow most nedes knowen that goode folk 5
ben alwey strong and myghti, and the schrewes ben feble, and
desert and naked of alle strengthes. And of thise thinges, certes,
everich of hem is declared and schewed by othere. For so as good
and yvel ben two contraries, yif so be that good be stedfast,
thanne scheweth the feblesse of yvel al opynly; and if thow 10
knowe clerly the freelnesse of yvel, the stedfastnesse of good is
knowen. But for as moche as the fey of my sentence schal ben the
more ferme and haboundant, I wil gon by the to weye and by the
tothir, and I wil conferme the thinges that ben purposed, now
on this side and now on that side. Two thinges ther ben in 15
whiche the effect of alle the dedes of mankynde standeth, that is to
seyn, wil and power; and yif that oon of thise two faileth, ther
nys nothing that may be doon. For yif that wille lakketh, ther
nys no wyght that undirtaketh to done that he wol nat doon; and
yif power faileth, the wil nys but in idel and stant for naught. 20
And therof cometh it that yif thou see a wyght that wolde geten
that he mai not geten, thow maist nat douten that power ne faileth
hym to have that he wolde."

"This is open and cler," quod I, "ne it ne mai nat be denyed
in no manere." 25

"And yif thou se a wyght," quod sche, "that hath doon that he
wolde doon, thow nilt nat douten that he ne hath had power to
doon it?"

"No," quod I.

"And in that that every wyght may, in that men may holden 30
hym myghti?"

"I confesse it wel," quod I.

"Remembreth the," quod sche, "that I have gaderid and
ischewid by forseide resouns that al the entencioun of the wil of
mankynde, which that is lad by diverse studies, hasteth to comen 35
to blisfulnesse."

"It remembreth me wel," quod I, "that it hath ben schewed."

"And recordeth the nat thanne," quod sche, "that blisfulnesse
is thilke same good that men requiren? so that whanne that
blisfulnesse is required of alle, that good also is required and 40
desired of alle?"

"It ne recordeth me noght," quod I, "for I have it gretly alwey ficched in my memorie."

"Alle folk thanne," quod sche, "goode and eek badde, enforcen 45 hem withoute difference of entencioun to comen to good."

"This is a verray consequence," quod I.

"And certein is," quod sche, "that by the getynge of good men ben ymakid gode."

"This is certein," quod I. 50

"Thanne geten gode men that thei desiren?"

"So semeth it," quod I.

"But wikkide folk," quod sche, "yif thei geten the good that thei desiren, thei ne mowe nat ben wikkid."

"So is it," quod I. 55

"Than so as the ton and the tothir," quod sche, "desiren good, and the gode folk geten good and not the wikkide folk, than is it no doute that the gode folk ne ben myghty and wikkid folk ben feble."

"Whoso that evere," quod I, "douteth of this, he ne mai nat 60 considere the nature of thinges ne the consequence of resouns."

"And over this," quod sche, "if that ther ben two thinges that han o same purpos by kynde, and that oon of hem pursuweth and performeth thilke same thing by naturel office, and the toother mai nat doon thilke naturel office, but folweth, by other manere 65 than is covenable to nature, hym that acomplisseth his purpos kyndely, and yit he ne acomplisseth nat his owene purpos—whethir of thise two demestow for more myghti?"

"Yif that I conjecte," quod I, "that thou wilt seie, algates yit I desire to herkne it more pleynly of the." 70

"Thou nilt nat thanne denye," quod sche, "that the moevement of goynge nys in men by kynde?"

"No, forsothe," quod I.

"Ne thou doutest nat," quod sche, "that thilke naturel office of goinge ne be the office of feet?" 75

"I ne doute it nat," quod I.

"Thanne," quod sche, "yif that a wight be myghti to moeve, and goth uppon his feet, and another, to whom thilke naturel office of feet lakketh, enforceth hym to gone crepinge uppon his handes,

which of thise two oughte to ben holden the more myghty by 80
right?"

"Knyt forth the remenaunt," quod I, "for no wight ne
douteth that he that mai gon by naturel office of feet ne be more
myghti than he that ne may nat."

"But the soverein good," quod sche, "that is eveneliche 85
purposed to the goode folk and to badde, the gode folk seken it by
naturel office of vertus, and the schrewes enforcen hem to getin it
by divers coveytise of erthly thinges, which that nys noon
naturel office to gete thilke same soverein good. Trowestow that
it be any other wise?" 90

"Nai," quod I, "for the consequence is open and schewynge of
thinges that I have graunted, that nedes goode folk moten be
myghty, and schrewes feble and unmyghti."

"Thou rennist aryght byforn me," quod sche, "and this is the
jugement, ryght as thise leches ben wont to hopin of sike folk, whan 95
thei aperceyven that nature is redressed and withstondeth to the
maladye. But for I se the now al redy to the undirstondynge, I
schal schewe the more thikke and contynuel resouns. . . ."

NOTE

The following are Chaucer's interpolations, not in the Latin original, which he
added to clarify passages for his readers. They were omitted from the text itself in
order to maintain the parallelism of the various versions.

METRUM I

9–10   imaked a knyght of the clere sterre (that is to seyn, whan the thought is
makid Godis knyght by the sekynge of cleer trouthe to comen to the verray know-
leche of God).

11   there as the schynynge nyght is ypainted (that is to sey, the nyght that is cloudeles; for on nyghtes that ben cloudeles it semeth as the hevene were peynted with
diverse ymages of sterres).

17   governeth the swifte wayn (that is to seyn, the circuler moevynge of the sonne).

21   her wol I fastne my degree (here wol I duelle).

PROSA II

30–31   "And in that that every wyght may, in that men may holden hym myghti?"
(As who seith, in so moche as man is myghty to doon a thing, in so mochel men halt
hym myghti; and in that he ne mai, in that men demen hym to ben feble.)

94–95   "and this is the jugement (that is to sein, I juge of the).

PROSA I: 2] cheere: appearance   3] foryeten: forgotten   4] forbrak: interrupted
6] gyderesse: conductress; verray: true (cf. Fr. *vrai*)   8] schewynge: evident;
hem: them (cf. NE colloq. *'em*)   9] thilke: (the ilke) the same, the very
20] meedes: rewards   21] abyeth: suffers   22] nys: (ne is) is not (cf. II, 27, 71

nilt: ne wilt); wyght: person, man   24] woot: knows   27] abaysschinge: bewilderment   28] wenest: supposest   29] ordene: well-regulated   30] meyne: household   31] heryed: honored   34] unaraced: unbroken   36] schrewes: scoundrels   46] fycchen: fix (cf. II, 44)   48] sledys: sledges, carriages.

METRUM I: 6] eschaufeth: burns   12] forleten: leave behind   13] pressen: press onward; wenden: go   16] atemprith: regulates   17] wayn: wagon   19] requerist: seekest.

PROSA II: 1] byhetist: promisest   4] moevid: moved, begun   7] certes: surely   12] fey: faith (Chaucer misconstrued the Latin *fides*, which in the context has the underlying meaning of "certainty"); sentence: opinion   35] studies: a too literal reading of the L. *studiis*, actually "desires"   51] that: i.e., that which   69] algates: nonetheless   75] goinge: i.e., walking   82] Knyt forth: a misconstruing of *contexe*, "infer"   89] Trowestow: dost thou believe   95] jugement: Chaucer misread *indicium*, "sign," as *iudicium;* leches: physicians.

QUESTIONS AND EXERCISES—MIDDLE ENGLISH

Parts of Speech and Morphology

Nouns

1. What is the usual inflection for the noun plural and genitive? What evidence is there that it was pronounced as a separate syllable? In which nouns in the passage has there been no change in this pronunciation since Chaucer's day, and what characteristics do these nouns have? Are the spelling variations of the usual plural ending significant?

2. Note the following nouns which do not have the usual ending: *resouns* (p. I, 8),[8] *tormentz* (p. I, 21), *felouns* (p. I, 22), *vertus* (p. I, 37), *governementz* (m. I, 16), *tirantz* (m. I, 23). What etymological background do they have in common? Does this help to explain this variation in the plural from the usual form?

3. What irregular plurals are present in the passage? Do they vary from ENE and NE usage? Note the form *folk(e)*, which recurs in the passage. What evidence can you find that Chaucer consistently construed it as a plural? Are there any other such nouns in the passages?

[8] Because our line numberings begin anew with each new prose or metrical section, in accord with standard editorial procedures in Chaucer texts, we have prefaced a *p.* or *m.* for ease of reference. Since we have not reprinted the second metrical passage, "II" will suffice for "Prose II."

Pronouns

1. Complete the chart below, filling in the pronoun forms (and variant forms) which are in the passage. The forms which are not found in this passage have been supplied.

	Singular			Plural		
	Nominative	*Genitive*	*Objective*	*Nominative*	*Genitive*	*Objective*
1				we	our(e)	us, ous 1
2				ye	your(e)	you, ye 2
3 {M F N					hir(e), her(e)	3

Save for spelling (which in part reflects The Great Vowel Shift) is there much change between ME and ENE pronouns? How do you account for this? What is the most significant difference in the pronoun usages of the two periods?

2. What factors appear to govern the use of *my/myn* and *thi (thy)/thyn*? Does this differ from ENE usage?

3. We have no usages of the second person plural pronouns, but does the use of the singular form, Boethius addressing Lady Philosophy and the reverse, compare with any of the ENE relationships illustrated in Shakespeare?

4. Does the third person plural, objective form bear any resemblance to informal modern usage? How does orthography obscure the resemblance?

Adjectives and adverbs

1. What endings do the adjectives have in agreement with the number of the noun they modify? Is the pattern consistent? Does the pattern hold for adjectives in the VP following *be*? Why do you suppose the pattern fell away by the ENE period?

2. There are very few instances of comparative forms for adjectives and adverbs, but how do those few in this passage compare with current usage?

3. What intensifiers occur with adjectives and adverbs in this passage? Which would now be considered substandard usage?

Note the use of *verray* as an adjective; describe the process by which it subsequently became an intensifier.

Verbs

1. Complete the chart below, filling in the personal endings for the verbs in both present and past tense forms. As before, the forms which do not occur in the passage are supplied.

Singular			Plural		
Present	*Past*		*Present*	*Past*	
1			-en	-en	1
2			-en	-en	2
3					3

There will be some deviations, either for strong verbs (those which do not form past tenses with a dental suffix) or for subjunctives. Ignore these for the moment. In general, what similarities exist between these personal endings and those in ENE? Does there seem to be a consistent change from ME to ENE?

2. What seems to have been the commonest way in ME of forming the past tense—that is, among the weak verbs? List the strong verbs with their past tense forms. Which of them have since become weak verbs? Describe the process by which these verbs changed from strong to weak. What verbs are irregular in present as well as past forms?

3. List all of the modals in the passage, with the different tense forms and personal endings which occur. Do any of them differ substantially from ENE usage? Which forms might be subjunctive? Note the form of the verb which follows the modal. How can you show that it is *not* the past participle form? What form is it? How would you have to alter the generative procedure for the Aux to accommodate this form?[9]

4. List all of the tense and person forms for *be*. How do these compare with the ENE forms?

---

[9] For a study in historical reconstructions of the rewriting of Aux, see Elizabeth Closs, "Diachronic Syntax and Generative Grammar," *Language* XLI (1965), 402–15.

5. What seems to have been the commonest way of forming the past participle in ME? How do these forms compare with their respective past tense forms? What significant process seems to have taken place with these forms between the ME and NE periods? Do the participle forms function with *have* in the Aux? What other uses do they have in ME? What evidences are there of the remains of a past participle prefix? How is the prefixed form used?

6. How are the present participles formed in the passages? What uses do the forms have in ME? Does the form occur as part of Aux, as it does in NE?

7. What inflection does the verb take after *to*, the infinitive marker in NE? Is this form consistent? Under what other circumstances does the form occur in the passages?

8. Study the following verb formations from the Chaucer passages:

thou . . . shalt mowen retourne (p. I, 47–48)
thow most nedes knowen (II, 5)
that nedes goode folk moten be myghty (II, 92–93)

How would you analyze these within a hypothetical reconstruction of the VP? Do any of these compare with like or similar forms in ENE?

9. We have seen the *-en* inflection used three different ways in ME: as marker for plural persons, for past participle, for infinitive. How does this tripling-up of the signal help to explain its subsequent decline in all of these categories and ultimate disappearance in two of them?

Sentence Structure

1. Chaucer's translation makes surprisingly great use of the passive transformation. Compare several instances of this form. Does it differ in any significant way from NE usage? What inference can you draw about the probable ENE usage?

2. Unfortunately, the passage makes little use of any interrogative transformation of whichever sort. Study the two clear

instances of the yes/no interrogative at II, 51, 89–90 (a problematical instance occurs at II, 57–59). What is the nature of the
transformational rearrangement, and how does it compare with
ENE usage? What do you infer might have been the device to
signal the interrogatives at II, 27–28, 30–31, 71–72, 74–75?

3. It is just possible that the Socratic dialogue does not
occasion many uses of the substantial interrogative. Anyhow,
study the two instances of this transformation at II, 68, 80–81.
In the same manner as in the preceding question, analyze these
structures, and compare them with the parallel passages in the
I. T. translation. Can you infer from these two ME examples the
prior operation of the yes/no transformation before the substantial
interrogative transformation?

4. Study the occurrences in the passages of the negative
transformation, limiting yourself for the time being to examples
paralleling the following:

> that ne hadde nat al outrely foryeten (p. I, 3)
> thei ne weren not al outrely unknowen (p. I, 11–12)
> I ne doute nat (II, 2)

How do these and like examples compare with ENE usage?
Obviously, the use of *ne* is the most significant difference. How
would you explain this form—that is, what purpose does it
serve? Have you encountered a similar form in any foreign
language? Explain the following forms in negative constructions:
nys (p. I, 22, etc.), *nilt* (II, 27, 71). What is the origin of the now-
archaic idiom *willy-nilly*?

5. Examine Chaucer's use of the *ne* form further. Does he use
it consistently with *not/nat*? With what other forms does he use
it? What do they have in common? How is *ne* used at p. I, 23
and 37? What difficulties are occasioned by the compound use
of *ne* at II, 2, 22–23, 27–28, 71–72? What possible reasons can you
give for the subsequent disappearance of this form before the
ENE period?

6. At II, 33–36 and 38–41, are two very problematical
passages. Analyze them, and make some attempt to explain
them. Why are they not true examples of an imperative

structure? In this connection, analyze the imperative structure at II, 82.

7. Review the passages for subjunctive structures, of which there are several—e.g., at p. I, 26–27, and II, 3–4 (as is the modal form *mowen* at p. I, 9). Examine them for their personal endings and for their contexts, and compare the latter with those which you found in Shakespeare and the I. T. translation. What are the contexual similarities between the ME and ENE structures?

8. The following examples from the passages are often explained away as "idiomatic expressions." Analyze each of them carefully.

> the thinges that thou hast seid me (p. I, 7)
> by me that have whilom yschewid it the, (p. I, 42)
> it remembreth me wel (m. I, 20; II, 37)
> I wondre me that . . . (II, 1)
> thou schalt . . . strengthen the with stedfast sadnesse. (p. I, 39–41)
> the schrewes enforcen hem to getin it (II, 87)
> yif the liketh thanne to looken on the derknesse (m. I, 21–22)
> God, of the whos reigne I speke, (p. I, 34–35)

Which of these exhibit features similar to those of ENE?

Other Features

1. Though phonology will not be stressed with ME (and OE), certain pronunciations can be inferred from the passages in the texts. What do the following spellings indicate about probable pronunciation?

> haboundant (II, 13)
> by the to weye and by the tothir (II, 13–14)
> the ton and the tothir (II, 56)
> the toother (II, 64)
> Trowestow (II, 89)
> o same purpos (II, 63)
> oon of hem (II, 63)

What generalizations can you draw about Chaucer's pronunciation from these? What explanations do some of them offer for certain regional or social dialect pronunciations in England and America?

2. In glancing over the passages of Chaucer's translation, what do you gather was his attitude (or that of his scrivener)— and by extension, the attitude of the period—toward spelling?

3. The following is a verse translation of Meter I in Book IV done in 1410 by John Walton. Very little is known of the translator, save that he was not a Londoner. He definitely referred to Chaucer's version as he translated and may have been led to adapt some aspects of his usage toward the emerging London standard. The text is taken from Eleanor P. Hammond (ed.), *English Verse Between Chaucer and Surrey* (Durham, N. C., 1927). The use of the letters *u* and *v* has been normalized.

Full swyft been my fetheres in þaire flight
Þat stieng into hyhe hevene ariseth
And when þei be into a mynde Ipight
Þe erthe þen it hateþ & despiseth
And setteþ all at noght as he deviseth   5
Þe speere of eyre he passeth all above
Behynde his bak he seeth þe cloudes hove

That mynde also þe spere of fuyre transcendeth
That is so hoot be movynge of þe hevene
And to þe sterred places he ascendeþ   10
Thurgh out þe speres of planetes sevene
And with þe sonne his wey he ioyneþ evene
So at þe laste he meteþ with þe old
Saturnus whos effectes ben so cold

So is þis sotill mynde made a knyght   15
Of god þat is þe sovereyn sterre clere
And so þe cercle of þe sterres bright
Þe whiche ye may behold on nyghtes here
With his recours he passeth all in fere
And in theire speres be holden wele   20
Þe manere of þeire movynge every dele

And well he wot þat goddes ben þai not
Þe hyest heven he leveth hym behynde
Till þat he have araysed up his þoght
Anone to hym þat auctour is of kynde   25
This worþi lyght he putteþ in his mynde
Þat of þis round world is lord & kyng
Þat kepeth & governeþ all þing

The swyft cours of sterres meveth he
Iuge of þinges bright & sovereyn   30
Hym self stedfaste evire in oo degre
If þis wey may reduce þe ageyn
Unto þi place þou schalt þi self seyn
Lo here it is þat I so longe have soght
My cuntre & til now I knewe it noght   35

Fro hennes I come & in þis place right
I thynke to abyden & to dwell
And if þe list to cast a doun þi sight
Into þis foule derk erthly selle
Be holden myght þou þere tyrantes felle   40
Whiche þat of wrecches ben Idrede full wyde
Out of this lond exiled for þere pryde

2] stieng: ascending   3] Ipight: penetrated, set   7] hove: hover   8] fuyre: fire
15] sotill: subtle, able   19] recours: course; fere: far   21] dele: bit, part   25] Anone
to: as far as; kynde: nature   31] oo: one   32] reduce: lead back   38] list: wish
39] selle: cell   40] felle: cruel.

What differences do you find between Walton's practices and Chaucer's, after making allowances for the exigencies of poetry? What evidence does the Walton version offer as to the pronunciation of final -e and the syllabication of inflectional endings? How trustworthy is this evidence? Recalling that Chaucer was a practicing poet at the time he made his translation, what do you think of his decision to do the Latin metrical passages in prose?

Middle English Dialects

We have already mentioned that the French overlordship of England, by imposing a system of virtual serfdom over the great

mass of English-speaking people in the island following the Conquest, led to a superimposition of isolation which inevitably
caused a widening of dialect differences. Dialects can be of
two main kinds: social, involving value judgments on matters of
class and culture; and regional, involving simply geography.
The third-class status of English at the beginning of the ME
period effectively took care of any social pretensions. To the party
in power, any kind of English speech eliminated any considerations of status. Regional dialects, however, were something else
again. Regardless of attempts to impose a linguistic standard,
there are bound to be regional differences in a language spoken
over a relatively large geographical area.

Prior to the Norman Conquest, regional dialects certainly
existed in England. In the next section, we will take up some of
the reasons for this, but it requires no great knowledge of history
to recognize that in medieval Europe communication over a wide
area, even in the best-governed of countries (which Anglo-Saxon
England most assuredly was not), is bound to be minimal.
During the greater part of the ME period, already-existing
dialect differences were widened and became more obvious, and
only with the reassertion of national and linguistic unity, focusing
upon London, was any attempt made to reverse the trend.

Map 8–1 shows the principal dialect areas of ME, and the
most prominent features, reflected in manuscripts, on which to
base the dialect boundaries.[10] The boundaries of dialect features,
called *isoglosses*, indicate the northern or southern limits of a
variation in pronunciation or inflectional form (or, in the instances
of lines D and F, the eastern limits). These lines represent a kind
of compromise, for the documents show some overlapping and
thus are drawn with an eye for geographical features.

Some of the isoglosses involving sounds may require further
explanation. Line A, for instance, represents the southern limit

---

[10] The basic source for the boundaries and the criteria for establishing them is
Samuel Moore, Sanford B. Meech, and Harold Whitehall, "Middle English Dialect
Characteristics and Dialect Boundaries: Preliminary Report of an Investigation
Based Exclusively on Localized Texts and Documents," *Essays and Studies in English
and Comparative Literature*, XIII (Ann Arbor, Mich., 1935), 1–60 (three accompanying
maps).

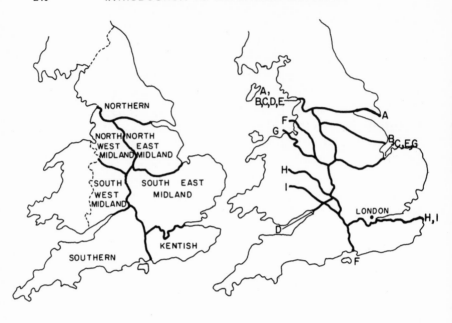

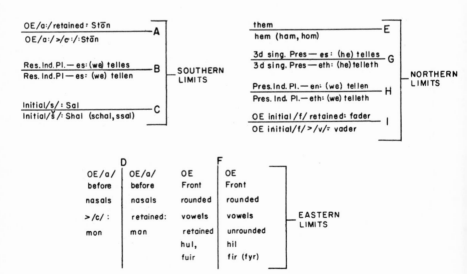

Map 8–1. ME Dialect Areas and Principal Dialect Features. (Based on Moore, Meech, and Whitehall.)

of the retention of the OE /aː/; south of that line, the sound was retracted to /ɔː/ (and ultimately raised to /oː/ or /ow/).[11] The term *limit* means that the unrounded /aː/, in this case, occurs no further south, though the rounded form, spelled *o* or *oo*, does occur north of the boundary, indicating that the unrounded form is regressive, ultimately nonstandard. Line I represents a similar regression, this time to the south, of an initial /v/ for the OE initial /f/. There was a like tendency, also in the south, to voice initial /s/ and /θ/, but these are not so obviously indicated in ME manuscripts. These dialect traits persisted in the southwest through the eighteenth century, as readers of the literature of the period will discover.

Lines D and F represent two westwardly regressive pronunciations. West of line D is the evidence of a retracting of OE /a/ before /m/ and /n/: *mon, nome*. Line F is more subtle, representing the eastern limit, admittedly based on scanty evidence, of the retention of front-rounded vowels in OE, phonemically represented as /y(ː)/ and /œ(ː)/;[12] whereas to the east, the sounds were unrounded to /i/ or /ɪ/, /e/, or /ɛ/. Unfortunately, the western spellings for these front-rounded sounds vary according to scribal ingenuity—*u, ui, ue, eo,* or *o,* often widely inconsistent with the same manuscript—and are thus not always reliable.

The remaining pronunciational isogloss is line B, which indicates the southern limit of an initial /s/ in *shall, should,* rather than /š/. The other lines represent relatively self-explanatory inflectional forms. It should be added here that though lines C and E appear to coincide, in actuality line E was slightly to the south of line C, but so slightly that the indication would only blur on the map. In practice, dialect variants are each of them independent forms and rarely do two isoglosses coincide more than briefly. However, working with documents rather than people forces the dialect geographer to merge his isogloss bundles much more than is usual.

---

[11] At a much later date, the /aː/ in Northern British (including Lowland Scots) was fronted and raised to /ɛː/ or /eː/.

[12] The symbols /y/ and /œ/ represent respectively the high- and mid-front *rounded* vowels, as sounded in French *tu* and *peur*.

The late ME focus upon London caused a lessening of the trend to greater dialect variation, though some has always remained despite the efforts of the universities, the clubs, and the BBC. The whole problem of regional dialects will be covered in greater detail in the next chapter. In the meantime, because regional dialect is one of the problems the student of ME literature must face, the following exercises are intended to acquaint him with a few of the details of the regional dialects of Middle English.

––––––

1. Taking the position of London as the focal point, study the implications of each of the isoglosses. Which indicate *regressive* dialect trends, those which continue to move further away from the focal point, or become nonstandard; and which are *aggressive*, moving toward the focal point and gradually supplanting the old forms?

2. Notice the geographical position of London, which straddles the boundary between the Southeast Midland and Kentish dialects, and is not too far east of the Southern dialect boundary. In developing what became the national standard, what would such a geographical position tend to cause in the selecting of standard forms? Go over the Chaucer translation to note his own usage. Does his own usage re-enforce your conclusion about the origins of the London standard? Which dialectal forms predominate?

3. The following are brief extracts from ME writings which can be fairly well located within the dialect area indicated. In addition to checking each extract against the isoglosses, analyze each for additional indications of the dialect of that particular area. In all the texts, the use of *u* and *v* has been normalized.

a. Kentish—Dan Michel, *Ayenbite of Inwyt* (1340):

þis boc is dan Michelis of Northgate, ywrite an Englis of his oȝene hand. þet hatte "Ayenbyte of Inwyt," and is of þe bochouse of saynt Austines of Canterberi. . . .

þis boc is ywrite
Vor Englisse men, þet hi wyte   5

Hou hi ssole hamzelve ssrive
And maki ham klene ine þis live.
Þis boc hatte huo þet writ
"Ayenbite of Inwyt." . . .
    Nou ich wille þet ye ywyte hou hit is ywent,   10
Þet þis boc is ywrite mid Engliss of Kent:
Þis boc is ymad vor lewede men,
Vor vader, and vor moder, and vor oþer ken,
Ham vor to berӡe vram alle manyere zen,
Þet ine hare inwytte ne bleve no voul wen.   15
"Huo ase god" is his name yzed,
Þet þis boc made. God him yeve þet bread
Of angles of hevene and þerto his red,
And ondervonge his zaule huanne þet he is dyad. Amen.

Ymende þet þis boc is volveld ine þe eve of þe holy apostles 20
Symon an Iudas of ane broþer of þe cloystre of sanynt Austin
of Canterberi ine þe yeare of oure lhordes beringe 1340.

1] dan: title of respect for priests 2] oӡene: own; Ayenbyte of Inwyt: remorse of conscience 3] bochouse: scriptorium 10] ywent: happened 12] lewede: unlearned 14] berӡe: protect 15] bleve: remains; wen: blemish 18] red: counsel 19] ondervonge: receive 20] volveld: completed 22] beringe: birth.

b. Southwest Midland—William Herebert, *Hostis Herodes impie* (c. 1330):

Herodes, þou wykked fo, whar-of ys þy dredinge?
And why art þou so sore agast of Cristes to-cominge?
Ne reveth he nouth erthlich god þat maketh ous hevene
    kynges.

Þe kynges wenden here way and foleweden þe sterre,
And sothfast lyӡth wyth sterre-lyth souhten vrom so verre,   5
And sheuden wel þat he ys god in gold and stor and mirre.

Crist y-cleped hevene lomb so com to seynt Ion
And of hym was y-wasӡe þat sunne nadde non,
To halewen our vollouth water þat sunne havet vordon.

A newe myhte he cudde þer he was at a feste: 10
He made vulle wyth shyr water six cannes by þe leste,
Bote þe water turnde in-to wyn þorou Crystes oune heste.

Wele, Louerd, boe myd þe, þat shewedest þe to-day
Wyth þe vader and þe holy gost wythouten ende-day.

3] reveth: robs; nouth: not 4] wenden: went 5] sothfast: true; lyȝth: light
6] sheuden: showed; stor: incense 7] y-cleped: called, named 8] sunne: sin
9] vollouth: baptism; vordon: undone, destroyed 10] cudde: made known
11] made vulle: caused to be filled; shyr: pure.

c. Northern—Thomas Castleford, *Chronicle* (*c.* 1350):

No sones had þis noble kyng Leyr,
Bot doughters he gat thre maydyns faire:
Gonorylle hyght þe aeldest maydyn,
Regan þe tothyr, so is it saydyn;
Cordoile þe therd syster scho hyght;   5
All thre fair to manys syght.
Ther fadyr, þe kyng Leir so fre,
Full mykyll he lofyd hys doughters thre;
Bot Cordoil hys yongest most dere
He lofed hyr most of ylkon sere.   10
Qwen kyng Leir turnyd into gret aeld
Noght longer þe kyngdome forto weld,
He þought, qwyls þat he myght lyve,
Devise hys landys and to þame gyfe,
Hys tresors and londys þame bekene,   15
And marye þame unto swylke men,
On qwome he wald lyke and wouch-safe
Þame wyth hys kyngdome for to hafe.
Bot for to wate þorowe knawyng sygne,
Qwylke þat war most worthy and dygne   20
Of hys landes hafe best and mast,
Of þame he þis wald prove and tast.
To ylkone sere of þame he yied,
And askyd þame anence þar led,
Qwylke of þame most in hert hym lofed;   25
Schew hym þe soth nedlynges behovyd.
He askyd hys doughter Gonoryll,
Scho suld hym scheu and say hyr wyll,
And sayd: "My doughter, say me nowe
Me in hert howe mykyll loffys þowe."   30
Gonoryll sayd: "Of wordys I nevyn
Wyttnese ber all þe goddes of heven:
I lofe þe mor anence my force

Thane þe saul restys in my cors.
Nothyng it is at mannes hert yiernys   35
Undyr þe mone ne eke þe sternys
That is to men thyng temporele
Os þowe in hert I lofe so wele.
Of all the thynges in þis werld here
Thayr may nothyng be me so dere."   40

10] sere: particularly 11] Qwen: when (qw indicates aspiration) 15] bekene: consign 19] wate: know 23] yied: went 24] anence: against 26] nedlyngs: necessarily 31] nevyn: declare, tell 35] yiernys: yearns 36] sternys: stars.

d. Northeast Midland—*Havelok* (*c.* 1300):

Herkneth to me, gode-men,
Wives, maydnes and alle men,
Of a tale þat ich you wile telle,
Wo-so it wile here and þerto duelle!
Þe tale is of Havelok imaked;   5
Wil he was litel, he yede ful naked.
Havelok was a ful god gome;
He was ful god in everi trome,
He was þe wicteste man at nede,
Þat þurte riden on ani stede.   10
Þat ye mowen nou yhere,
And þe tale ye mowen ylere.
At þe beginning of ure tale
Fil me a cuppe of ful god ale,
And y wile drinken, her y spelle.   15
Þat Crist us shilde alle fro helle!
Krist late us hevere so to do,
Þat we moten comen him to!
And with þat it mote ben so,
Benedicamus domino!   20
Here y schal biginnen a rym;
Krist us yeve wel god fyn!
Þe rym is maked of Havelok,
A stalworþi man in a flok.
He was þe beste man at nede,   25
Þat may riden on ani stede.

4] duelle: remain 7] gome: man 8] trome: troop, company 9] wicteste: bravest 10] þurte: needed 15] her: ere, before; spelle: tell, relate 22] fyn: end 24] stalworþi: stalwart; flok: group.

e. Southeast Midland—*The Book of Margery Kempe* (*c.* 1436):

A schort tretys of a creature sett in grett pompe and pride
of þe world, whech sythen was drawen to ower lord be gret
poverte, sekenes, schamis, and gret reprevys in many divers
contres and places, of whech tribulacyons sum schal ben
schewed aftyr, not in ordyr as it fellyn but as þe creatur cowd   5
han mend of hem whan it were wretyn, for it was xx ʒer and
mor fro tym þis creatur had forsake þe world and besyly
clef onto ower lord or þis boke was wretyn, not-wythstondyng
þis creatur had greet cownsel for to don wryten hir tribulacyons and hir felingys, and a whyte frer proferyd hir to   10
wryten frely yf sche wold. And sche was warnyd in hyr spyrit
þat sche xuld not wryte so sone. And many ʒerys aftyr
sche was bodyn in hyr spyrit for to wrytyn. And þan ʒet it
was wretyn fyrst be a man whech cowd neiþyr wel wryten
Englysch ne Duch, so it was unable for to be red but only be   15
specyal grace, for þer was so mech obloquie and slawndyr of
þis creatur þat þer wold fewe men beleve þis creatur. And
so at þe last a preste was sor mevyd for to wrytin þis tretys,
and he cowd not wel redyn it of a iiij ʒere togedyr. And
sythen be þe request of þis creatur and compellyng of hys   20
owyn consciens he asayd agayn for to rede it, and it was
mech mor esy þan it was afortyme. And so he gan to wryten
in þe ʒer of owr lord a mccccxxxvi on þe day next aftyr
Mary Maudelyn aftyr þe informacyon of þis creatur.

2] sythen: since   3] reprevys: reproofs   6] mend of: called to mind   8] clef:
cleaved, clung; or: ere, before   10] whyte frer: White Friar, a member of the
Carmelite order   13] to wryten: i.e., dictate, for this remarkable woman was illiterate
18] mevyd: moved   21] asayd: tried.

f. London—*Petition of the Mercers to Parliament* (1386):

To the moost noble and worthiest lordes, moost ryghtful
and wysest conseille to owre lige-lorde the kyng, compleynen,
if it lyke to yow, the folk of the mercerye of London as a
membre of the same citee of many wronges subtiles and also
open oppressions, ydo to hem by long tyme herebifore passed.   5
Of which oon was: Where the eleccion of mairaltee is to be
to the fremen of the citee bi gode and paisible avys of the
wysest and trewest at o day in the yere frelich, there nought-
withstondyng the same fredam or fraunchise Nicholas

Brembre wyth his upberers purposed hym the yere next   10
after John Northampton mair of the same citee with stronge
honde as it is ful knowen, and thourgh debate and strenger
partye ayeins the pees bifore purveyde was chosen mair in
destruccion of many ryght. For in the same yere the forsaid
Nicholas with-outen nede ayein the pees made dyverse   15
enarmynges bi day and eke bi nyght, and destruyd the
kynges trewe lyges, som with open slaughtre, some bi false
emprisonementz, and some fledde the citee for feere, as it is
openlich knowen.

6] mairaltee: mayoralty   7] fremen: freemen (i.e., members of the various guilds,
and thus "free of the company" or guild)   8] frelich: freely   10] upberers: supporters
13] ayeins: against   16] enarmynges: armed disturbances.

4. Probably the earliest attempt in English literature to record
regional dialect consciously for literary effect is in Chaucer's
Reeve's Tale, in which the two Cambridge scholars, John and
Aleyn, are depicted as northerners. The following extract[13] from
the tale recounts their conversation with Symond (Symkyn), the
unscrupulous miller, and subsequent speech:

Aleyn spak first, "Al hayl, Symond, y-fayth!
Hou fares thy faire doghter and thy wyf?"
   "Aleyn, welcome," quod Symkyn, "by my lyf!
And John also, how now, what do ye heer?"   4025
   "Symond," quod John, "by God, nede has na peer.
Hym boes serve hymself that has na swayn,
Or elles he is a fool, as clerkes sayn.
Oure manciple, I hope he wil be deed,
Swa werkes ay the wanges in his heed;   4030
And forthy is I come, and eek Aleyn,
To grynde oure corn, and carie it ham agayn;
I pray yow spede us heythen that ye may."
   "It shall be doon," quod Symkyn, "by my fay!
What wol ye doon whil that it is in hande?"   4035
   "By God, right by the hopur wil I stande,"

13 *The Works of Geoffrey Chaucer*, ed. F. N. Robinson. Reprinted by permission of
the publisher, Houghton Mifflin Company. Line numbers follow Robinson's numbering for the "A" group of tales.

Quod John, "and se how that the corn gas in.
Yet saugh I nevere, by my fader kyn,
How that the hopur wagges til and fra."
    Aleyn answerde, "John, and wiltow swa?   4040
Thanne wil I be bynethe, by my croun,
And se how that the mele falles doun
Into the trough; that sal be my disport.
For John, y-faith, I may been of youre sort;
I is as ille a millere as ar ye."   4045

*   *   *

"Now, Symond," seyde John, "by seint Cutberd,
Ay is thou myrie, and this is faire answerd.
I have herd seyd, 'man sal taa of twa thynges
Slyk as he fyndes, or taa slyk as he brynges.'   4130
But specially I pray thee, hooste deere,
Get us som mete and drynke, and make us cheere,
And we wil payen trewely atte fulle.
With empty hand men may na haukes tulle;
Loo, heere oure silver, redy for to spende."   4135

*   *   *

He poked John, and sayde, "Slepestow?
Herdestow evere slyk a sang er now?   4170
Lo, swilk a complyn is ymel hem alle,
A wilde fyr upon thair bodyes falle!
Wha herkned evere slyk a ferly thyng?
Ye, they sal have the flour of il endyng.
This lange nyght ther tydes me na reste;   4175
But yet, nafors, al sal be for the beste. . . ."

4027] boes: (it) behooves 29] manciple: college steward 30] werkes: aches;
wanges: molars 33] heythen: hence 4129] taa: take 30] Slyk: such 34] tulle:
lure 4171] complyn: mournful ballad; ymel: among 73] ferly: strange 76]
nafors: nonetheless.

How well does Chaucer represent the northern dialect traits,
as indicated by the isoglosses on the map? Is he completely
consistent in his representation? What other dialect characteristics are given in the clerks' dialogue?

OLD ENGLISH (c. 500–1100)

The Germanic Invasion of England

Approximately halfway through the fifth century A.D., some Germanic tribesmen from the northwest coast of Europe came to England at the request of the inhabitants, Romanized Celts no longer under the protection of the legions, to help them beat off an invasion of Picts and Scots. Liking what they saw, the Germanic tribesmen—custom assigns them the names of Angles, Saxons, and Jutes—returned in force, dispossessed the inhabitants, forced them back into the western extremities of Wales and Cornwall or back to the coast of France, and took over the land themselves. Within the space of a century, virtually every vestige of the Celtic–Roman civilization on the island was erased, and the new Germanic language of the Anglo-Saxons was established westward to the Severn, and northward beyond the Humber.

The displacing language was Germanic, and despite the borrowings from the French and elsewhere later on, English has always been classified as a member of the Germanic group of languages, a subcategory of the Indo-European family. This group includes the modern languages of German, Yiddish, Dutch, Flemish, and Frisian, and the Scandinavian languages, as well as English. These languages, the results of successive splitting off from the main body of Germanic tribes in central Europe before the era of recorded history, share a good many features with the other Indo-European languages. But they also maintain certain features which serve to differentiate them from the other language groups in the "family" and classify them as Germanic.

Distinctive Features of Germanic Languages

The most significant feature is the shifting of consonant sounds which has come to be known as "Grimm's Law".[14] This shift

---

[14] Briefly stated, "Grimm's Law" records the changes of certain classes of Indo-European consonants in Germanic languages. Specifically, the voiced aspirated stops /b^h, d^h, g^h/ in IE (Indo-European) became the like voiced stops /b, d, g/ in Gmc (Germanic), passing through an intermediate fricative stage. For instance, Skt (Sanskrit) *bhrater* > L (Latin) *frater* > *brother*. The IE voiceless stops /p, t, k/ became the respective voiceless fricatives /f, θ, x/ in Gmc: L *piscus* > *fish*. In initial positions,

occurred in pre-history, after the Germanic tribes broke away from the main migrations of the other Indo-European peoples and became isolated from them. In like manner, the Germanic languages share certain vowel shiftings dating from roughly the same time, and it is possible, from studying these progressive sound shifts, to make generalizations about the divisions within the Germanic languages, as dialects gradually became separate languages. We should add that each group within the Indo-European family shares certain sound-shift features as they in turn split off from the hypothetical main body.

Another feature of the Germanic languages is the general moving of the stress within a word to the first syllable, unless that syllable is a prefix. This is still a very active trait in English, for after a period of time most borrowed words undergo a shift of stress. In England, for instance, the word *garage* is usually pronounced to rime with *carriage*, and perhaps this pronunciation will eventually become standard in America. It is possible to gauge the length of time that a borrowed word has been in the language by noting whether or not it has undergone this fronting of stress. Even some prefixed words have acquired this feature: note the stress in *pérfèct* (adjective) as against *pèrféct* (verb).

Other distinctive features of the Germanic languages include matters of grammatical form. All have just two inflected tenses, past and present (or "nonpast"). The remainder of the forms are all phrasal, involving in English the modal, phase, and aspect portions of the Aux, with cognate forms in the other Germanic languages. Further, the Germanic languages developed quite early a "weak" past tense form, based upon a dental suffix. This form is used with all new verbs introduced into the languages, and the stock of "strong" verbs, which form their past tenses by means of an internal vowel change (called *Ablaut*), is continually being depleted by an analogical process. Finally, alone of the

---

the back-velar fricative /x/ became /h/: L *centum* > *hund(red)*. Lastly, the IE voiced stops /b, d, g/ became in Gmc the respective voiceless stops /p, t, k/: L *dou* > *two*, L *genu* > *knee* (loss of initial *k*- is an ENE development.) Exceptions to these result from environmental pressures, such as an initial *s*-, or from a preceding stressed syllable. Instances of the latter are carefully detailed in what is now called "Verner's Law."

Indo-European groups of languages, the Germanic languages developed a double series of "strong" and "weak" declensions of adjectives, the weak being used when preceded by a pronominal element (which became the English determiner fillers), the strong when there was no such element preceding the adjective. Lest you fear that you've missed something in our discussions of Modern English, I hasten to add that this feature dropped out of English early in the ME period, though it still lingers to haunt students of German.

All of these features were legacies of the early Germanic tribes after they made the break from the mainstream of the Indo-European peoples. Sound changes are theoretically inevitable when in the course of progressive isolation dialects become distinct languages, and the grammatical characteristics are likewise expected to vary under the same circumstances. Yet, just as the origin of language remains a mystery, so does the reason for the development of these specific characteristics. It is possible for scholars to reconstruct hypothetical descriptions of the original Proto-Germanic, but more than this we cannot do.

Germanic Migrations

We can, however, reconstruct the successive breaking up of the Germanic peoples, with the subsequent development of their respective languages. Philologists have posited three basic central European dispersals of the Germanic tribes—to the east, the north, and the west. **East Germanic** is principally attested by the now-extinct Gothic language, known to us primarily through a fourth-century translation of a portion of the Gospels. **North Germanic,** which takes its earliest extant form in Old Norse, with its rich literature, is the ancestor of the modern Scandinavian languages—Swedish, Danish, Norwegian, and Icelandic. **West Germanic** underwent another division, into High and Low German, so-called in terms of their relative proximity to the North Sea or the Alps, without any disparaging connotation in the use of "low." **High German** has developed into modern Standard German, and also Yiddish, which began its separate linguistic development in the fifteenth century and is distinctly Germanic, despite its Hebraic alphabet and borrowing of Hebrew words. **Low German** is the ancestor of *Plattdeutsch*, the dialect of north-west Germany, and of modern Dutch, Flemish, and Frisian. And because the Angles, Saxons, and Jutes originally lived along the North Sea Coast, it is the ancestor of English, too.

Anglo-Saxon England and the Scandinavian Invasions

The Germanic invaders of the island managed to force a complete cultural, ethnic, and linguistic turnover, the last being something that the earlier Roman invaders could not do. They destroyed the existing Romanized Christian culture of the Britons, and painfully, slowly, attempted to establish their own. But what is won by the sword must be defended by the sword as well. The Germanic invaders, now well enough established to be called Anglo-Saxons,[15] if not English, set up a weak system of petty kingdoms in the island, small states which were frequently warring with each other. Despite the re-establishment of Christianity on the island, this situation did not improve, and it obviously made England a tempting target for further invasion.

The first invasions were Scandinavian plundering expeditions. Beginning in 787, according to the *Anglo-Saxon Chronicle*, and continuing for about the next sixty years, these hit-and-run raids had little political effect, but they did succeed in destroying forever the flourishing cultural renaissance fostered by the monasteries in the northern kingdom of Northumbria. About 850, however, a well-organized army invaded the northern part of England fully intending to stay, and soon had swept down to occupy everything north of the Thames, and most of Kent as well. Despite the odds, the subsequent invasion of the south-western kingdom of Wessex was beaten back under the inspired and humane leadership of Alfred, the hero-king of Wessex, who

---

[15] *Anglo-Saxon* stems from the Roman and Christian means of differentiating between the Saxons on the island of Britain and the mainland Saxons. The first element is not related to the tribe of *Angles*, though the folk etymology stemming from *Angle-land* (later *England*), the districts of East and West *Anglia*, and Pope Gregory's "not Angles, but Angles" is certainly understandable. Because there are unwarranted racial overtones in the compound "Anglo-Saxon" (cf. WASP), linguists prefer to use "Old English" to designate the language.

was able to establish a kind of "concord" with the Danes (the generic name given the invaders). Under the terms of the agreement, the Danes were permitted to remain in the occupied area to the north and east of the Thames and Wessex, the so-called *Danelaw*. The Danes also accepted, on paper at least, the overlordship of Alfred and his successors, and agreed to be baptized as Christians.

The agreement was subject to some stress and strain, ending around 950 with fairly secure English control over the Danelaw and assimilation of the Danes into the English mainstream. Thus, in 991 and thereafter, both Dane and Englishman were threatened by a new Norse invasion. This time, the islanders were not successful in putting down the invasion. Lacking an inspiring leader, they preferred to pay tribute, rather than fight. Ultimately, the Norse chased the English king, Athelred (wrongly called "Unready," a mistranslation of *unrædlic* "poorly counseled"), from his throne and country, and from 1014 to 1042, England was ruled by Norse kings. The re-establishment of the English line with Athelred's son Edward, whose French upbringing while in exile left the country open to incursions from the Norman French, culminated, despite the efforts of his successor Harold, in 1066 and All That.

I stress these Scandinavian invasions because of their influence upon the linguistic development in the island during this Old English period. The Anglo-Saxons had not been so long away from the continent but what they could, without too much difficulty, understand and communicate with these Danish and Norse invaders. Of particular importance is the fact of the Danish settlement of Northumberland and the East Midlands, which was not a transitory occupation, but a permanent settlement. This influenced the language of the area, and had its effect as well on the dialects as they developed in the ME period. One notable pronunciation variant is the Norse /sk/ for OE /š/: *shirt* and *skirt* once referred to the same garment, the latter being the Scandinavian word. Another easy test of Norse influence is the Scandinavian /k/ for West Saxon /č/, reflected today in northern *kirk* as against southern *church*. Likewise, the northern /g/ ultimately won out over southern /j/ in initial positions, as in *give* (ME *yeve*). And we saw in the preceding section that the northern -(*e*)*s* ending forced out the southern -(*e*)*th* for the third person indicative, present tense inflection. All of these northern forms reflect the Scandinavian presence in that area over an extended period of time.

Alfred's Translation of Boethius

Although the Old English period was a troubled age in English history, marked with few moments of tranquility, it would be wrong to think of it as a dark age, without culture. It is a mistake to picture the Anglo-Saxon as a warrior continually whooping it up in the mead-hall between bouts of arson and pillage. One of the cultural high points, in fact, was the reign of Alfred, justly called "the Great," as king of Wessex (871–899). After pacifying the Danes, he turned his attention during the last decade of his reign to re-establishing the Anglo-Saxon cultural life which had fallen into decay. To help strengthen education and the Church in England, he ordered several Latin works to be translated and circulated throughout his kingdom, one of which was Boethius's *Consolation of Philosophy*.[16] Tradition has it that this translation was done by Alfred himself, and recent scholarship has found no reason to dispute tradition in this instance. For our investigation of this, the earliest period of the English language, we will turn to the passages from Alfred's translation of this work.

ALFRED'S BOETHIUS (*c.* 900)

[Text: Cotton MS. Otho A. vi. compared with Bodleian MS. 180 (2079); ed. Sedgefield (1899). Metrical version *Anglo-Saxon Poetic Records*, V, ed. Krapp (1932). All abbreviations spelled out.]

XXXVI.

	When the Wisdom		then	this	song	very		pleasantly		and
i. Ða	se Wisdom	ða	ðis	leoð	swiðe	lustbærlice	and

---

[16] The other works were Gregory's *Dialogues* and *Pastoral Care*, Bede's *Ecclesiastical History of England*, Orosius's *Universal History* (with interpolated accounts of the explorers Ohthere and Wulfstan), and St. Augustine's *Soliloquies*. Another Alfredian contribution was the *Anglo-Saxon Chronicle*, a chronological history of the Germanic

reasonably   sung   had then had I up-to-then
gesceadwislice ásungen hæfde, ða hæfde ic ða giet

some   recollection in my mind of-the sadness that I
hwylchwugu gemynd on minum mode ðære unrotnesse þe ic

before had and said O Wisdom thou that art messenger
ær hæfde, and cwæð: Eala Wisdom, ðu þe eart boda

and harbinger of-the true light how wonderful to-me seems
and forerynel ðæs soðan leohtes, hu wundorlic me ðincð 5

that which thou to-me explainest because I understand that all that
þæt ðæt þu me recst; forðæm ic ongite þæte eall ðæt

thou to-me before explained to-me explained God through thee and I it
þu me ær reahtes me reahte God þurh ðe, and ic hit

knew also before to some extent but me had this sadness
wisse eac ær be sumum dæle; ac me hæfde þios unrotnes

hindered that I it had altogether forgotten and that is
amerredne, þæt ic hit hæfde mid ealle forgiten. And þæt is

also of-my sadness the greatest part that I wonder why
eac minre unrotnesse se mæsta dæl, þæt ic wundrige forhwy 10

the good God should-let any evil be or if it yet be
se gooda God léte ænig yfel bion, oððe gif hit þeah bion

should and he it to-permit should-wish why he it therefore soon
scyle, and he hit geþafian wille, forhwy he hit þōn sona

not wreck lo thou mightest thyself perceive that that is to
ne wrece. Hwæt, þu meaht ðe self ongitan þæt ðæt is to

wonder-about and also another thing to-me seems yet (a)greater
wundrianne, and eac oðer ðincg me ðincð giet mare

wonder that is that folly and wickedness now rule over
wundor; þæt is þæte dysig and unrihtwisnes nu rixsað ofer 15

all-the earth   and the wisdom and also other virtues
eallne middangeard, and se wisdom and eac oðre cræftas

have(not) no praise nor no honor in this world but
nabbað nan lof ne nænne weorðscipe on ðisse worulde, ac

lie despised even as dung under (a)privy and evil men
licgað forsewene swa swa miox under feltune; and yfele men

---

settlement and Norse invasions. Copies were placed in several cathedral chapter-houses, in the hope that they would be continued. The copy at Peterborough was continued to the middle of the twelfth century, giving valuable linguistic evidence of the transition from OE to ME.

in every land are now honored and the good have
on ælcum lande sindon nu weorþe and þa goodan habbað

manifold punishments who can forbear that he that not
manigfeald witu.   Hwa mæg forberan þæt he þæt ne 20

lament and of-such spectacles not wonder-at that always such evil
siofige and swelcre wæfðe ne wundrige, ðæt te æfre swylc yfel

happen should under of-the almighty God's power now
geweorðan sceolde under ðæs ælmihtgan Godes anwalde, nu

we know that he it knows and every good desires
we witon þæt he hit wat and ælc good wile?

then said he [i.e., Wisdom] if it so is as thou sayest
ii. Da cwæð he: Gif hit swa is swa ðu sægst,

then is that more-terrible than any other terror and is
ðonne is þæt egeslicre ðonne ænig oðer broga, and is 25

(an)endless wonder the most-like that in a-certain king's court
endeleas wundor, ðæm gelicost ðe on sumes cyninges hirede

be golden vats and silver despised and wooden one
sien gyldenu fatu and selfrenu forsewen, and treowenu mon

might-prize is(not) it not even as thou thinkest but if thou all that
weorðige. Nis hit no swa swa ðu wenst; ac gif ðu eall ðæt

remember wilt that we before spoke-of with the God's help
gemunan wilt þæt we ær spræcon, mid ðæs Godes fultume

that we now about speak then might thou remember that the
ðe we nu embe sprecað, ðonne meaht ðu ongitan þæt ða 30

good are always controlling and the evil have(not) no
gódan beoð symle waldende, and þa yfelan nabbað nænne

power and that the virtues neither are never without praise
anwald; and ðæt þa cræftas ne bioð næfre buton heringe

nor without reward nor the vices never — are unpunished
ne buton edleane, ne þa unðeawas næfre ne bioð unwitnode,

but the good are always prosperous and the evil unprosperous
ac ða goodan bioð symle gesælie, and þa yfelan ungesælige.

I to-thee may reveal of-the very many reasons that thee might
Ic ðe mæg eowian ðæs swiðe manega bisena, ða ðe magon 35

encourage to that which thou hast-not what thou long lament But
getrymian to ðon ðæt þu nast hwæt þu leng siofige. Ac

I thee wish now yet to-show the way that thee might-lead to
ic þe wille nu giet getæcan ðone weg ðe ðe gelæt to

the   heavenly   city   that thou before from came   since   thou
þære heofonlican byrig þe ðu ær   of come, siððan ðu

remembrest through my   teaching what   the   true   happiness is
ongitst þurh mine lare   hwæt sio soðe gesælð bið,

and where she [i.e., happiness] is   but I shall first-of-all thy mind
and hwær hio   bið. Ac ic sceal ærest ðin mod 40

provide-with-wings that it   might by-it thee more-easily up raise
gefeðeran,   ðæt hit mæge hit ðe yð   up ahebban

before when it to-fly   begin   into the heights   that it might
ær ðon hit fleogan onginne on ða heanesse, þæt hit mæge

healthy and untroubled fly   to its home and leave-behind all
hal and orsorh fleogan to his earde, and forlætan ælce

of-the troubles   that it now endure   Place it   in my
ðara gedrefednessa ðe hit nu ðrowað. Sitte him on minum

chariot   let-run it   in my   path I (will) be its guide
hrædwæne; ðocrige him on minne weg; ic bio his ladðeow. 45

       When the wisdom   then this discourse explained had   then
iii. Ða se Wisdom ða þis spell   areaht hæfde, ða

       began he to-sing and said
       ongon he singan and cwæð:

       I   have   wings   (a) bird swifter (than)
       Ic hæbbe fiðru   fugle swiftran,

       with them I fly   can   far from earth
       mid ðæm ic fleogan mæg   feor fram eorðan

       above (the) lowly roof   of-sky   this
       ofer heane   hrof   heofones þisses,   50

       but there I now must   (the) mind provide-with-wings
       ac ðær ic nu moste   mod   gefeðran,

       thy   spirit   with-wings my
       ðinne ferðlocan   feðrum minum,

       until thou might   from-this earth
       oððæt ðu meahte   þisne middangeard

       every earthy thing   entirely   despise
       ælc eorðlic ðing,   eallunga forsion.

       (Thou) mightest over (the) firmament   straight
       Meahtes   ofer rodorum   gereclice   55

       with-wings fly   far up above
       feðerum lacan,   feor up ofer

(the) clouds fly   look   afterwards
wolcnu windan,   wlitan siððan

from-above over all   (Thou) mightest also travel
ufan   ofer ealle.   Meahtes   eac faran

above the   fire   that (for) many years
ofer ðæm fyre   ðe fela   geara

traveled long between   air and firmament
for   lange betweox   lyfte and rodere,   60

as   to-it at (the) beginning   (the) father ordained
swa him æt frymðe   fæder   getiode.

Thou mightest   thee afterwards   with the   sun
Ðu meahtest ðe siððan   mid ðære sunnan

travel   between   (the) other stars
faran betweox   oðrum   tunglum.

(Thou) mightest then full quickly   at the   firmament from-above
Meahtest   ðe full recen   on ðæm rodere ufan

afterwards arrive   and then   forthwith
siððan   weorðan,   and ðonne samtenges   65

at the very-cold   one   star
æt ðæm ælcealdan   anum steorran,

which highest is   of-all-the stars
se   yfmest is   eallra   tungla,

that   Saturn   people
ðone Saturnus   sundbuende

call   under   (the) heavens   he is the cold-one
hatað under heofonum;   he is se cealda

of-all-the stars,   highest   wandreth
eallisig tungl,   yfemest wandrað   70

over all   high   (the) other stars
ofer eallum ufan   oðrum   steorran.

Afterward thou then   which up ever hast
Siððan ðu ðonne   ðone up a hafast

forth traveling-over   thou might   pass-beyond
forð oferfarenne,   ðu meaht feorsian;

then   art thou afterward   immediately over above
ðonne bist ðu siððan   sona   ofer uppan

(the) firmament swiftly-moving   If   thou rightly might-travel
rodere   ryneswiftum.   Gif ðu on riht færest   75

thee the   highest   heaven   behind   (thou) leavest
ðe ðone hehstan heofon   behindan lætst

then   might   thou afterward   of-true light
ðonne meaht ðu siððan   soðes leohtes

have   thy   share   thence a   king
habban þinne dæl,   ðonan an cyning

far-and-wide reigns   over (the) firmament up
rume   ricsað   ofer roderum   up

and in   (the) same-way   (of) all creation
and under swa same   eallra gesceafta   80

(the) world governeth   that is (a) wise king
weorulde waldeð.   Þæt is wis   cyning,

that is he that governs   over   (the) nations
þæt is se ðe waldeð   giond werðioda

of-all (the) other   of-(the) earth kings
ealra oðra   eorðan   cyninga,

who with his bridle   curbed   hath
se mid his bridle   ymbebæted hæfð

(the) orbit   of-all   (the) earth and heaven
ymbhwyrft ealne   eorðan and heofones.   85

he his reign   well controls
He his gewaldleðer   wel gemetgað,

who governs ever   through the strong   might
se stioreð a   þurg ða strongan meaht

with-the chariot   of-heaven and earth
ðæm hrædwæne   heofones and eorðan.

He alone judge   is steadfast
Se an dema   is gestæððig,

unchangeable,   beautiful and famous
unawendendlic,   wlitig and mære.   90

If   thou happenest   on (the) way right
Gif ðu weorðest   on wege   rihtum

up to the   native-place   that is (a) noble place
up to ðæm earde,   þæt is æðele stow,

yet   thou them   still   forgotten might-have
ðeah ðu hi nu geta   forgiten hæbbe,

if   thou ever again   there once should-come
gif ðu æfre eft   þær an cymest,

then wilt thou say and soon say
ðonne wilt þu secgan and sona cweðan: 95

This is entirely my own home
"Ðis is eallunga min agen cyð,

native-place and home I was before hence
eard and eðel, Ic wæs ær hionan

come and brought-forth thru this powerful might
cumen and acenned ðurh ðisses cræftigan meaht.

Will-not I ever hence out depart
Nylle ic æfre hionan ut witan,

but I always here quiet will
ac ic symle her softe wille 100

with (the) father's will fast stand
mid fæder willan fæste stondan."

If that then ever again (it) should-happen
Gif ðe ðonne æfre eft geweorðeð

that thou wilt or must (the) world gloomy
þæt ðu wilt oððe most weorolde ðiostro

again examine thou mightiest easily see
eft fandian, ðu meaht eaðe gesion

unjust of-(the) earth kings
unrihtwise eorðan cyningas 105

and the proud other kingdoms
and þa ofermodan oðre rican

that this weary people most-wrongly torment
ðe þis werige folc wryst tuciað,

that they always are very wretched
þæt hi symle bioð swiðe earme,

weak of-every thing
unmehtige ælces ðinges

equally the same that this wretched people
emne ða ilcan þe þis earme folc 110

(for) some time now most fears
sume hwile nu swiðost ondrædæð.

 then said I O Wisdom much is that and
iv. Ða cwæð ic: Eala Wisdom, micel is ðæt and

wonderful that thou promisest and I also nothing — might-doubt
wundorlic þæt ðu gehætst, and ic eac nauht ne tweoge

that thou it   might   perform   But I   thee entreat   that thou me   no
ðæt ðu hit mæge gelæstan. Ac ic þe halsige ðæt ðu me no

longer — hinder but show   me   the   path   because   thou might
leng ne lette, ac getæc me þone weg; forðæm þu meaht

understand that for-me desirest the   path   then said   he   thou shalt
ongitan þæt me lyst   ðæs weges. Ða cwæð he: Þu scealt   5

first-of-all understand that the good   have   always power   and
ærest   ongitan þæt ða goodan habbað symle anweald, and

the evil   never   none   nor no   virtue   because   of-them none
þa yfelan næfre nanne, ne nænne cræft; forðæm hiora nan

— understand that good   and   evil   are   always foes   if
ne ongit   þæte good and yfel bioð symle gewinnan. Gif

the good   then   always have   power   then   have(not) the
ða goodan ðonne symle habbað anwald, þonne nabbað þa

evil   never   none   because   the   good   and   the   evil   are
yflan næfre nænne; forðæm þæt good and þæt yfel sint   10

very-much in-opposition   but I   to thee would   yet   about either
swiðe   unsamwræde. Ac ic ðe   wolde giet be   ægðrum

of-them something   more-clearly explain   that thou may   the
ðara hwæthwugu sweotolor gereccan, þæt ðu mæge ðy

better believe   what I   to-thee at-one time   might-explain about the
bet gelefan ðe ic ðe   oðre hwile recce   be   ðæm

one   at-another time   about the   other   two   things (there)are that
oðrum, oðre   hwile be   ðæm oðrum. Twa ðing sindon ðe

each   man's   mind   toward move   that is   the   will
ælces monnes ingeðonc to   fundað, þæt is ðonne willa   15

and   power   if   then   to-anyone of-the two   of which   (a)lack
and anwald; gif ðonne hwæm ðara twega hwæðres wana

be   then   — may   he with the   other   not-at-all   accomplish
bið, þonne ne mæg he mid ðæm oðrum nanwuht fullfremman.

because   none will(not) begin   that which he will-not except   he
Forðæm nan nyle   onginnan þæt þæt he nyle, buton he

need   must   and although he all   might-desire he not may   if   he
nede scyle; and ðeah   he eall wille,   he ne mæg, gif he

of-the thing   (the)power has-not   about that   thou might   clearly
ðæs ðinges anwald næfð. Be   ðæm ðu meaht sweotole   20

understand if   thou any   man   seest   to-desire of-that which he
ongitan, gif ðu ænigne mon gesihst wilnian ðæs   ðe   he

has-not that there be of-power　(a)lack　then said　I　that is true
næfð, ðæt þā bið anwaldes wana. Ða cwæð ic: Þæt is soð;

nor may I this deny　then said　he　if　thou then　anyone
ne mæg ic þæs oðsacan. Ða cwæð he: Gif ðu ðonne hwone

seest　that can　do　that which he　to-do wishes　nor thee then
gesihst ðe mæg don þæt þæt he don wile, ne ðe ðonne

not-at-all — (it)doubts that that-one have　power　then said　I
nauht ne tweoð þæt se　hæbbe anwald. Ða cwæð ic:　25

nor (it)doubts me of-this not-at-all then said　he　each man is
Ne tweoð　me ðæs nauht. Ða cwæð he: Ælc mon bið

controlling of-that that he　controls has(not) he　no　power　of-that
waldend ðæs ðe he welt; næfð he nanne anweald þæs

that he　not controls then said　I　of-this I am　in-agreement then
ðe he ne welt. Ða cwæð ic: Þæs ic eom geðafa.　Ða

said　he　whether　thou now still　might　remember　what I to-thee
cwæð he: Hwæðer þu nu giet mæge gemunan þæt ic ðe

before explained that was　that　each　man's　mind　desires　to
ær　reahte; þæt wæs þæte ælces monnes ingeðanc wilnað to　30

the　true　happiness to　come　though they differently of-them
þære soðan gesælðe to cumanne, ðeah hi ungelice hiora

deserved　then said　I　that I　remember sufficiently clearly
earnien. Ða cwæð ic: Þæt ic geman; genog　sweotole

to-me is that said　then said　he　remembrest thou that I to-thee
me is ðæt gesæd. Ða cwæð he: Gemunst ðu þæt ic ðe

before said　that it　were　all　one good　and happiness whosoever
ær　sæde þæt hit wære eall an good and gesælða; se

that happiness seeks he seeks good　then said　I　that I have
þe gesælða secð, he secð good. Ða cwæð ic: Þæt ic hæbbe　35

sufficiently fast　in　mind　then said　he　all　men
genog　fæste on gemynde. Ða cwæð he: Ealle men

whether good　or evil　desire　to come　to good　though
ge　goode ge yfele wilniað to cumanne to goode, þeah

they of-it variously might-desire then said　I　that is true that thou
hi his mislice wilnien. Ða cwæð ic: Þæt is soð þæt þu

sayest　then said　he　sufficiently clear　that is that therefore are
sægst. Ða cwæð he: Genog　sweotol þæt is ðæt te forðy sint

good　men　good　that they good find　then said　I
góde men goode, ðe hi gód gemetað. Ða cwæð ic:　40

sufficiently evident it   is   then said   he   the good   obtain   the
Genog   open hit is. Ða cwæð he: Þa goodan begitað þæt

good   that they desire   then said   I   so   to-me (it) seems then
good þæt hi wilniað. Ða cwæð ic: Swa me   ðyncð. Ða

said   he   the evil   were(not) not evil   if   they might-obtain that
cwæð he: Þa yfelan næron na yfele gif hi gemetten ðæt

good   that   they desire   but therefore they are   evil when they it
good ðæt hi wilniað; ac forðy hi sint yfle þe hi hit

not obtain   and   therefore they it   not obtain which they it   rightly
ne metað, and forðy hi hit ne metað ðe   hi hit on riht   45

not seek   then said   I   so   it is as   thou sayest   then said
ne secað. Ða cwæð ic: Swa hit is swa ðu sægst. Ða cwæð

he   therefore   it   is no   doubt that   the good   are   always
he: Forðæm hit is nan tweo þæt ta goodan beoð symle

controlling   and the evil   have(not)   no   power   therefore
waldende, and þa yflan nabbað nænne anwald; forðy

the good   that good rightly   seek   and   the evil   wrongly
ða goodan ðæt gód on riht secað, and ða yflan on woh.

then said   I   whosoever that not believes that this truth be   then
Ða cwæð ic: Se   ðe ne wenð þæt ðis soð sie, ðonne   50

— believes he of-no   truth
ne gelyfð he names soðes.

          then said   he   which   believest-thou now   if   two
v. Ða cwæð he: Hwæðer wenstu   nu? gif twegen

men   move   toward a   place   and have   equally-great
men fundiað to   anre stowe, and habbað emnmicelne

desire toward to come   and (the)one has   of-his feet (the) power
willan to   to cumenne, and oðer   hæfð his fota anweald

that he might go   where he wish   even as   to-all   men
þæt he mæg gan ðær he wile, swa swa eallum monnum   55

natural   (it)were that   they might   (the)other has-not of-his feet
gecynde wære þæt hi meahten, oðer   næfð his fota

(the) power that he   might   go   and   desires   nevertheless to
geweald þæt he mæge gan, and wilnað ðeah   to

travel   and begins   to-creep   on the   same path   which
feranne, and onginð creopan on þone ilcan weg; hwæðer

of-the two   seems to-thee mightier   then said   I   is-not that
ðara twega þincð ðe   mehtigra? Ða cwæð ic: Nis þæt

similar   he is   mightier   who that goes   than   he that creeps
gelic; se bið mehtigra se   ðe gæð þonne se ðe criepð,   60

because   he might come   more-easily thither where he wish   than
forðæm he mæg cuman eð   ðider ðe   he wile þonne

the other   say   (what)else that   thou wish   that knows any   man
se oðer; saga elles   þæt ðu wille, ðæt wat ælc mon.

then said   he   in-such like is   to-the good   and to-the evil
Ða cwæð he: Swa ilce bið ðæm goodum and ðæm yflum;

both   of-them desire   of   nature   that   he   come   to the
ægþer heora wilnað for gecynde þæt he cume to ðæm

highest good   but the good   might come   whither he   wishes
hehstan goode. Ac se gooda mæg cuman ðider he wilnað,   65

because   he of-it rightly   wishes   and the evil not might come   to
forðæm he his on riht wilnað, and se yfla ne mæg cuman to

that   which he wishes   because   they it   wrongly seek   I   know-not
ðæm þe   he wilnað, forðæm hi hit on wog secað. Ic nat

nevertheless else   what   (it) might seem   then said   I   nor (it)seems
ðeah þe elles hwæt ðince.   Ða cwæð ic: Ne ðincð

to-me   not-at-all otherwise from thy   discourse   then said   he
me   nauht oðres of ðinum spellum.   Þa cwæð he:

sufficiently right   thou it   understandest and   that is also (a)sign of-thy
Genog rihte ðu hit ongitst,   and þæt is eac tacn þinre   70

health even as   of-physicians (the)custom is that they say   when
hælo; swa swa læca   gewuna is þæt hi cweðað ðonne

they (a)sick   man   see   if   they some   unserious   sign   on
hi siocne mon gesioð, gif hi hwilc ungefæglic tacn on

him   see   to-me (it)seems now that   thy   nature   and   thy
him gesioð. Me ðincð nu þæt þin gecynd and ðin

custom   should-contend very   strenuously against the   folly
gewuna flite   swiðe swiðlice wid   ðæm dysige.

QUESTIONS AND EXERCISES—OLD ENGLISH

Parts of Speech and Morphology

Nouns

1. Old English is a *highly inflected* language; that is, the grammatical meaning and syntactic arrangement of the sentence elements are signaled primarily by inflectional endings, rather

than by function words or word order. The term is of course relative; OE is certainly more highly inflected than the later states of the language, but not as highly inflected as Latin. The inflections are particularly numerous for the nouns and the ancillary elements of the NP.

The OE nouns in theory could take five case endings, the selection determined by use, each case having a singular and plural form: *nominative* (sentence subject, complement of *be*), *genitive* (possessive), *dative* (indirect object, object of prepositions *to*, *for*, direct object of a few verbs taking the dative rather than accusative), *accusative* (direct object), and *instrumental* (object of preposition). Early in the OE period the dative and instrumental cases had merged completely, except in the masculine singular declension. There were three main declensions of OE nouns, confusingly denominated *masculine*, *feminine*, and *neuter*. These terms have no reference to NE natural gender, but are meant to be descriptive of grammatical categories: masculine nouns take the nominative singular article *se*; feminine, *seo* or *sio*; and neuter, *þæt*. In this respect, they resemble German nouns, which can be classified by their articles *der*, *die*, *das*; or French, with *le* and *la*. It would be very useful if foreign language grammars for English-speaking students could get away from using English natural gender terminology to describe purely grammatical categories.

In the passages above, analyze the *singular* nouns, and try to categorize as many as you can by both gender and case. Record *all* the elements of the NP when making up your chart. As a help to classification, *dæl*, *weg*, and *fyr* are masculine; *sunne* and nouns ending in *-nes* are feminine; and *good* and *yvel* (the qualities, not the adjectives) are neuter. Consider the dative and instrumental to be one case. It also helps to know that the singular endings for masculine and neuter nouns are generally identical: the principal difference is in the articles. What impediments to classification by declension do you find? Are all the forms consistent?[17]

---

[17] The use of a dictionary might be helpful for this exercise. Henry Sweet's *Student's Dictionary of Anglo-Saxon* (Oxford, 1896), still in print, is the least expensive and easiest to use. Most libraries have John R. Clark Hall's *Concise Anglo-Saxon Dictionary* (4th ed.; Cambridge, 1960); and some might even have the monumental Bosworth–Toller *Anglo-Saxon Dictionary* (Oxford, 1882–1920).

2. In like manner, analyze the *plural* noun instances. This time, consider the nominative and accusative, as well as the dative-instrumental, to be one case. Record *all* the elements of the NP.

3. From the above analyses, indicate what you believe to be the inflectional form and the article form for each of the cases in all genders and numbers. On the chart below, we have filled in the forms which do not occur:

		Singular			*Plural*			
	M	F	N	M	F	N		
N								N–A
G			ðæs -es	ðara		ðara -a		G
D–I				ðæm -um	ðæm	ðæm -um		D–I
	(instr.: ðy)							
A		ða -e						

Which of the forms in the chart are the probable ancestors of those which we use today? Describe the process by which they have come down to us, to the exclusion of the others.

4. Note the use of articles other than as the NP determiner. What light does this throw on the way the article was regarded in OE? How do you account for the rapid decline of the definite article into the single form *the*?

5. What other elements besides the articles listed above appear in the determiner portion of the NP in the translation passages? Which of them have come down to us, and which have dropped out of use?

6. Complete the following chart of forms for the OE pronouns. The forms which do not appear in the translation have been supplied:

		Singular				*Plural*			
				3					
	1	*2*	M	F	N	*1*	*2*	*3*	
N								ge		N
G				hire		ure	eower		G
D–I				hire		us	eow	him	D–I
A			hine	hie		us	eow		A

Study these forms, noting which ones have come down to us in very much the same form (the second person plural nominative *ge* was pronounced very much like /jeː/; the diphthong *eo* was pronounced /eːə/ or /ɛːə/). What has happened to the accusative and dative forms, with respect to the subsequent history of the pronoun? How do you account for the variations in the forms of the first and second person singular genitives? Why has the pronoun retained more case forms than the noun?

Adjectives and adverbs

1. It was mentioned earlier that it was a general feature of the Germanic languages to have a double declension of adjectives: a "weak" form when preceded by a determiner element (originally pronominal), and a "strong" form in its absence. The declensions called for agreement between adjective and noun headword in gender, case, and number. The adjective form following *be* was originally a "strong" nominative.[18]

Classify the adjectives in the translation, according to their gender, case, and number, in the two declensions. Even though your inventory is incomplete, what do you notice about a good many of the inflectional endings? How does this help to explain the eventual disappearance of these forms?

2. What means did the OE adjective (and adverb) have for comparison? What examples do you find of this in the passages? Do any of the intensifiers show a resemblance to the use of *more* and *most* today?

3. What means did the OE speaker have of forming adjectives from nouns and verbs? Analyze the adverbs in the passages. How were adverbs formed from adjectives? What common adverbial ending is in part derived from this noun + adjectival ending + adverbial ending combination?

Verbs

1. Old English verbs come in two distinct classes, "weak" and "strong." The former, a Germanic characteristic, formed the

---

[18] The terms *strong* and *weak* were borrowed as literal translations of the German *stark* and *schwach*, a legacy of the philologists.

past tense with a dental suffix, whereas the latter formed it by an internal vowel change (*Ablaut*) identical with NE *sing, sang, sung*. Sometimes the "weak" verb participle may have a dental suffix, but not always, by any means. Some "weak" verbs may have vowel gradation accompanying the dental suffix, but this does not change their "weak" status.

Identify the verbs according to these two categories. Further, for the "strong" verbs, classify the form as to whether it is an infinitive stem (including all present stems), first or third person singular past, plural past, or past participle. This is the commonest means of showing vowel gradation.

Note: The OE "strong" verbs have traditionally been classified into seven different types, according to their gradation *and* their Proto-Germanic originals.[19] We will not go into this classification here, save to say that some types show remarkable similarity to their NE forms:

writan   wrāt   writon   writen   "write"   (type I)
brecan   bræc   brǣcon   brocen   "break"   (type II)

These paradigms show respectively the infinitive, the first and third singular past form, the plural past, and past participle, including the endings. The macrons marking the lengthened vowels are usually included in these paradigms, though they don't ordinarily occur in OE manuscripts.

Which of the strong verbs in the passages have remained "strong" and which have become "weak"? How do you account for the obstinacy of the few remaining strong verbs in English?

2. Analyze each verb, this time to classify it according to person and number (all plurals can be lumped together). Are there differences between the present and past personal endings? Which endings carried over into ME? Note the subjunctives (I've tried to indicate them in the translation) and classify them separately. You might begin by classifying the verbs that occur most often: (*a-/ge-)reccan* "explain" (i, 7; iii, 46; iv, 12, 13, 30) and *gemunan* "remember" (iv, 29, 32, 33).

---

[19] This traditional classification has recently been challenged by a descriptively more viable classification: see Samuel R. Levin, "A Reclassification of the Old English Strong Verbs," *Language*, XL (1964), 156–61.

3. Note each instance of the modals, *have*, and *be*, and classify it by person, number, and tense. Again, classify the subjunctives separately. Which forms seem to be the ancestors of the like-functioning NE forms, and which have since disappeared?

4. Analyze the Aux portion of the VP. Which form does the modal govern? Which form does *have* govern? What is the commonest ending for the main verb following *have*? What changes would have to be written into Aux to account for the whole VP in OE? How would you account for the ordering of the VP?

Sentence Structure

1. By far the commonest transformation which occurs is the negative. Note every instance of sentence negation in our passages. What elements are similar to those in ME? Does the *ne* element function in precisely the same way as in ME? What change in attitude toward this element seems to have taken place between Alfred's time and Chaucer's?[20] Note the forms *nyle* (iv, 18), *næfð* (iv, 20), *nis* (ii, 28), *nat* (v, 67), and *nast* (ii, 36). What operation has taken place here? How does it compare with similar ME practices?

2. So very few instances of other transformations occur in the passages of the OE translation that we cannot draw definitive conclusions about them. However, analyze the following instances, and compare them with those in ME, ENE, and NE:

    a. Imperative (ii, 44–45, 45; iv, 4; v, 62).
    b. Yes/no interrogative (none occur directly, but there is an indirect occurrence at iv, 33–35).
    c. Substantial interrogative (i, 20–23; v, 52, 58–59).

3. At least two examples of idiomatic expressions in their embryo state, since fossilized, occur in these passages:

    a. *me ðincð* (or *ðyncð*). What are the successive states of this form in ME and ENE? How do we (and possibly the

---

[20] On occasion, I have been forced in the translation of the OE Boethius passages to take no "official" notice of the negative element to avoid misleading the reader. In these passages (see ii, 33, etc.) the omission is indicated by a dash in the translation. The lone exceptions are when the elements are contracted, as in i, 17.

Elizabethans) interpret it? Compare the OE verbs *ðencan* "think, consider" (past, *ðohte*) and *ðyncan* "seem" (past, *ðuhte*). How does this help to explain the later confusion?

b. *ðy bet* (iv, 12–13). The direct ancestor of "all the better to see you with, my dear," and "the more, the merrier." What are the components of the idiom? What led to the use subsequently of the definite article in the current idiom?

4. Highly inflected languages are traditionally assumed to rely entirely on the inflectional forms as structural signals. Word order therefore becomes a rhetorical device, rather than grammatical—resulting in a good deal of modern scholarship just to uncover the rhetorical connotations of word placement. To test this with OE, analyze the ordering of words and word groups in an extended prose passage of the Alfred translation. Does a general pattern begin to emerge? What implication does this have for the later state of the language? Would the Norman Conquest have had any effect upon this tendency?

Summation

We cannot pretend to have covered the history of the English language in the space of this one chapter. The field is vast, and if this weren't difficult enough, the student faces additional problems. On the one hand, there is a relative shortage of good OE manuscripts;[21] and though ME manuscripts are in greater supply, their usefulness is often circumscribed by problems of dialect and faulty scribal transmission. Overshadowing all historical study of English is the problem of phonological development, which, for what are hopefully good and sufficient reasons, we barely touched upon. However, it will suffice if from this overview you can understand in general terms something of the development of English: its origins and the kinds of changes which have culminated in its present state.

[21] This situation was not helped any by a fire which destroyed roughly one-third of the contents of the Cottonian Library in 1731—at the time the finest antiquarian collection in England. Of the surviving manuscripts, the Alfred Boethius translation was partly destroyed, and the unique *Beowulf* manuscript was slightly singed and has since become extremely fragile. Scholars have often had to rely upon transcriptions made prior to the fire. The entire surviving collection has since formed the nucleus of the manuscript holdings of the British Museum.

To this end, therefore, there is one more exercise. Review the material which we have covered, this time in regular chronological order. In this review, make generalizations about the changes which have occurred in grammatical signals—that is, in the inflectional endings, function words, and word order. Trace the importance and the uses of these signaling devices at the various stages we have arbitrarily set in the historical development of English.

To help fill in some of the gaps, appended below are two examples of the English language at transition points in its development. The first is the entry for the year 1100 in the *Anglo-Saxon Chronicle* kept at Peterborough, recounting the death of King William Rufus, the son of William the Conqueror. The second is the passage of the last battle between Mordred and Arthur in Thomas Malory's *Morte d'Aurthur*, written between 1460 and 1470. Use these extracts as a means of checking your conclusions.

From *The Anglo-Saxon (Peterborough) Chronicle:*

1100. On þison geare se cyng Willelm heold his hired to Cristesmæssa on Gleaweceastre, and to Eastron on Winceastre, and to Pentecosten on Westmynstre. And to þam Pentecosten wæs gesewen innan Barrucscire æt anan tune blod weallan of eorþan, swa swa mænige sædan þe hit geseon   5
sceoldan. And þæræfter on morgen æfter Hlammæssedæge wearð se cyng Willelm on huntnoðe fram his anan men mid anre fla ofsceoten and syððan to Winceastre gebroht and on þam biscoprice bebyrged. Þæt wæs þæs þreotteðan geares þe he rice onfeng. He wæs swiðe strang and reðe ofer his   10
land and his mænn and wið ealle his neahheburas and swiðe ondrædendlic. And þurh yfelra manna rædas þe him æfre gecweme wæran and þurh his agene gitsunga he æfre þas leode mid here and mid ungylde tyrwigende wæs. Forþan þe on his dagan ælc riht afeoll, and ælc unriht for gode and   15
for worulde up-aras. Godes cyrcean he nyðerade. And þa biscoprices and abbotrices þe þa ealdras on his dagan feollan, ealle he hi oððe wið feo gesealde oððe on his agenre hand heold and to gafle gesette, forþan þe he ælces mannes

gehadodes and læwedes yrfenuma beon wolde. And swa   20
þæt þæt dæges þe he gefeoll, he heafde on his agenre hand
þæt arcebisceoprice on Cantwarbyrig and þæt bisceoprice
on Winceastre and þæt on Searbyrig and ·xi· abbotrices
ealle to gafle gesette. And, þeah þe ic hit læng ylde, eall
þet þe gode wæs lað and rihtfullan mannan, eall þæt wæs   25
gewunelic on þisan lande on his tyman. And forþi he wæs
forneah ealre his leode lað and gode andsæte, swa swa his
ænde ætywde; forþan þe he on middewardan his unrihte
buten behreowsunge and ælcere dædbote gewat.

Freely translated:

    1100. In this year King William held his court on Christmas
at Gloucester, and on Easter at Winchester, and on Pentecost at
Westminster. And on that Pentecost at a town in Berkshire
blood was seen welling up out of the earth, as many said that
could have seen it. And afterwards, on the morning after
Lammas-day [August 1], King William while hunting was shot
with an arrow by one of his men and thereafter was brought to
Winchester and interred at the bishopric. This was on the
thirteenth year after he succeeded to the kingdom. He was very
severe and ruthless over his realm and his subjects and against
all his neighbors, and very terrible. And through the advice of
evil men who were agreeable to him, and through his own greed,
he was ever afflicting the nation with the army and with excessive
taxes. So that in his days every right decayed, and every injustice rose up before God and the world. He humiliated God's
Church. And the bishoprics and abbacies whose leaders died in
his days, all of them he either sold for money or held in his own
possession and let out for rent, so that he would be every man's
beneficiary, whether cleric or lay. And thus on the day that he
died, he held in his own possession the Archbishopric of Canter-
bury and the Bishopric of Winchester and of Salisbury and eleven
abbacies, all let out for rent. And, although I delayed it long,
all that was hateful to God and honorable men, it was all customary in this country in his time. And therefore he was loath-
some to nearly all his nation and hateful to God, as it appeared
at his end; for he died in the midst of his injustice without
repentence and any penance.

From Thomas Malory, *Morte d'Arthur*:

And thus they fought all the longe day, and never stynted
tylle þe noble knyȝtes were layde to the colde erthe. And
ever they fought stylle tylle hit was nere nyȝt, and by than
was þere an hondred thousand leyde dede uppon the erthe.
Than was kynge Arthure wode wrothe oute of mesure, whan   5
he saw hys people so slayne frome hym. And so he loked
aboute hym and cowde se no mo of all hys oste and good
knyȝtes leffte, no mo on lyve but two knyȝtes: the tone was
sir Lucan de Buttler and hys brother sir Bedwere; and
yette they were full sore wounded.   10

'Jesu mercy!' seyde the kynge, 'where ar all my noble
knyȝtes becom? Alas, that ever I shulde se thys doleful day;
for now,' seyde kynge Arthur, 'I am com to myne ende.
But wolde to god,' seyde he, 'that I wyste now where were
that traytoure sir Mordred that hath caused all thys   15
myschyff.'

Than kynge Arthur loked aboute and was ware where
stood sir Mordred leanyng uppon hys swerde amonge a grete
hepe of dede men.

'Now gyff me my speare,' seyde kynge Arthure unto sir   20
Lucan, 'for yondir I have aspyed þe traytoure that all thys
woo hath wrought.' 'Sir, latte hym be,' seyde sir Lucan,
'for he ys unhappy. And yf ye passe this unhappy day, ye
shall be ryȝt well revenged. And, good lord, remembre ye
of your nyȝtes dreme and what the spyryte of sir Gawayne   25
tolde you to-nyȝt, and yet god of hys grete goodnes hath
preserved you hyddirto. And for goddes sake, my lorde,
leve of thys; for, blyssed be god, ye have won the fylde.
For yet we ben here three on lyve, and with sir Mordred ys
nat one on lyve. And therefore if ye leve of now, thys   30
wycked day of desteny ys paste.'

'Now tyde me dethe, tyde me lyff,' seyde the kyng, 'now
I se hym yondir alone, he shall never escape myne hondes!
For at a bettir avayle shall I never have hym.' 'God spyede
you well!' seyde sir Bedyvere.   35

Than the kynge gate his speare in bothe hys hondis, and
ran towarde sir Mordred, cryyng and saying: 'Traytoure,
now ys thy dethe-day com!' And whan sir Mordred saw

kynge Arthur, he ran untyll hym with hys swerde drawyn
in his honde, and þere kyng Arthur smote sir Mordred undir   40
the shylde with a foyne of hys speare, thorowoute the body
more than a fadom. And whan sir Mordred felte that he
had hys dethys wounde, he threste hymselff with the myȝt
that he had upp to the burre of kyng Arthurs speare, and
ryȝt so he smote hys fadir, kynge Arthure, with hys swerde   45
holdynge in both hys hondys, uppon the syde of the hede,
that the swerde perced the helmet and the tay of the brayne.
And þerewith Mordred daysshed downe starke dede to the
erthe.

BIBLIOGRAPHY

The general area of the history of the English language is particularly
rich in studies and monographs of all kinds. The materials which are mentioned here, only a very few of the available resources, indicate those considered
the most useful to the interested beginning student.

The two best general histories of the English language, widely used in
both graduate and undergraduate courses, are Albert C. Baugh, *A History of
the English Language* (2d ed.; New York: Appleton-Century-Crofts, 1957);
and Thomas Pyles, *The Origins and Development of the English Language* (New
York: Harcourt, Brace & World, Inc., 1964). The first is an "external"
history, concentrating primarily on the outside factors which influenced the
development of English, whereas the latter is principally a descriptive history
of the changes which occurred in the language. A more recent addition to the
subject is Robert D. Stevick, *English and Its History: The Evolution of a Language*
(Boston: Allyn and Bacon, Inc., 1968), with its especially full material on
phonology. A helpful guide to the historical phonology and morphology of
English is Samuel Moore and Albert H. Marckwardt, *Historical Outlines of
English Sounds and Inflections* (rev. ed.; Ann Arbor, Mich.: George Wahr
Publishing Company, 1951).

There is no descriptive grammar of Early Modern English. The closest
thing to one is Margaret Schlauch, *The English Language in Modern Times
(Since 1400)* (Warsaw: Państwowe Wydawnictwo Naukowe, 1962; distributed
by Oxford University Press). This work contains a detailed description of
English development following the death of Chaucer, with plenty of illustrative
material. Two excellent brief Middle English reference grammars are Edith
E. Wardale, *An Introduction to Middle English* (London: Routledge and Kegan
Paul Ltd., 1937); and Karl Brunner, *An Outline of Middle English Grammar*,
trans. G. K. W. Johnston (Cambridge, Mass.: Harvard University Press,
1963). A more advanced, detailed reference grammar is Fernand Mossé,

A Handbook of Middle English, trans. James A. Walker (Baltimore: The Johns Hopkins Press, 1952).

For Old English, a good introduction to the rudiments of the language is Samuel Moore and Thomas A. Knott, *The Elements of Old English* (10th ed.; Ann Arbor, Mich.: George Wahr Publishing Company, 1955). The best student's reference is Randolph Quirk and C. L. Wrenn, *An Old English Grammar* (New York: Holt, Rinehart and Winston, Inc., 1955), especially useful for its full treatment of syntax and of affix forms.

An excellent collection of Old and Middle English texts suitable for both linguistic and literary study is Rolf Kaiser (ed.), *Medieval English* (5th impression; West Berlin: privately printed, 1961). A companion volume of notes and glossary is in progress. For the literary background of medieval England, see Stanley B. Greenfield, *A Critical History of Old English Literature* (New York: New York University Press, 1965); and David M. Zesmer, *Guide to English Literature: From Beowulf Through Chaucer and Medieval Drama* (New York: Barnes and Noble, Inc., 1961). Both studies contain excellent bibliographies for further study.

9

The Dialects of English

"I knowed you wasn't Oklahomy folks. You talk queer kinda—that ain't no blame, you understan'."

"Ever'body says words different," said Ivy. "Arkansas folks says 'em different, and Oklahomy folks says 'em different. And we seen a lady from Massachusetts, an' she said 'em differentest of all. Couldn' hardly make out what she was sayin'."

JOHN STEINBECK, *The Grapes of Wrath*

LANGUAGE AND DIALECT

Like the Joads and the Wilsons, all of us recognize and take for granted the fact of regional varieties of English. Though we tend to think of our own speech as standard, and refer to the "accents" of others, regional speech in itself is not a crucial factor with us. As soon as the term *dialect* is used, however, we find that misconceptions abound. Too many people think of dialect as "illiterate speech" (an interesting contradiction of terms) or "folksy," or something manifested by Snuffy Smith and the denizens of the Great Smokies. However most people may think of it, of one thing they are sure: *they* don't speak a dialect.

Even though we covered this ground in Chapter 1, it is important that we go over it again, if only to avoid further misunderstanding. We noted that any definition of *language* must

276

show its special attributes: that it is vocal, systematic, arbitrary, symbolic, and noninstinctive—a human activity used for social interaction and cultural transmission. Further, it is an *abstract* concept partly because we cannot point to any single instance of *The* language, and partly because no grammatical description can possibly pin down all of the utterances which we are capable of making. On the other hand, *dialect* is the tangible manifestation of language, the social, cultural, and especially regional variations of this abstraction. Yet none of these variations, which can include differences in sounds, in grammatical signals, and in vocabulary, is so extreme as to eliminate mutual intelligibility.

With these distinctions and definitions in mind, we can clarify some misconceptions. Dialect is not necessarily nonstandard or substandard. This is obvious simply because all of us speak a dialect. Nor is a dialect "folksy," or something manifested elsewhere. These attitudes reflect a kind of linguistic chauvinism, the notion that what *I* speak is standard and that the failure to speak as *I* do is nothing but sheer perversity. Finally, a common view that dialect is "corruption of the language" does not hold up under scrutiny. Many dialectal usages which are now no longer standard, as the forms *holp* or *holpen* for *helped*, were at one period of our language history the standard forms.[1] There is good evidence that dialectal usages, especially those commonly considered substandard, are actually more conservative than the standard usages. It's an interesting point to ponder—who is actually corrupting what?

We have already briefly considered the social and cultural variations of English, but in our previous discussions we have tacitly and conveniently assumed that all of us speak English more or less alike. This is a useful assumption when discussing the grammatical system of English or the mainstream of its historical development. But we must now recognize the fact of regional varieties of Standard English. Throughout this chapter, this will be the primary meaning of *dialect* (recognizing that it

---

[1] See, for example, in the King James Version, Psalm 86:17 and Luke 1:54, not to mention *Henry IV, Part I*, I, iii, 13. For present-day dialect use of this form, see E. Bagby Atwood, *A Survey of Verb Forms in the Eastern United States* (Ann Arbor, Mich., 1953), pp. 16–17 and fig. 13.

isn't possible to exclude social and cultural varieties of usage completely). This in no way conflicts with our basic definition of dialect as the tangible manifestation of the abstraction *language*. After all, every spoken utterance reveals evidences of regional variation.

THE HISTORY OF DIALECT STUDY

Because there is a good deal of interest in dialect study today, we should sketch briefly the background of this study. Dialect study, better known as linguistic geography, got its start in an off-hand way with dialect word lists of uneven worth compiled in the eighteenth and nineteenth centuries, usually by people with an amateur's interest and an attitude of romantic condescension.[2] Systematic study began late in the nineteenth century in Germany, with the first of several efforts to plot the geographical distribution of dialect forms.

This first effort was the *Deutscher Sprachatlas*, begun in 1876 under the direction of Georg Wenker. The object of the study was to determine the distribution of dialect pronunciations over Germany, and to this end questionnaires were mailed out to village schoolmasters with the request that they transcribe the local pronunciation of forty-four prepared sentences. The returns were overwhelming—over 40,000 responses—but dishearteningly uneven. First of all, the skills of the schoolmasters in transcribing speech were too varied; but even more important, vocabulary items themselves varied greatly. A *Pferd* in one part of Germany is another German's *Ros*. This questionnaire method proved wholly insufficient for its original purpose, but it did expose riches of another sort in the lexicon, hitherto unexplored.[3]

The deficiencies of the Wenker method were corrected by Jules Gillièron in his *Atlas linguistique de la France* (1902–1910). He

[2] It was under the influence of this attitude that dialect study was done in England, and the first fruits of this study, Joseph Wright's *English Dialect Dictionary* (6 vols.; Oxford, 1898–1905), suffer from this defect. Even today, dialect study in England tends to seek out the quaint and archaic.

[3] The whole *Sprachatlas* was never published, though portions began to appear, beginning in 1881, and there have been several articles and monographs based on it. The files of the atlas are kept at the University of Marburg.

selected a single fieldworker, Edmond Edmont, whom he carefully trained in the techniques of close, accurate transcription. Supplied with a questionnaire of 2,000 items, Edmont pedaled all over France on his bicycle, ultimately making 600 complete field records. This method eliminated any guesswork, especially in phonological studies, and because the interviews were carefully arranged and planned, the results were conclusive, even though there were considerably fewer samplings than in the German atlas. The one drawback was that the interviews were limited to rural areas or small communes—no urban studies were made at all. This deficiency was noted by the Swiss dialectologists Karl Jaberg and Jakob Jud, and in their atlas of Italian and southern Swiss dialects (1925–1940), they included at least one interview in each urban area.

This has been the theoretical development of dialect geography study. The argument still ranges along the Wenker-Gilliéron axis, some studies emphasizing mailed questionnaires, others using fieldworkers. The tendency has been of late to compromise, to elicit vocabulary responses via the mailed questionnaire, while the fieldworker at first hand transcribes the phonological and grammatical details. The fieldworker's task has been made much easier by the tape recorder, on which he can transcribe conversation and anecdotes by the subject for further study at his leisure.

DIALECT STUDY IN AMERICA

In the United States and Canada, systematic linguistic geography work was established in 1930 as the American Linguistic Atlas Project, under the auspices of the American Council of Learned Societies, though important work with dialects had been done since 1894 by the American Dialect Society. The American Linguistic Atlas Project, headed by Hans Kurath and the late Bernard Block, was set up at first under the Gilliéron method, but of late, ancillary vocabulary studies have been accomplished by questionnaires.

The United States and Canada are obviously much too large for one fieldworker to do any kind of adequate job. Over the years, the atlas project has trained a number of fieldworkers to gather and transcribe responses, using a worksheet of over 850 items.[4] Though there are bound to be minor discrepancies between the transcriptions of the workers—a deficiency which can be corrected now by tape recordings—their training and practice make their results as close as human efforts can be. However, training is only part of their qualifications. They must be able to listen, yet elicit the desired response. They must do rapid, accurate, close transcription—though at least one worker claims to be able to keep it all in his head for several hours! They must approach each interview without preconceptions of any kind, showing no surprise at an unusual response, certainly not prejudging the subject. Finally, to quote one of the leading fieldworkers, Professor Raven I. McDavid, Jr., they must be able to "blend in with the scenery." A promising interview can be handicapped by an intimidating, authoritarian fieldworker.[5]

The key to every linguistic atlas interview, however, is the subject himself, the *informant*. These people are picked as carefully as the fieldworkers are. In general, they must be natives of the locale, and it is helpful if their parents were also natives of the area. With the exception of short trips elsewhere, they should have lived in the same area all of their lives.[6] It goes without

[4] In some areas, shorter worksheets of from five to seven hundred items are used, depending upon the objectives of the survey and the number of vocabulary items to be elicited. For a complete review of possible worksheet items, with comments on eliciting certain responses, see Frederic G. Cassidy and Audrey R. Duckert, "A Method for Collecting Dialect," *Publications of the American Dialect Society (PADS)*, 20 (November, 1953).

[5] For a popular account of the "romance" of dialect field work, see Gledhill Cameron, "Some Words Stop at Marietta, Ohio," *Collier's* (June 25, 1954).

[6] There is still a good deal of argument about the length of time outside one's native district and nature of the absence before it has some effect upon his speech. Temporary visits are no problem, of course, and most fieldworkers do not worry about absence while in college, provided the informant returns home after graduation. One big worry is the common experience of military service, which some scholars feel has the effect of modifying dialect traits. However, it is this writer's experience that the nature of the military, with its insistence upon uniformity, forces the individual to hang on to whatever is left of his individuality—and what is more individual than his dialect? The new communications media probably have less effect upon dialect than is commonly assumed, for watching films or television is primarily a passive

saying that they should be willing and able to help—an interview lasts several hours, sometimes stretching into days. Finally, because the American Linguistic Atlas Project has been trying to make up for more than fifty years of delay, most of the informants are elderly, their ages ranging from sixty to ninety.

Each informant is carefully classified into one of three cultural types:

    I. Old-fashioned, rustic, poorly educated, usually quite old.
    II. Younger, better educated—at least two years of high school.
    III. Cultured, well educated—college graduates, as a rule.

During the early period of the atlas fieldwork, type III was used for control purposes, primarily in urban areas, but in recent years, the regional directors of the project have come to use more of them. Obviously, these classifications will vary somewhat from one region to another; therefore, included with each atlas interview is a brief biographical sketch of the informant, whose anonymity is always preserved. As a further check against their results, the fieldworkers and directors also compile a history of the region, noting in particular the date and manner of first settlement, principal occupations, and the geographical origin of the early settlers.

The information from each interview is carefully collected and filed. After a steady accumulation of data, sufficient to make a significant regional survey, the whole range of responses for each item is plotted on a map. By means of a process too complicated to give in detail, the boundaries between different responses are marked off by isogloss lines. When a significant number of these isoglosses coincide fairly closely or parallel one another, they will set up the boundary line for major or minor dialect areas.

American Dialect Areas

Until the findings of the Linguistic Atlas Project were made known, the standard dialect division in America, based upon a

---

activity. On the other hand, the mobility of the average American is making the dialect geographer's work harder than ever, and will probably prove to be the biggest single factor in the submergence of many dialect traits.

rather subjective and cursory observation of postvocalic /-r/, was into four areas: New England, Northern, Southern, and General American. The last area apparently took in the Midwest from the Ohio River valley northward, and everything west of the Mississippi River except Texas and Louisiana. However, the now-completed survey of the eastern United States, on the basis of vocabulary items, shows the three-part division into **Northern, Midland,** and **Southern,** with Midland being further subdivided into North and South Midland. These areas are shown on Map 9-1, with their eighteen minor subdialect areas.

These dialect boundaries must be taken as approximations. You cannot point to any given imaginary line on the land and say, "Here begins the Midland dialect region." These boundaries mark the line of greatest divergence, but there's bound to be some slippage. For one thing, no two isoglosses will ever coincide completely over their entire length; at best, they will parallel one another fairly well. Also, we cannot rely upon these boundaries remaining the same for any extended period of time. Already, with the remarkable mobility of our society, higher educational standards, and the improvements in communications, sharp dialectal differences are fading away. Undoubtedly we will have to reassess these boundaries before long, but in the meantime, they do give us a good basic frame of reference upon which to build certain conclusions.

We should look more closely at some of the subdialect areas on this map to note some of the considerations which go into determining them. For instance, the principal differences between areas 1 and 2 of the Northern dialect region is the difference, respectively, between rural and urban. Area 2 is definitely focused upon the metropolitan center of Boston. A famous verification of this is in the use of *tonic* instead of *soda pop* or *soft drink*, which usage seems to have been influenced by the bottlers and distributors of Boston, and nowhere else. The further one gets from Boston, the less apt one is to hear the term, which is not in general or customary use in Providence or Portland.

Area 3, southwestern New England, is an instance of settlement differences. Whereas areas 1 and 2 are expansions out of the

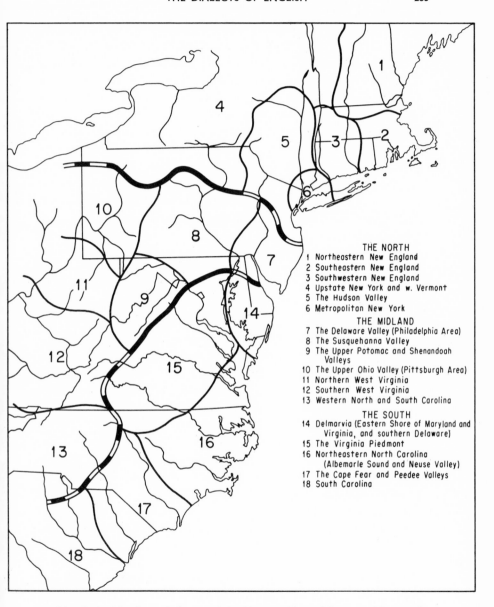

Map 9–1. The Speech Areas of the Eastern United States. (Copyright 1949 by the University of Michigan Press. Reprinted from *A Word Geography of the Eastern United States* by Hans Kurath, by permission of the University of Michigan Press.)

Plymouth and Massachusetts Bay colonies, area 3 expanded from New Haven northward, entry to the north being facilitated by the Connecticut River. Throughout the colonial period, the focal point continued to be New Haven and Hartford, and the principal educational institution was Yale, rather than Harvard. Likewise, area 5, the Hudson Valley, shows, at least in the old-fashioned speech, the effect of the Dutch settlement in the colonizing of the region, and the continuing influence of the *patroons* even after English domination.

Area 6, metropolitan New York, however, represents the overlay of the metropolis upon this original Dutch settlement. This is the immediate area of pronunciations like /lɔ̀ŋ-gáilənd/ *Long Island*, with the distinctly articulated *g*, and /bəid/, which so many tourists are positive that they heard pronounced "boid." Both of these usages have attracted unwarranted attention to themselves, and as a result, upwardly mobile speakers of types II and III go out of their way to avoid them. Our brief survey of the Northern dialect is completed with area 4, upstate New York and western Vermont. This area, which extends westward into the Great Lakes region and beyond, is inhabited by people who retain the final /-r/, unlike those in areas 1, 2, and 3, and who sit on the back *stoop* when they're not out tapping the trees in their sugar *bush*.

The Midland area is conveniently divided further into the North Midland (areas 7, 8, 10, 11) and South Midland (9, 12, 13), though more recent field work has disclosed the probability of re-designating areas 10 and 11 as West Midland. Area 7 comes under a strong metropolitan influence, like area 2, this time from Philadelphia. Parts of this area, but especially area 8, the Susquehanna Valley, are prone to Germanisms, the influence of the so-called Pennsylvania Dutch: a *toot*, pronounced /tʊt/, for a paper bag, *smearcase* for cottage cheese, and the expression "The milk is all."[7] Area 10 is dominated by Pittsburgh, a focal point

---

[7] The term *Dutch* comes from *Deutsch*, and was a common appellation for anyone or anything German until World War I—as a Dutch comic, or Honus ("the Dutch-man") Wagner, immortal infielder for Pittsburgh. How the meaning was specialized to refer only to the Netherlands (whose citizens, by the way, detest the word) is a mystery.

for the westward expansion after independence. The South Midland region is influenced primarily by varying degrees of cultural isolation due to its physical geography. Throughout the area, almost everyone *packs* the groceries home, speaks of a sugar *tree* in reference to a grove, and, if unfortunate, gets *dogbit*. The general boundaries of the Midland region were determined by the isoglosses shown in Map 9–2. These isoglosses enclose the areas in which three Midland vocabulary items are commonly heard.

The interesting, and to some people, surprising, thing about the Southern dialect is the relatively restricted area of its extent. Common to this whole area is the loss of the postvocalic /-r/, which, unlike the New England usage, is not used even intrusively between vowels. Here, too, one does not often hear a historical final /-r/ before an initial vowel, as seen in Map 9–3, though this "linking" /-r/ occurs regularly in New England, especially in area 1. Other general pronunciations are the /e/ in *Mary*, and /mɪz/ for both *Mrs.* and *Miss.* Area 14, the Delmarvia Peninsula, once featured the now-dying use of *'mongst-ye* among type I informants, rather than *you* (plural) or *you-all*.[8] Area 15, the Virginia Piedmont, with its complicated focus on Richmond and Baltimore, and complex mixture of rural and cultivated urban population, still retains the Elizabethan and seventeenth-century /əu/ diphthong in *about, house.* Finally, area 18, South Carolina and northern Georgia, contains such usages as *groundnuts* for peanuts (or the more generally Southern *goobers*), *fatwood* for kindling, a usage attributed to the quinine industry there, plus numerous Africanisms among type I Negro informants, as *cooter* /kútə/ "turtle," and *buckra* "white man" (from West African *mba-kara* "he who governs").

Some idea of specific localisms can be gotten from Map 9–4, which shows the responses in the eastern United States for *doughnut*,

---

[8] *You-all* is common throughout the South and much of the Midland region, and every educated user of the form insists that it is plural. That is, the greeting "How're you-all?", though addressed to one person, is meant to include his friends-and-relations as well. However, an acquaintance of mine reports that in Georgia, a back-country sheriff's deputy asked him, "What time you-all got?", and my friend carefully noted that no one else was present. Could it be that the deputy intended the alleged plural form to be a mark of respect, analogous to the Elizabethan usage of *you* vs. *thou*?

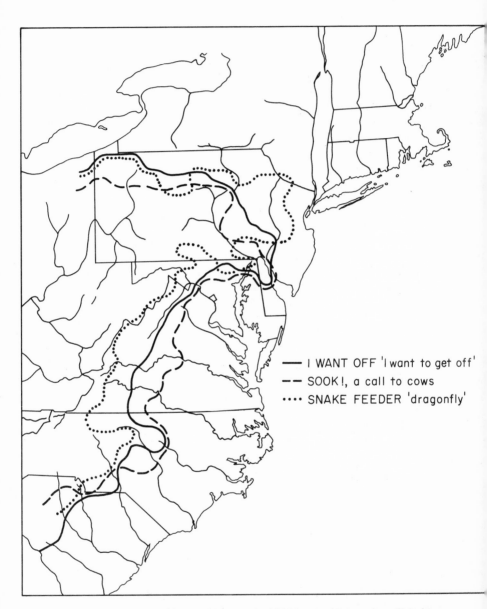

Map 9–2. The Midland. (Copyright 1949 by the University of Michigan Press. Reprinted from *A Word Geography of the Eastern United States* by Hans Kurath, by permission of the University of Michigan Press.)

which is the general term in use everywhere for this bakery product. The variant *fried-cake* is limited to upstate New York (area 4) and its westward extension. Though some instances of *fried-cake* occur in southern New England, the more usual variant is *cruller*, which extends into metropolitan New York, the Philadelphia area, and further south, with lessening intensity. Northern New England has some instances of *nut cake*; and *ring* was the response on Nantucket Island. Two indications of foreign settlement are evidenced: the Dutch *olicook* in the Hudson Valley, and the German *fat-cake*, in the Pennsylvania German area. Finally, the German influence may be responsible for the occurrence of *cookie* (from *Fettkuchen*, which is also the source for *fat-cake*) in eastern North Carolina, as well as the isolated instance of *fat-cake* there. Some informants make a differentiation between the pastry made with raised and unraised dough: in general, *cruller* tends to refer to the former, whereas the other variants refer to the latter.[9]

All of this is nothing more than the barest overview, and the reader is invited to look over the published material which has resulted from this material, particularly the monumental *Linguistic Atlas of New England*, three volumes (in six parts) of large folio maps, 734 of them, with the responses from each of the informants hand-lettered on the basic plates. This arduous and expensive undertaking could not be done again; succeeding atlases have been limited to coded representations of morphological and vocabulary responses, as in Maps 9-3 and 9-4 below, with pronunciation represented by charts. In addition to the New England project, the completed work in the eastern United States has been published, and is mentioned in the bibliography. The completed field work for the Great Lakes region (Michigan, Wisconsin, Ohio, Indiana, Illinois, and Kentucky) and the Upper Midwest (Minnesota, Iowa, North and South Dakota, and Nebraska) has not been published in tabulated form, but general

[9] The distinction which I learned while growing up in central Michigan was that *doughnuts* were made from dough with yeast, whereas *fried-cakes* were made from cake dough without leavening. This distinction seems not to be general, however; even among bakery employees I have questioned informally, only one (from Iron Mountain, Michigan) was aware of the distinction.

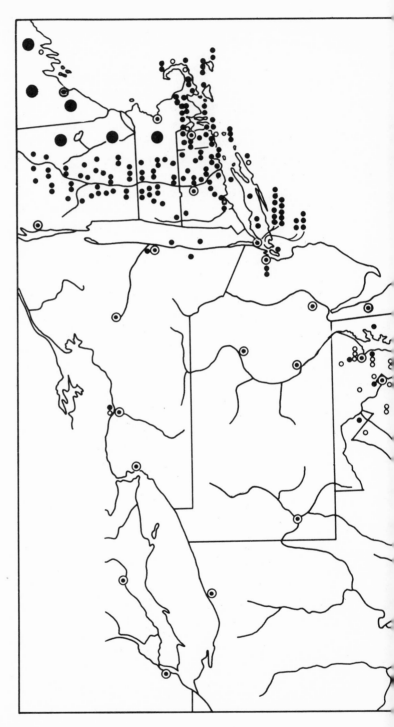

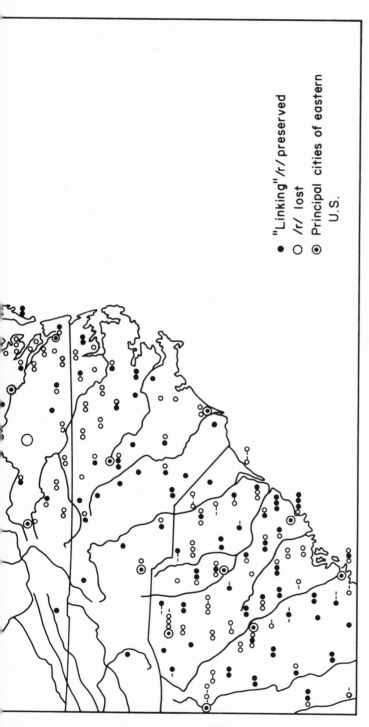

Map 9–3. Treatment of Historical /-r/ in the Phrase *Your Aunt* by Speakers Who Lack Postvocalic /-r/ in *Door, Barn.* (Copyright © 1961 by the University of Michigan Press. Reprinted from *The Pronunciation of English in the Atlantic States* by Hans Kurath and Raven I. McDavid, Jr., by permission of the University of Michigan Press.)

● "Linking" /r/ preserved
○ /r/ lost
◉ Principal cities of eastern
   U.S.

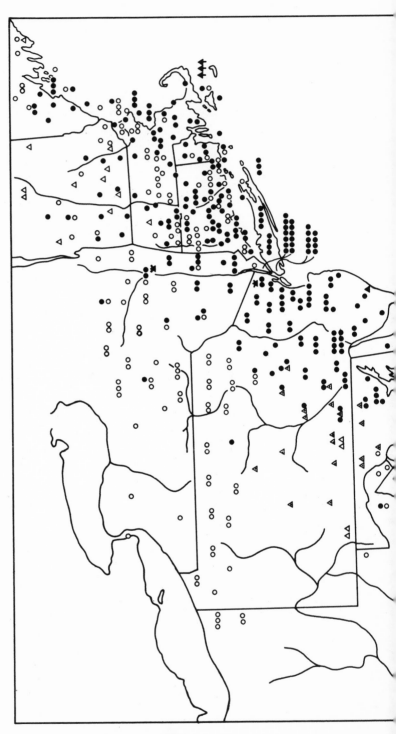

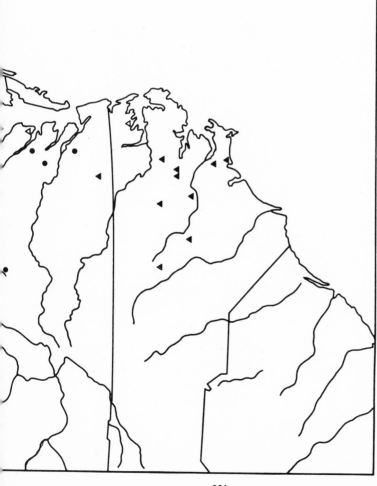

○ FRIED-CAKE

● CRULLER

△ NUT CAKE

♦ RING

✖ OLICOOK

▲ FAT-CAKE

◁ COOKIE

Map 9–4. Doughnut. (Copyright 1949 by the University of Michigan Press. Reprinted from A Word Geography of the Eastern United States by Hans Kurath, by permission of the University of Michigan Press.)

findings have been published, as has the somewhat more limited field work in Texas and Colorado.

The findings of all of these studies have been utilized in the preparation of Map 9–5, tentatively showing the major dialect areas of the United States. The broken lines represent what can honestly be called educated guesses, based upon only very vague information. The tentative line dividing Midland from Southern, as it moves along the Mississippi River, is based upon the author's personal observation, subject to correction, that Memphis, Tennessee, represents a northernmost point of the Southern dialect along the river. The other tentative line, dividing Northern from Midland west of the Dakotas, is pure conjecture. However, field work in the Gulf States, the Rocky Mountains, the Far West, and the Southwest is under way, and currently in various stages of completion.

The Future of the Atlas Project

The initial project of the Linguistic Atlas of the United States and Canada, as represented here, has several built-in defects, most of which were anticipated and compensated for as well as possible. The first is the hugeness of the task. The work thus far has taken forty years, and completion is only a dimly seen hope ahead. During this time, editors and fieldworkers have come and gone, with resultant inconsistencies. Moreover, the principal purpose has been to try to reconstruct the dialect areas rising out of the settlement of this country, hence the predominant use of type I informants and basically rural terminology.[10] The search for genuinely old-fashioned informants becomes progressively harder as time goes on; and as communications improve, travel becomes easier, and the nation itself becomes increasingly urbanized, such informants will soon disappear altogether. As if

---

[10] Among the vocabulary items elicited by fieldworkers are terms for haying, kinds of farm outbuildings, fences and walls, parts of buggies and wagons (and means of hitching animals to them), farm implements, animal sounds, calls to animals, food staples and garden produce, insects, and kinds of amusements. Some of these are reproduced in exercise 4. Because substandard usages are generally more conservative, type I informants can often give some significant information about what was once standard morphology and syntax.

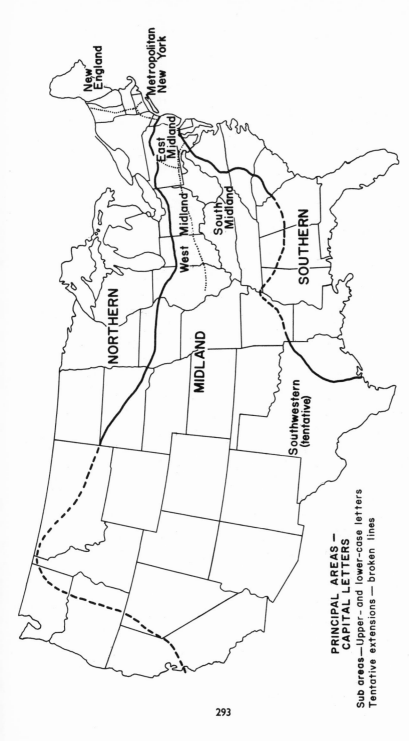

PRINCIPAL AREAS —
CAPITAL LETTERS

Sub areas—Upper- and lower-case letters
Tentative extensions — broken lines

New England

Metropolitan
New York

East
Midland

West Midland

South
Midland

NORTHERN

MIDLAND

SOUTHERN

Southwestern
(tentative)

Map 9–5. Principal Dialect Areas of the United States. (Based on the work of Kurath, Atwood, Marckwardt, and Shuy.)

293

in anticipation of this eventuality, work has already begun on a definitive *Dictionary of American Regional English*, directed by Professor Frederic G. Cassidy of the University of Wisconsin.[11]

This points up a change of emphasis in atlas work. Whereas past results are no doubt valid for fifty to seventy-five years ago, they are less useful today. They do not truly represent the current scene, which is certainly neither rural nor old-fashioned and unsophisticated. Many things have come to pass which make the *fills/thills* and *singletree/whiffletree* problems purely academic. But linguistic geographers and dialectologists are aware of this fact. Already, several studies have appeared on metropolitan speech and the pronunciation and vocabulary of persons in bilingual and biracial areas. Some of these findings have proved useful in the inner-city education system, where teachers have had to deal with the linguistic difficulties of the child of the ghetto, the Appalachian worker, and the immigrant whose native language is not English.

The changing emphasis in linguistic geography means a search for new dialect touchstones. Rather than corn bread and cottage cheese, the fieldworker now looks for more modern gastronomic delights. For instance, is that popular supersandwich consisting of an Italian loaf cut lengthwise and filled with various meats, cheeses, greens, and relishes called a *hero*, a *grinder*, a *submarine*, or a *poor-boy*—and does the informant differentiate between the hot and cold variety? Another possibility is the nomenclature of the soda fountain, especially the malts and shakes. Dialectologists are always searching for items which have only local names, without any generally known term. For instance, the patch of lawn between the sidewalk and the street is variously called a *treelawn*, *park*, *parkway*, *boulevard*, *berm*, and probably lots of other things, all of which is grist for the mill. Finally, it will be interesting to learn whether government-enforced nomenclature really sticks. Once the various superhighways are completed, we will be able to see whether the official names of *Turnpike*, *Toll Road*, and *Tollway* will remain standard in the locale, or whether some

11 For a description of this project, see Professor Cassidy's "American Regionalism and the Harmless Drudge," *PMLA*, LXXXII, 3 (June, 1967), 12–19.

regional or national term like *Thruway, Interstate,* or just *The Highway* will come along to topple them.

DIALECT STUDY AND THE TEACHER OF ENGLISH

In the meantime, the work of the linguistic geographers has some significance for everyone. Primary among the points which they have repeatedly brought out is that *dialect* does not of itself have a pejorative connotation, but rather signifies simply what we speak. Teachers would do well to apprise themselves of the features of the dialect in the area where they teach, and they should also recognize that the dialect of the newcomer should be neither the subject of magisterial ridicule nor ruthlessly expunged. Generally speaking, attempts to alter the local dialect in the classroom seldom work, and are usually strongly resisted; if left alone, the "outlander" will modify his dialect in conformity with the usage of his peers, to whatever extent he deems necessity. Many a perfectly legitimate dialect form has run afoul of the prescriptive handbooks, however. Teachers should therefore recognize the fallibility of such guides. As Map 9–6 shows, *hadn't ought* for *ought not* covers the entire Northern region, and the prohibition against it is therefore just foolishness. If the feature is common to all speakers in the area, the ban is ineffective, and if it isn't part of the dialect, there's no point in wasting time on it.

For the interesting fact is that Americans are remarkably tolerant of dialect.[12] Until recently in England, as one grew upwardly mobile, the dialectal features in his speech were expunged and replaced with something called "Public School English" or "Received Standard English." Not so in America: provided that one avoids such social shibboleths as *ain't, I seen,* and *he don't,* he can retain as much of the pronunciation, syntax, and vocabulary of his dialect as he likes, as Presidents Kennedy and Johnson have effectively demonstrated. We recognize that

---

[12] The average American would probably speak favorably of someone's "accent"; as we have said before, "dialect" has an unfavorable connotation. But regardless of terminology, the attitude is the same.

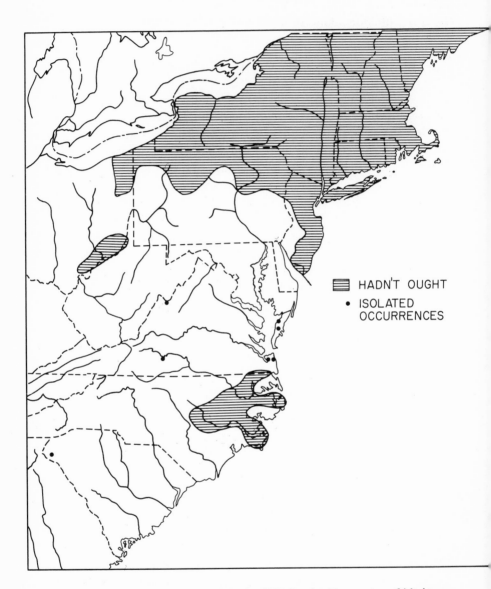

Map 9–6. *Ought Not.* (Copyright 1953 by the University of Michigan Press. Reprinted from *A Survey of Verb Forms in the Eastern United States* by E. Bagby Atwood, by permission of the University of Michigan Press.)

dialects exist and that they are not impediments in themselves to one's well-being. In fact, we find the subject interesting and often play at dialect identification with an amateur's enthusiasm. They certainly don't trouble us; as Pa Joad put it, "You talk queer kinda—that ain't no blame, you understan'."

QUESTIONS AND EXERCISES

1. Review the basic points in this chapter by considering the following questions:

    a. Why are nonstandard usages more conservative generally than their cognate standard usages?

    b. What factors have given the term *dialect* a bad connotation amongst the general populace?

    c. What factors led to the establishment, probably during the colonial period, of the three principal American dialects?

    d. The basic dialect areas were established by means of vocabulary studies. Could this lead to inconsistencies, as the lines are extended inland? Could a phonological investigation lead to an entirely different set of findings?

    e. What factors might contribute to the establishment of a *dialect island*—an isolated community of speakers of one dialect completely surrounded by another? An example is Marietta, Ohio, a Northern enclave in a Midland area (see Map 9–6). Why is this different from the isolated use of a single Northern dialect term in a Midland area (as the term *stone boat* around St. Louis)? What might be the causes of instances like the latter?

2. What geographical and historical considerations can you give for the following dialect boundaries or areas:

    a. New England—inland northern boundary.

    b. Midland—southern boundary.

    c. The westward spread of Midland from a very small coastal area.

    d. The westward spread (limited in width) of Northern.

    e. The coastal spread of Southern.

3. What limitations can you find in the encounter between fieldworker and informant? How can the fieldworker minimize them? Do any of these limitations demonstrate the superiority of the mailed questionnaire?

4. The following are a few of the items which fieldworkers elicit from informants. Note your own responses as objectively as possible, then compare them with the responses of those from other parts of the country. When you find a usage which you know, but do not use, try to pin it down as to area and category of speaker.

a. Pronunciation:

(1) *catch*: with /ɛ/ or /æ/?
(2) *cot* and *caught*: do you differentiate, and if so, how?
(3) *fog*: with /a/ or /ɔ/?
(4) *Mary, merry, marry*: do you differentiate between the vowels?
(5) *roof*: with /u/ or /ʊ/? (likewise, *hoof, root*)
(6) *creek*: with /i/ or /ɪ/?
(7) *route*: with /u/ or /au/?
(8) *humor*: with or without an initial /h-/? (likewise, *humble*)
(9) *Missouri, Cincinnati*: with final /-ə/ or /-i/?
(10) *deer* or *dear*: with or without final /-r/?
(11) *Cuba is*: with or without intrusive intervocalic /-r-/?
(12) *greasy*: with /s/ or /z/?
(13) *wheel, whip*: with or without initial /h-/?

b. Morphology:

(1) *dream*; past, p. part.
(2) *learn*; past, p. part.
(3) *plead*; past
(4) *dive*; past, p. part.
(5) *here* (is/are) *your clothes*; contracted to /-z/ or /-ər/
(6) *you* (oughtn't/hadn't ought) *to do it*
(7) *I've never* (heard/heard tell) *of it*
(8) *we used to do it*; negative

c. Vocabulary:

(1) TOWNSHIP OFFICER: selectman, trustee, supervisor, reeve, councilman.

(2) A Time of Day: quarter before eleven, quarter of eleven, quarter till eleven, quarter to eleven, 10:45.

(3) Rain with Thunder and Lightning: tempest, thunder-shower, thunderstorm, electric(al) storm, electric(al) shower, storm.

(4) Window Covering on Rollers: blinds, curtains, roller shades, shades, window blinds, window shades.

(5) Overlapping Horizontal Boards on Outside of House: clapboards, siding, weatherboards, weather-boarding.

(6) Devices at Edges of Roof to Carry off Rain: eaves, eave spouts, eave(s)troughs, gutters, rain troughs, spouting, spouts, water gutters.

(7) Large Porch with Roof: gallery, piazza, porch, step, steps, portico, stoop, veranda.

(8) Small Porch, Often with No Roof: platform, porch, step, steps, portico, stoop, veranda.

(9) Bread in Loaves, Made of White Flour: bread, light-bread, loaf bread, wheat bread, white bread, yeast bread, riz bread.

(10) Bread Made of Corn Meal: corn bread, corn dodger(s), pone, corn pone, hoe cake(s), johnny cake, pone bread, bread.

(11) Fried, Round, Flat Cakes Made with White Flour: battercakes, flannel cakes, flapjacks, flitters, fritters, pancakes, griddle cakes, hot cakes, slapjacks, wheat cakes.

(12) Corn Eaten on Cob: corn-on-the-cob, garden corn, green corn, mutton corn, roasting ears, sugar corn, sweet corn.

(13) Tree That Produces Sugar and Syrup: hard maple, rock maple, sugar maple, sugar tree.

(14) Place Where Sap Is Gathered: maple grove, maple orchard, sap bush, sap orchard, sugar bush, sugar camp, sugar lot, sugar grove, sugar-maple grove, sugar orchard, sugar place, sugar-tree grove.

(15) A Rustic: backwoodsman, clodhopper, country gentle-man, country jake, countryman, hayseed, hick, hoosier, yokel, hillbilly, jackpine savage, mossback, mountain-boomer, pumpkinhusker, railsplitter, cracker, redneck,

yahoo, sharecropper, stump farmer, swamp angel, sod-buster (etc.).

(16) SICK————: at his stomach, in his stomach, on his stomach, to his stomach, of his stomach, with his stomach.

(17) TO ABSENT ONESELF FROM SCHOOL: bag school, bolt, hook jack, lay out, lie out, play hooky, play truant, run out of school, skip class, slip school, slip off from school.

(18) TO COAST LYING DOWN FLAT: belly-booster, belly-bump, belly-bumper, belly-bunker, belly-bunt, belly-bust, belly-buster, belly-down, belly-flop, belly-flopper, belly-grinder, belly-gut, belly-gutter, belly-kachug, belly-kachunk, belly-whack, belly-wop, belly-wopper, belly-slam.

(19) TO HIT THE WATER FLAT WHEN DIVING: belly-flop, belly-blooper, belly-bust, belly-buster.

(20) CHILD WHO TELLS ON CLASSMATES OR OTHER CHILDREN: tattler, snitcher, newstoter, tattletale, telltale, squealer.

Dialect in Literature

The second segment of the exercises for this chapter is concerned with dialect in literature. Though there have been several studies made of this area, they are seldom made available to the student or teacher in usable form. Therefore, we will give considerable attention to two examples of dialect in American literature and two examples of dialect in British literature, plus some additional problems concerning the whole subject of literary dialect.

The two American examples include the *Bigelow Papers* of James Russell Lowell, an example of the rural dialect of the "north of Boston" New Englander, and the Uncle Remus stories of Joel Chandler Harris, an example of the Negro dialect of central Georgia. Both examples have been hailed as generally accurate representations of their own particular area and type of speaker. The other two examples are more general: the writing of literary Scots dialect, and the first extensive stage representation of various British dialects, Shakespeare's *Henry V*. Not only will we be concerned with the dialect traits of the characters in literature, but we will also study the techniques used to develop dialect in literature, and its general effectiveness.

Examples of American dialect in literature

James Russell Lowell

From THE BIGLOW PAPERS

FIRST SERIES

No. 1

A Letter

From Mr. Ezekiel Biglow of Jaalam to the Hon. Joseph T. Buckingham, editor of the Boston Courier, inclosing a Poem of his son, Mr. Hosea Biglow.

Jaylem, june 1846.

Mister Eddyter,—Our Hosea wuz down to Boston last week, and he see a cruetin Sarjunt a struttin round as popler as a hen with 1 chicking, with 2 fellers a drummin and fifin arter him like all nater. the sarjunt he thout Hosea hed n't gut his i teeth cut cos he looked a kindo 's though he 'd jest com down, so he cal'-lated to hook him in, but Hosy wood n't take none o' his sarse for all he hed much as 20 Rooster's tales stuck onto his hat and eenamost enuf brass a bobbin up and down on his shoulders and figureed onto his coat and trousis, let alone wut nater hed sot in his featers, to make a 6 pounder out on.

wal, Hosea he com home considerabal riled, and arter I'd gone to bed I heern Him a thrashin round like a short-tailed Bull in fli-time. The old Woman ses she to me ses she, Zekle, ses she, our Hosee 's gut the chollery or suthin anuther ses she, don't you Bee skeered, ses I, he's oneya makin pottery ses i, he 's ollers on hand at that ere busynes like Da & martin, and shure enuf, com mornin, Hosy he com down stares full chizzle, hare on eend and cote tales flyin, and sot rite of to go reed his varses to

Parson Wilbur bein he haint aney grate shows o' book larnin himself, bimeby he cum back and sed the parson wuz dreffle tickled with 'em as i hoop you will Be, and said they wuz True grit.

Hosea ses taint hardly fair to call 'em hisn now, cos the parson kind o' slicked off sum o' the last varses, but he told Hosee he did n't want to put his ore in to tetch to the Rest on 'em, being they wuz verry well As thay wuz, and then Hosy ses he sed suthin a nuther about Simplex Mundishes or sum sech feller, but I guess Hosea kind o' did n't hear him, for I never hearn o' nobody o' that name in this villadge, and I've lived here man and boy 76 year cum next tater diggin, and thair aint no wheres a kitting spryer 'n I be.

If you print 'em I wish you'd just let folks know who hosy's father is, cos my ant Keziah used to say it 's nater to be curus ses she, she aint livin though and he 's a likely kind o' lad.

Ezekiel Biglow

Thrash away, you'll *hev* to rattle
   On them kittle-drums o' yourn,—
'T aint a knowin' kind o' cattle
   Thet is ketched with moldy corn;
Put in stiff, you fifer feller,
   Let folks see how spry you be,—
Guess you'll toot till you are yeller
   'Fore you git ahold o' me!

Thet air flag's a leetle rotten,
   Hope it aint your Sunday's best;—
Fact! it takes a sight o' cotton
   To stuff out a soger's chest:
Sence we farmers hev to pay fer 't,
   Ef you must wear humps like these,
S'posin' you should try salt hay fer 't,
   It would du ez slick ez grease.

'T would n't suit them Southun fellers,
    They're a dreffle graspin' set,
We must ollers blow the bellers
    Wen they want their irons het:
May be it's all right ez preachin',
    But *my* narves it kind o' grates,
Wen I see the overreachin'
    O' them nigger-drivin' States.

Them thet rule us, them slave-traders,
    Haint they cut a thunderin' swarth
(Helped by Yankee renegaders),
    Thru the vartu o' the North!
We begin to think it 's nater
    To take sarse an' not be riled;—
Who 'd expect to see a tater
    All on eend at bein' biled?

Ez fer war, I call it murder,—
    There you hev it plain an' flat;
I don't want to go no furder
    Than my Testyment fer that;
God hez sed so plump an' fairly,
    It's ez long ez it is broad,
An' you 've gut to git up airly
    Ef you want to take in God.

'T aint your eppyletts an' feathers
    Make the thing a grain more right;
'T aint afollerin' your bell-wethers
    Will excuse ye in His sight;
Ef you take a sword an' dror it,
    An' go stick a feller thru,
Guv'ment aint to answer for it,
    God'll send the bill to you.

Wut's the use o' meetin'-goin'
      Every Sabbath, wet or dry,
Ef it 's right to go amowin'
      Feller-men like oats an' rye?
I dunno but wut it 's pooty
      Trainin' round in bobtail coats,—
But it 's curus Christian dooty
      This 'ere cuttin' folks's throats.

They may talk o' Freedom's airy
      Tell they 're pupple in the face,—
It's a grand gret cemetary
      Fer the barthrights of our race;
They jest want this Californy
      So 's to lug new slave-States in
To abuse ye, an' to scorn ye,
      An' to plunder ye like sin.

Aint it cute to see a Yankee
      Take sech everlastin' pains,
All to get the Devil's thankee
      Helpin' on 'em weld their chains?
Wy, it 's jest ez clear ez figgers,
      Clear ez one an' one make two,
Chaps thet make black slaves o' niggers
      Want to make wite slaves o' you.

Tell ye jest the eend I 've come to
      Arter cipherin' plaguy smart,
An' it makes a handy sum, tu,
      Any gump could larn by heart;
Laborin' man an' laborin' woman
      Hev one glory an' one shame.
Ev'y thin' thet 's done inhuman
      Injers all on 'em the same.

'T aint by turnin' out to hack folks
    You 're agoin' to git your right,
Nor by lookin' down on black folks
    Coz you 're put upon by wite;
Slavery aint o' nary color,
    'T aint the hide thet makes it wus,
All it keers fer in a feller
    'S jest to make him fill its pus.

Want to tackle *me* in, du ye?
    I expect you 'll hev to wait;
Wen cold lead puts daylight thru ye
    You 'll begin to kal'late;
S'pose the crows wun't fall to pickin'
    All the carkiss from your bones,
Coz you helped to give a lickin'
    To them poor half-Spanish drones?

Jest go home an' ask our Nancy
    Wether I 'd be sech a goose
Ez to jine ye,—guess you 'd fancy
    The etarnal bung wuz loose!
She wants me fer home consumption,
    Let alone the hay 's to mow,—
Ef you 're arter folks o' gumption,
    You 've a darned long row to hoe.

Take them editors thet 's crowin'
    Like a cockerel three months old,—
Don't ketch any on 'em goin',
    Though they *be* so blasted bold;
Aint they a prime lot o' fellers?
    'Fore they think on 't guess they'll sprout
(Like a peach thet 's got the yellers),
    With the meanness bustin' out.

Wal, go 'long to help 'em stealin'
  Bigger pens to cram with slaves,
Help the men thet 's ollers dealin'
  Insults on your fathers' graves:
Help the strong to grind the feeble,
  Help the many agin the few,
Help the men thet call your people
  Witewashed slaves an' peddlin' crew!

Massachusetts, God forgive her,
  She 's akneelin' with the rest,
She, thet ough' to ha' clung ferever
  In her grand old eagle-nest;
She thet ough' to stand so fearless
  W'ile the wracks are round her hurled,
Holdin' up a beacon peerless
  To the oppressed of all the world!

Ha'n't they sold your colored seamen?
  Ha'n't they made your env'ys w'iz?
Wut 'll make ye act like freemen?
  Wut 'll git your dander riz?
Come, I 'll tell ye wut I 'm thinkin'
  Is our dooty in this fix,
They 'd ha' done 't ez quick ez winkin'
  In the days o' seventy-six.

Clang the bells in every steeple,
  Call all true men to disown
The tradoocers of our people,
  The enslavers o' their own;
Let our dear old Bay State proudly
  Put the trumpet to her mouth,
Let her ring this messidge loudly
  In the ears of all the South:—

"I'll return ye good fer evil
 Much ez we frail mortils can,
But I wun't go help the Devil
 Makin' man the cus o' man;
Call me coward, call me traiter,
 Jest ez suits your mean idees,—
Here I stand a tyrant-hater,
 An' the friend o' God an' Peace!"

Ef I 'd *my* way I hed ruther
 We should go to work an' part,
They take one way, we take t' other,
 Guess it would n't break my heart:
Men hed ough' to put asunder
 Them thet God has noways jined;
An' I should n't gretly wonder
 Ef there 's thousands o' my mind.

June 17, 1846

Joel Chandler Harris

THE WONDERFUL TAR-BABY STORY

From *Uncle Remus: His Songs and Sayings* (1880)

"Didn't the fox *never* catch the rabbit, Uncle Remus?" asked the little boy the next evening.

"He come mighty nigh it, honey, sho's you bawn—Brer Fox did. One day atter Brer Rabbit fool 'im wid dat calamus root, Brer Fox went ter wuk en got 'im some tar, en mix it wid some turkentime, en fix up a contrapshun wat he call a Tar-Baby, en he tuck dish yer Tar-Baby en he sot 'er in de big road, en den he lay off in de bushes fer ter see wat de news wuz gwineter be. En he didn't hatter wait long, nudder, kaze bimeby here come Brer Rabbit pacin' down de road—lippity-clippity, clippity-lippity— dez ez sassy ez a jay-bird. Brer Fox, he lay low. Brer Rabbit come prancin' 'long twel he spy de Tar-Baby; en den he fotch up on his behime legs like he wuz 'stonished. De Tar-Baby, she sot dar, she did, en Brer Fox, he lay low.

" 'Mawnin'!' sez Brer Rabbit, sezee—'nice wedder dis mawnin', ' sezee.

"Tar-Baby ain't sayin' nuthin', en Brer Fox, he lay low.

" 'How duz yo' sym'tums seem ter segashuate?' sez Brer Rabbit, sezee.

"Brer Fox, he wink his eye slow, en lay low, en de Tar-Baby, she ain't sayin' nuthin'.

" 'How you come on, den? Is you deaf?' sez Brer Rabbit, sezee. 'Kaze if you is, I kin holler louder,' sezee.

"Tar-Baby stay still, en Brer Fox, he lay low.

" Youer stuck up, dat's w'at you is,' says Brer Rabbit, sezee, 'en I'm gwineter kyore you, dat's w'at I'm a gwineter do,' sezee.

"Brer Fox, he sorter chuckle in his stummuck, he did, but Tar-Baby ain't sayin' nuthin'.

" 'I'm gwineter larn you howter talk ter 'specttubble fokes ef hit's de las' ack,' sez Brer Rabbit, sezee. 'Ef you don't take off dat hat en tell me howdy, I'm gwineter bus' you wide open,' sezee.

"Tar-Baby stay still, en Brer Fox, he lay low.

"Brer Rabbit keep on axin' 'im, en de Tar-Baby, she keep on sayin' nuthin', twel present'y Brer Rabbit draw back wid his fis', he did, en blip he tuck 'er side er de head. Right dar's whar he broke his merlasses jug. His fis' stuck, en he can't pull loose. De tar hilt 'im. But Tar-Baby, she stay still, en Brer Fox, he lay low.

" 'Ef you don't lemme loose, I'll knock you agin,' sez Brer Rabbit, sezee, en wid dat he fotch 'er a wipe wid de udder han', en dat stuck. Tar-Baby, she ain't sayin' nuthin', en Brer Fox, he lay low.

" 'Tu'n me loose, fo' I kick de natal stuffin' outen you,' sez Brer Rabbit, sezee, but de Tar-Baby, she ain't sayin' nuthin'. She des hilt on, en den Brer Rabbit lose de use er his feet in de same way. Brer Fox, he lay low. Den Brer Rabbit squall out dat ef de Tar-Baby don't tu'n 'im loose he butt 'er cranksided. En den he butted, en his head got stuck. Den Brer Fox, he sa'ntered fort', lookin' des ez innercent ez wunner yo' mammy's mockin'-birds.

" 'Howdy, Brer Rabbit,' sez Brer Fox, sezee. 'You look sorter stuck up dis mawnin',' sezee, en den he rolled on de groun', en

laft en laft twel he couldn't laff no mo'. 'I speck you'll take dinner wid me dis time, Brer Rabbit. I done laid in some calamus
root, en I ain't gwineter take no skuse,' sez Brer Fox, sezee."

Here Uncle Remus paused, and drew a two-pound yam out
of the ashes.

"Did the fox eat the rabbit?" asked the little boy to whom the
story had been told.

"Dat's all de fur de tale goes," replied the old man. "He
mout, en den agin he moutent. Some say Jedge B'ar come 'long
en loosed 'im—some say he didn't. I hear Miss Sally callin'.
You better run 'long."

HOW MR. RABBIT WAS TOO SHARP FOR
MR. FOX

"Uncle Remus," said the little boy one evening, when he had
found the old man with little or nothing to do, "did the fox kill
and eat the rabbit when he caught him with the Tar-Baby?"

"Law, honey, ain't I tell you 'bout dat?" replied the old
darkey, chuckling slyly. "I 'clar ter grashus I ought er tole you
dat, but ole man Nod wuz ridin' on my eyeleds 'twel a lettle mo'n
I'd a dis'member'd my own name, en den on to dat here come
yo' mammy hollerin' atter you.

"W'at I tell you w'en I fus' begin? I tole you Brer Rabbit wuz
a monstus soon beas'; leas'ways dat's w'at I laid out fer ter tell
you. Well, den, honey, don't you go en make no udder kalkala-
shuns, kaze in dem days Brer Rabbit en his fambly wuz at de
head er de gang w'en enny racket wuz on han', en dar dey stayed.
'Fo' you begins fer ter wipe yo' eyes' bout Brer Rabbit, you wait
and see whar'bouts Brer Rabbit gwineter fetch up at. But dat's
needer yer ner dar.

"W'en Brer Fox fine Brer Rabbit mixt up wid de Tar-Baby,
he feel mighty good, en he roll on de groun' en laff. Bimeby he
up'n say, sezee:—

" 'Well, I speck I got you dis time, Brer Rabbit,' sezee:
'maybe I ain't, but I speck I is. You been runnin' roun' here
sassin' atter me a mighty long time, but I speck you done come ter
de een' er de row. You bin cuttin' up yo' capers en bouncin' 'roun'

in dis naberhood ontwel you come ter b'leeve yo'se'f de boss er de
whole gang. En den youer allers some'rs whar you got no biz-
ness,' sez Brer Fox, sezee. 'Who ax you fer ter come en strike up
a 'quaintence wid dish yer Tar-Baby? En who stuck you up dar
whar you iz? Nobody in de roun' worril. You des tuck en jam
yo'se'f on dat Tar-Baby widout waitin' fer enny invite,' sez Brer
Fox, sezee, 'en dar you is, en dar you'll stay twel I fixes up a
bresh-pile and fires her up, kaze I'm gwineter bobbycue you dis
day, sho,' sez Brer Fox, sezee.

"Den Brer Rabbit talk mighty 'umble.

" 'I don't keer w'at you do wid me, Brer Fox,' sezee, 'so you
don't fling me in dat brier-patch. Roas' me, Brer Fox,' sezee, 'but
don't fling me in dat brier-patch,' sezee.

" 'Hit's so much trouble fer ter kindle a fier,' sez Brer Fox,
sezee, 'dat I speck I'll hatter hang you,' sezee.

" 'Hang me des ez high as you please, Brer Fox,' sez Brer
Rabbit, sezee, 'but do fer de Lord's sake don't fling me in dat
brier-patch,' sezee.

" 'I ain't got no string,' sez Brer Fox, sezee, 'en now I speck
I'll hatter drown you,' sezee.

" 'Drown me des ez deep ez you please, Brer Fox,' sez Brer
Rabbit, sezee, 'but don't fling me in dat brier-patch,' sezee.

" 'Dey ain't no water nigh,' sez Brer Fox, sezee, 'en now I
speck I'll hatter skin you,' sezee.

" 'Skin me, Brer Fox,' sez Brer Rabbit, sezee, 'snatch out my
eyeballs, t'ar out my years by de roots, en cut off my legs,' sezee,
'but do please, Brer Fox, don't fling me in dat brier-patch,'
sezee.

"Co'se Brer Fox wanter hurt Brer Rabbit bad ez he kin, so he
cotch 'im by de behime legs en slung 'im right in de middle er de
brier-patch. Dar wuz a considerbul flutter whar Brer Rabbit
struck de bushes, en Brer Fox sorter hang 'roun' fer ter see w'at
wuz gwineter happen. Bimeby he hear somebody call 'im, en
way up de hill he see Brer Rabbit settin' cross-legged on a chink-
apin log koamin' de pitch outen his har wid a chip. Den Brer
Fox know dat he bin swop off mighty bad. Brer Rabbit wuz
bleedzed fer ter fling back some er his sass, en he holler out:

" 'Bred en bawn in a brier-patch, Brer Fox—bred en bawn in a brier-patch!' en wid dat he skip out des ez lively ez a cricket in de embers."

---

1. We should make the following preliminary observations about these two pieces:

   a. That the authors are attempting, within the limitations of the conventional alphabet, to give an accurate presentation of the respective dialects.

   b. That their spellings are a consistent, systematic representation of the dialect pronunciation.

   c. That where the spellings differ from conventional orthography, the pronunciation usually (but not always) differs from the author's own, and is presumed to differ from the reader's as well.

With these in mind, draw up a list of the phonemes represented by the spellings, noting as well spellings which indicate consonant omissions. For instance, in the first stanza of the Lowell poem, we would note the following:

> *ketched, thet, hev*: $/\varepsilon/$ for $/\mathrm{æ}/$
> *kittle*: $/\mathrm{I}/$ for $/\varepsilon/$
> *knowin'*: $/\mathrm{n}/$ for $/\mathrm{ŋ}/$
> *o'*: $/\mathrm{ə}/$, omission of $/\mathrm{v}/$

2. The linguistic atlas survey verifies the observation that in New England generally the postvocalic $/\text{-r}/$ is not pronounced, yet the spellings *feller* and *yeller* occur in the same first stanza. What does this indicate was the poet's own pronunciation of the *-er* spelling? Since the postvocalic $/\text{-r}/$ is likewise not pronounced throughout the South, do any similar spellings occur in Harris's tale? Does Lowell give any indication of the linking or intrusive $/\text{-r-}/$?

3. Note the following spellings:

> Lowell: *wuz, Sarjunt, i* (eye), *wood n't, tales* (tails), *enuf, ses, Bee* (be), *stares* (stairs), *reed* (read), etc.
> Harris: *contrapshun, sez, duz, stummuck, fokes* (folks), *laft, laff*, etc.

How *do* you pronounce the words indicated by these spellings? This "phenomenon" is called *eye dialect*. What does an eye-dialect spelling tell us about the author's (and reader's) attitude toward the speaker?

4. In the Harris story, the "little boy's" speech is indicated in conventional orthography, yet he is presumably the son of the plantation owner and therefore speaks the Southern dialect. What does this tell us about Harris's attitude toward the little boy's pronunciation and Uncle Remus's?[13]

5. Both works give consistent indications of the grammatical practices in these dialects, especially of verb forms. Note some of these practices and generalize from them.

6. What do these works indicate about the following:

    a. The limitations of the conventional alphabet for dialect writing.
    b. The attitude of the author toward speakers of the dialect.
    c. The effect upon the contemporary reader.

Why do you imagine that dialect writing as a literary form is much less prevalent now? How does the Steinbeck passage which heads this chapter differ from these earlier works?

Scots dialect in literature

The following poems include Robert Burns's famous bit of sectarian malice (written in 1785 about an actual person), and three poems by contemporary exponents of the so-called Scottish Renaissance.

Robert Burns

HOLY WILLIE'S PRAYER

O Thou, wha in the Heavens dost dwell,
Wha, as it pleases best thysel',
Sends ane to heaven and ten to hell,
    A' for thy glory
And no for ony guid or ill
      They've done afore thee!

---

[13] In some of the *Biglow Papers*, a similar situation occurs when Parson Wilbur appends some highly pedantic notes in standard spelling to Hosea's dialect poems. The notes to the above poem were omitted as irrelevant to our study.

I bless and praise thy matchless might,
Whan thousands thou hast left in night,
That I am here afore thy sight,
   For gifts an' grace
A burnin' an' a shinin light,
   To a' this place.

What was I, or my generation,
That I should get sic exaltation?
I, wha deserve most just damnation,
   For broken laws,
Sax thousand years 'fore my creation,
   Thro' Adam's cause.

When frae my mither's womb I fell,
Thou might hae plunged me in hell,
To gnash my gums, to weep and wail,
   In burnin lakes,
Where damned devils roar and yell,
   Chain'd to their stakes;

Yet I am here a chosen sample,
To show thy grace is great and ample;
I'm here a pillar in thy temple,
   Strong as a rock,
A guide, a buckler, an example
   To a' thy flock.

O Lord, thou kens what zeal I bear,
When drinkers drink, and swearers swear,
And singin there and dancin here,
   Wi' great an' sma':
For I am keepit by thy fear
   Free frae them a'.

But yet, O Lord! confess I must
At times I'm fash'd wi' fleshy lust;
An' sometimes too, wi' warldly trust,
      Vile self gets in;
But thou remembers we are dust,
      Defil'd in sin.

O Lord! yestreen, thou kens, wi' Meg—
Thy pardon I sincerely beg;
O! may't ne'er be a livin' plague
      To my dishonour,
An' I'll ne'er lift a lawless leg
      Again upon her.

Besides I farther maun allow,
Wi' Lizzie's lass, three times I trou—
But, Lord, that Friday I was fou,
      When I cam near her,
Or else thou kens thy servant true
      Wad never steer her.

May be thou lets this fleshly thorn
Beset thy servant e'en and morn
Lest he owre high and proud should turn,
      That he's sae gifted;
If sae, thy hand maun e'en be borne,
      Until thou lift it.

Lord, bless thy chosen in this place,
For here thou hast a chosen race;
But God confound their stubborn face,
      And blast their name,
Wha bring thy elders to disgrace
      An' public shame.

Lord, mind Gawn Hamilton's deserts,
He drinks, an' swears, an' plays at cartes,
Yet has sae mony takin arts
      Wi' grit an' sma',
Frae God's ain priest the people's hearts
      He steals awa'.

An' when we chasten'd him therefor,
Thou kens how he bred sic a splore
As set the warld in a roar
      O' laughin' at us;
Curse thou his basket and his store,
      Kail and potatoes.

Lord, hear my earnest cry an' pray'r,
Against that presbytery o' Ayr;
Thy strong right hand, Lord, make it bare
      Upo' their heads;
Lord, weigh it down, and dinna spare,
      For their misdeeds.

O Lord my God, that glib-tongu'd Aiken,
My very heart and soul are quakin',
To think how we stood sweatin, shakin,
      An' piss'd wi' dread,
While he, wi' hingin lips and snakin,
      Held up his head.

Lord in the day of vengeance try him;
Lord, visit them wha did employ him,
And pass not in thy mercy by them,
      Nor hear their pray'r:
But, for thy people's sake, destroy them,
      And dinna spare.

But, Lord, remember me and mine
Wi' mercies temp'ral and divine,
That I for gear and grace may shine
      Excell'd by nane,
And a' the glory shall be thine,
      Amen, Amen!

Hugh MacDiarmid[14]

THE WATERGAW

Ae weet forenicht i' the yow-trummle
I saw yon antrin thing,
A watergaw wi' its chitterin' licht
Ayont the on-ding;
An' I thocht o' the last wild look ye gied
Afore ye dee'd!

There was nae reek i' the laverock's hoose
That nicht—an' nane i' mine;
But I hae thocht o' that foolish licht
Ever sin' syne;
An' I think that mebbe at last I ken
What your look meant then.

THE BONNIE BROUKIT BAIRN
(for Peggy)

Mars is braw in crammasy,
Venus in a green silk goun,
The auld mune shak's her gowden feathers,
Their starry talk's a wheen o' blethers,
Nane for thee a thochtie sparin',
Earth, thou bonnie broukit bairn!
—But greet, an' in your tears ye'll droun
The haill clanjamfrie!

[14] Reprinted with permission of The Macmillan Company from *The Collected Poems of Hugh MacDiarmid.* Copyright 1948, © 1962 by Christopher Murray Grieve.

R. Crombie Saunders

HAD I TWA HERTS[15]

Had I twa herts an you but ane
    Whan we were twin'd, still for your sake
That I micht loe yet be alane
    Ae hert wud thrive, the ither break.

Had I twa tongues tae speak o thee
    I culdna let a morrow come
An hear na o your cheritie
    From ane—the ither wud be dumb.

Had I fower een an twa tae close
    Wi greetan o a hert forlorn,
The ither twa wud see a rose
    Ahint the gairden o your scorn.

But I am ane an sae maun find
    An answer tae the mysterie;
Dee an forget, or livan mind
    Aa times my troublit historie.

    1. After reading through these poems, what basic difference do you find between the Burns poem on the one hand, and the MacDiarmid and Saunders poems on the other? What attitude toward a potential audience does this difference indicate on the part of the poets? What seems to be Burns's position on the writing of Scots dialect?[16]

    2. Some Scots dialect spellings have a pattern of their own which must be learned: *guid* (good), for example, is pronounced

---

[15] R. Crombie Saunders, *XXI Poems*. Reprinted by permission.

[16] I have not appended a glossary to the poems on purpose. However, glossary notes may be found at the end of this sequence of questions—but don't peek until you've pondered this first question.

with a front-rounded vowel, as indicated by the "silent" *i* after *u*. (A similar pronunciation is indicated by *mune*.) Given this problem, and the further problem of unfamiliar sounds, as in *licht*, what sounds can you derive from the spellings?

3. Though the sampling is too slight for generalizing, what grammatical patterns are indicated here, especially with the verbs again? Why is Burns less thorough in this respect than the contemporary writers?

4. In what respects does the Saunders poem differ from those by MacDiarmid? Note that each poet indicates his scorn of Standard Southern British in a different way. How do they differ in their treatment of present participles, and which is historically more accurate?

5. When all is said and done, what is missing from these poems, regardless of the writers' accuracy? Could phonetic transcription help? Is this a general failing in dialect literature?

BURNS: *sic*, such; *ken*, know; *fash'd*, beset; *maun*, may; *fou*, drunk; *steer*, tough; *splore*, disturbance; *gear*, merit; *kail*, cabbage.

MACDIARMID: (1) *forenicht*, dusk; *yow-trummle*, "eve-tremble," cold spell in July after sheep-shearing; *antrin*, occasional, momentary; *watergaw*, indistinct rainbow; *chitterin'*, shivering; *ayout*, beyond; *on-ding*, rainfall; *reek*, smoke; *laverock*, lark; *syne*, since, ago.

(2) *braw*, handsome; *crammasy*, crimson; *wheen o'blethers*, bunch of nonsense; *broukit*, neglected; *greet*, cry; *clanjamfrie*, collection of people.

SAUNDERS: *akint*, beyond.

Conventional and stage dialect

1. The following extracts from Shakespeare's *Henry V*, the "international" episode of the four captains (III, ii) and Fluellen's comparison of Henry V and Alexander the Great (IV, vii), represent one of the earliest extensive uses of dialect on the English stage. Stage dialect had been done before—at least as early as the *Second Shepherd's Play*, and Shakespeare himself used dialect briefly in *Merry Wives of Windsor* and later in *King Lear*, but never in so ambitious a way, introducing, as he does, representatives of each of the four kingdoms of Great Britain.

From William Shakespeare, *The Life of Henry the Fifth* (First Folio Text):

[From Act III]

Enter Gower.

Gower. Captaine *Fluellen*, you must come presently to the Mynes; the Duke of Gloucester would speake with you.

Flu. To the Mynes? Tell you the Duke, it is not so good to come to the Mynes: for looke you, the Mynes is not according to the disciplines of the Warre; the concauities of it is not sufficient: for looke you, th'athuersarie, you may discusse vnto the Duke, looke you, is digt himselfe foure yard vnder the Countermines: by *Cheshu*, I thinke a will plowe vp all, if there is not better directions.

Gower. The Duke of Gloucester, to whom the Order of the Siege is giuen, is altogether directed by an Irish man, a very valiant Gentleman yfaith.

Welch. It is Captaine *Makmorrice*, is it not?

Gower. I thinke it be.

Welch. By *Cheshu* he is an Asse, as in the World, I will verifie as much in his Beard: he ha's no more directions in the true disciplines of the Warres, looke you, of the Roman disciplines, then is a Puppy-dog.

Enter Makmorrice, and Captaine Iamy.

Gower. Here a comes, and the Scots Captaine, Captaine *Iamy*, with him.

Welch. Captaine *Iamy* is a maruellous falorous Gentleman, that is certain, and of great expedition and knowledge in th'aunchiant Warres, vpon my particular knowledge of his directions: by *Cheshu* he will maintaine his Argument as well as any Militarie man in the World, in the disciplines of the Pristine Warres of the Romans.

Scot. I say gudday, Captaine *Fluellen*.

Welch. Godden to your Worship, good Captaine *Iames*.

Gower. How now Captaine *Mackmorrice*, haue you quit the Mynes: haue the Pioners giuen o're?

Irish. By Chrish Law tish ill done: the Worke ish giue ouer, the Trompet sound the Retreat. By my Hand I sweare, and my fathers Soule, the Worke ish ill done: it ish giue ouer: I would haue blowed vp the Towne, so Chrish saue me law, in an houre. O tish ill done, tish ill done: by my Hand tish ill done.

Welch. Captaine *Mackmorrice*, I beseech you now, will you voutsafe me, looke you, a few disputations with you, as partly touching or concerning the disciplines of the Warre, the Roman Warres, in the way of Argument, looke you, and friendly communication: partly to satisfie my Opinion, and partly for the satisfaction, looke you, of my Mind: as touching the direction of the Militarie discipline, that is the Point.

Scot. It sall be vary gud, gud feith, gud Captens bath, and I sall quit you with gud leve, as I may pick occasion: that sall I mary.

Irish. It is no time to discourse, so Chrish saue me: the day is hot, and the Weather, and the Warres, and the King, and the Dukes: it is no time to discourse, the Town is beseech'd: and the Trumpet call vs to the breech, and we talke, and be Chrish do nothing, tis shame for vs all: so God sa' me tis shame to stand still, it is shame by my hand: and there is Throats to be cut, and Workes to be done, and there ish nothing done, so Christ sa' me law.

Scot. By the Mes, ere theise eyes of mine take themselues to slomber, ayle de gud seruice, or Ile ligge i' th' grund for it; ay, or goe to death: and Ile pay 't as valorously as I may, that sal I suerly do, that is the breff and the long: mary, I wad full faine heard some question tween you tway.

Welch. Captaine *Mackmorrice*, I thinke, looke you, vnder your correction, there is not many of your Nation.

Irish. Of my Nation? What ish my Nation? Ish a Villaine, and a Basterd, and a Knaue, and a Rascall. What ish my Nation? Who talkes of my Nation?

Welch. Looke you, if you take the matter otherwise then is meant, Captaine *Mackmorrice*, peraduenture I shall thinke you doe not vse me with that affabilitie, as in discretion you ought to vse me, looke you, being as good a man as your selfe, both in the disciplines of Warre, and in the deriuation of my Birth, and in other particularities.

Irish. I doe not know you so good a man as my selfe: so Chrish saue me, I will cut off your Head.

Gower. Gentlemen both, you will mistake each other.

Scot. A, that's a foule fault.   *A Parley.*

Gower. The Towne sounds a Parley.

Welch. Captaine *Mackmorrice*, when there is more better

oportunitie to be required, looke you, I will be ṣo bold as to tell you, I know the disciplines of Warre: and there is an end.

Exit.

[From Act IV]

Enter Fluellen and Gower.

Flu. Kill the poyes and the luggage, 'Tis expressely against the Law of Armes, tis as arrant a peece of knauery marke you now, as can bee offert in your Conscience now, is it not?

Gow. Tis certaine, there's not a boy left aliue, and the Cowardly Rascalls that ranne from the battaile ha' done this slaughter: besides they haue burned and carried away all that was in the Kings Tent, wherefore the King most worthily hath caus'd euery soldiour to cut his prisoners throat. O 'tis a gallant King.

Flu. I, hee was porne at *Monmouth* Captaine *Gower*: What call you the Townes name where *Alexander* the pig was borne?

Gow. *Alexander* the Great.

Flu. Why I pray you, is not pig, great? The pig, or the great, or the mighty, or the huge, or the magnanimous, are all one reckonings, saue the phrase is a litle variations.

Gower. I thinke *Alexander* the Great was borne in *Macedon*, his Father was called *Phillip* of *Macedon*, as I take it.

Flu. I thinke it is in *Macedon* where *Alexander* is porne: I tell you Captaine, if you looke in the Maps of the Orld, I warrant you sall finde in the comparisons betweene *Macedon* & *Monmouth*, that the situations looke you, is both alike. There is a Riuer in *Macedon*, & there is also moreouer a Riuer at *Monmouth*, it is call'd Wye at *Monmouth*: but it is out of my praines, what is the name of the other Riuer: but 'tis all one, tis alike as my fingers is to my fingers, and there is Salmons in both. If you marke *Alexanders* life well, *Harry of Monmouthes* life is come after it indifferent well, for there is figures in all things. *Alexander* God knowes, and you know, in his rages, and his furies, and his wraths, and his chollers, and his moodes, and his displeasures, and his indignations, and also being a little intoxicates in his praines, did in his Ales and his angers (looke you) kill his best friend *Clytus*.

Gow. Our King is not like him in that, he neuer kill'd any of his friends.

Flu. It is not well done (marke you now) to take the tales out of my mouth, ere it is made and finished. I speak but in the figures, and comparisons of it: as *Alexander* kild his friend *Clytus*, being in his Ales and his Cuppes; so also *Harry Monmouth* being in his right wittes, and his good iudgements, turn'd away the fat Knight with the great belly doublet: he was full of iests, and gypes, and knaueries, and mockes, I haue forgot his name.

Gow. Sir *Iohn Falstaffe.*

Flu. That is he: Ile tell you, there is good men porne at *Monmouth.*

Gow. Heere comes his Maiesty.

Answer the following questions relating to the preceding extracts from *Henry V*:

a. Enumerate the phonological, morphological, and vocabulary conventions of Fluellen the Welshman, MacMorris the Irishman, and Jamy the Scot. What traits of character are given to each man?

b. Which of these conventions and traits seem to be based on actual dialect, and which cater to preconceived notions of how "those people" ought to speak and behave?

c. What dialect conventions and character traits—as viewed by Hollywood and the television industry—do the following nationalities have: English, French, German, Italian, Russian, Japanese, Mexican? How much truth is there in these stock characters? How did such stereotyping originate in each case?

d. The Irish stage character seems to have changed considerably, if Captain MacMorris is any model of the Elizabethan Irishman. What changes have taken place, with respect to both dialect and character traits, in the stage Irishman since 1600? What other national and ethnic groups have undergone a similar change, and what factors are responsible for this?

2. The following extracts are samples of dialect writing by several authors. In each instance, list the phonological, morphological, and vocabulary traits of the dialect, indicate which traits seem real and which merely conventional, and comment on the effectiveness of the piece.

a. From William Shakespeare, *King Lear* (IV, vi, 235–51), First Folio Text (1623):

[Edgar is disguised as a Southern peasant.]

Steward. Wherefore, bold Pezant,
Dar'st thou support a publish'd Traitor? Hence,
Least that th'infection of his fortune take
Like hold on thee. Let go his arme.
Edgar. Chill not let go Zir,
Without vurther 'casion.
Stew. Let go Slave, or thou dy'st.
Edg. Good Gentleman goe your gate, and let poore volke passe: and 'chud ha' bin zwaggerd out of my life, 'twould not ha' bin zo long as 'tis, by a vortnight. Nay, come not neere th'old man: keepe out che vor' ye, or ice try whither your Costard, or my Ballow be the harder; chill be plaine with you.
Stew. Out Dunghill.
Edg. Chill picke your teeth Zir: come, no matter vor your foynes.

b. From John Dunton, *An Hue and Cry After Conscience: or the Pilgrim's Progress by Candle-Light, in Search After Honesty and Plain-Dealing* (1685):

We were no sooner in the Street, but we stumbled upon a plain Country Fellow in a gray homespun Coat, a Girdle near as big as a Horse-collar about his Wast, and a steepled Crownd Hat, much in fashion in the days of Queen *Dick*, his Shooes were clouted, and his Stockings you wou'd have taken for *Roman* Buskins. At sight of this Man my heart began to leap, for thought I, this must be *Plain-dealing*, or the Devil's in't: . . . . And with that pulling his Hat out of his Eyes, I perceived *Ignorance* on his forehead, wherefore I found I was mistaken; yet *Discovery* tipping him on the Elbow urged him to discourse.

Discovery. *Friend, whether are you Travelling?*
Ignorance. Whay waud whoo knaw? If whoo won tall a Body, that whoo will tall whoo whare whoo dwall.
Disc. *I suppose in the Country Friend, but it matters not where, so be it you can inform us where* Honesty *and* Plain-dealing *have taken up their Quarters.*

Ign. What won you say *Haunestay* and *Plaun-Daulin,* thoat's whaint? No marry dant oy.

Disc. *We thought you might. But again have you not heard of 'em?*

Ign. Oy marry han I, but oy cou'd n'are zee aum.

Disc. *That's hard, I thought they might be taking the Air in the Country, seeing they have absented themselves from the Town of late.*

Ign. Deer zer dy, oys knaw nauthing on aum, aw oys can zay to the mauter oys heard, oys Vather zay oance they caume doan an liggd in whoos Hause.

Disc. *And pray did you hear how he entertained them?*

Ign. Yeas varily, whoo zay whoo at virst waus varey loffing to 'aum, but whoo perceving whoo waud now let whoo remave the Land-Maurks, naw ne maws a zwath of whoo's Naughbers Grass, or remave his zhocks a Caun an Haw to whoos awn gront, naw ner pauster whoos Horses in his Naubours gront, when whoo waus a sleap ne anter the meausur of whoos Caun, and manny zuch Mauters, whoo won ha naw mawr to done with whoo, but zent whoo a pauking, and then whoo done aw this, and a graut dale mawr as well as whoos Naubour's.

Disc. *And since that time you have not heard of 'em.*

Ign. Naw ne oy, moyn Vather chaurg oy, on whoos Bleasing that oy's ha nauthing to done wiw whoo ne mawr oy's ha naw.

c. From Henry Fielding, *The History of Tom Jones, a Foundling* (1749), Book VI, Chapter 2:

. . . "'Fore George!" cries the squire [Western], "now you mind me on't, I remember it all. It is certainly so, and I am glad on't with all my heart. I knew Sophy was a good girl, and would not fall in love to make me angry. I was never more rejoyced in my life; for nothing can lie so handy together as our two estates. I had this matter in my head some time ago: for certainly the two estates are in a manner joined together in matrimony already, and it would be a thousand pities to part them. It is true, indeed, there be larger estates in the kingdom, but not in this county, and I had rather bate something than marry my daughter among strangers and foreigners. Besides, most o' zuch great estates be in the hands of lords, and I heate the very name of *themmun.* Well but, sister, what would you advise me to do; for I tell you women know these matters better than we do?"—"Oh, your humble servant, sir," answered the lady: "we are obliged to you for allowing us a capacity in anything. Since you are pleased, then, most politic sir, to ask my advice, I think you may propose the match to Allworthy yourself. There is no indecorum in the proposal's coming from the parent of either side. King Alcinous, in Mr. Pope's Odyssey, offers his daughter to Ulysses. I need not caution so politic a person not to say that your daughter is in love; that would indeed be against all rules."—"Well," said the squire, "I will propose it; but I shall certainly lend un a flick, if he should refuse me."

d. From Charles Dickens, *Hard Times*, Book I, Chapter 13. The setting for the novel, "Coketown," was based on Manchester (Lancashire):

"Thou 'rt not fearfo';" he [Stephen Blackpool] said it in a low voice, as they went out at the door; "to leave me alone wi' her!"

As she [Rachael] looked at him, saying, "Stephen?" he went down on his knee before her, on the poor mean stairs, and put an end of her shawl to his lips.

"Thou art an Angel. Bless thee, bless thee!"

"I am, as I have told thee, Stephen, thy poor friend. Angels are not like me. Between them, and a working woman fu' of faults, there is a deep gulf set. My little sister is among them, but she is changed."

She raised her eyes for a moment as she said the words; and then they fell again, in all their gentleness and mildness, on his face.

"Thou changest me from bad to good. Thou mak'st me humbly wishfo' to be more like thee, and fearfo' to lose thee when this life is ower, and a' the muddle cleared awa'. Thou 'rt an Angel; it may be, thou hast saved my soul alive!"

She looked at him, on his knee at her feet, with her shawl still in his hand, and the reproof on her lips died away when she saw the working of his face.

"I coom home desp'rate. I coom home wi'out a hope and mad wi' thinking that when I said a word o' complaint I was reckoned a onreasonable Hand. I told thee I had had a fright. It were the Poison-bottle on table. I never hurt a livin' creetur;

but happenin' so suddenly upon 't, I thowt, 'How can *I* say what I might ha' done to myseln, or her, or both!' "

She put her two hands on his mouth, with a face of terror, to stop him from saying more. He caught them in his unoccupied hand, and holding them, and still clasping the border of her shawl, said hurriedly:

"But I see thee, Rachael, setten by the bed. I ha' seen thee, aw this night. In my troublous sleep I ha' known thee still to be there. Evermore I will see thee there. I nevermore will see her or think o' her, but thou shalt be beside her. I nevermore will see or think o' anything that angers me, but thou, so much better than me, shalt be by th' side on 't. And so I will try t' look t' th' time, and so I will try t' trust t' th' time, when thou and me at last shall walk together far awa', beyond the deep gulf, in th' country where thy little sister is."

e. From Charles Dickens, *Great Expectations*, Chapter 7:

"Why, didn't you ever go to school, Joe, when you were as little as me?"

"Well, Pip," said Joe, taking up the poker, and settling himself to his usual occupation, when he was thoughtful, of slowly raking the fire between the lower bars: "I'll tell you. My father, Pip, he were given to drink, and when he were overtook with drink, he hammered away at my mother most onmerciful. It were a'most the only hammering he did, indeed, 'xcepting at myself. And he hammered at me with a wigour only to be equalled by the wigour with which he didn't hammer at his anwil.—You're a-listening and understanding, Pip?"

"Yes, Joe."

" 'Consequence, my mother and me we ran away from my father several times; and then my mother she'd go out to work, and she'd say, 'Joe,' she'd say, 'now, please God, you shall have some schooling, child,' and she'd put me to school. But my father were that good in his hart that he couldn't abear to be without us. So, he'd come with a most tremenjous crowd and make such a row at the doors of the houses where we was, that they used to be obligated to have no more to do with us and to give us up to him. And then he took us home and hammered us. Which, you see, Pip," said Joe, pausing in his meditative raking of the fire, and looking at me, "were a drawback to my learning."

"Certainly, poor Joe!"

"Though mind you, Pip," said Joe, with a judicial touch or two of the poker on the top bar, "rendering unto all their doo, and maintaining equal justice betwixt man and man, my father were that good in his hart, don't you see?"

I didn't see; but I didn't say so.

"Well!" Joe pursued, "somebody must keep the pot a-biling, Pip, or the pot won't bile, don't you know?"

I saw that, and said so.

" 'Consequence, my father didn't make objections to my going to work; so I went to work at my present calling, which were his too, if he would have followed it, and I worked tolerable hard, I assure *you*, Pip. In time I were able to keep him, and I kept him till he went off in a purple leptic fit. And it were my intentions to have had put upon his tombstone that Whatsume'er the failings on his part, Remember reader he were that good in his hart."

Joe recited this couplet with such manifest pride and careful perspicuity, that I asked him if he had made it himself.

"I made it," said Joe, "my own self. I made it in a moment. It was like striking out a horseshoe complete, in a single blow. I never was so much surprised in all my life—couldn't credit my own ed—to tell you the truth, hardly believed it were *my* own ed. As I was saying, Pip, it were my intentions to have had it cut over him; but poetry costs money, cut it how you will, small or large, and it were not done. Not to mention bearers, all the money that could be spared were wanted for my mother. She were in poor elth, and quite broke. She waren't long of following, poor soul, and her share of peace come round at last."

f. From Charles Dickens, *Mugby Junction*, Chapter 3:

Another time, a merry, wideawake American gent . . . says, very loud and good-tempered: 'I tell Yew what 'tis, ma'arm. I la'af. Theer! I la'af. I Dew. I oughter ha' seen most things, for I hail from the Onlimited side of the Atlantic Ocean, and I haive travelled right slick over the Limited, head on through Jeerusalemm and the East, and likeways France and Italy, Europe Old World, and am now upon the track to the Chief

Europian Village; but such an Institution as Yew, and Yewer young ladies, and Yewer fixing's solid and liquid, afore the glorious Tarnal I never did see yet! And if I hain't found the eighth wonder of monarchial Creation, in finding Yew, and Yewer young ladies, and Yewer fixin's solid and liquid, all as aforesaid, established in a country where the people air not absolute Loo-naticks, I am Extra Double Darned with a Nip and a Frizzle to the innermostest grit! Wheerfur—Theer!—I la'af! I Dew ma'arm. I la'af!'

g. From George Eliot, *Adam Bede*, Chapter 1:

[The setting is based on Staffordshire.]

"Come, Ben," said Adam, rather sternly, "you let the words o' the Bible alone; you're going too far now."

"What! are *ye* a-turnin' roun', Adam! I thought ye war dead again th' women preachin', a while agoo?"

"Nay, I'm not turnin' noway. I said nought about the women preachin': I said, You let the Bible alone: you've got a jest-book, han't you, as you're rare and proud on? Keep your dirty fingers to that."

"Why, y' are gettin' as big a saint as Seth. Y' are goin' to th' preachin' to-night, I should think. Ye'll do finely t' lead the singin'. But I don' know what Parson Irwine 'ull say at his gran' favright Adam Bede a-turnin' Methody."

"Never do you bother yourself about me, Ben. I'm not a-going to turn Methodist any more nor you are—though it's like enough you'll turn to something worse. Mester Irwine's got more sense nor to meddle wi' people's doing as they like in religion. That's between themselves and God, as he's said to me many a time."

"Ay; ay; but he's none so fond o' your dissenters, for all that."

"Maybe; I'm none so fond o' Josh Tod's thick ale, but I don't hinder you from making a fool o' yourself wi't."

There was a laugh at this thrust of Adam's, but Seth said, very seriously,

"Nay, nay, Addy, thee mustna say as anybody's religion's like thick ale. Thee dostna believe but what the dissenters and the

Methodists have got the root o' the matter as well as the church folks."

"Nay, Seth, lad; I'm not for laughing at no man's religion. Let 'em follow their consciences, that's all. Only I think it 'ud be better if their consciences 'ud let 'em stay quiet i' the church—there's a deal to be learnt there. And there's such a thing as being over-speritial; we must have something beside Gospel i' this world. Look at the canals, an' th' aqueducs, an' th' coal-pit engines, and Arkwright's mills there at Cromford; a man must learn sommat beside Gospel to make them things, I reckon. But t' hear some o' them preachers, you'd think as a man must be doing nothing all's life but shutting's eyes and looking what's a-going on inside him. I know a man must have the love o' God in his soul, and the Bible's God's word. But what does the Bible say? Why, it says as God put his sperrit into the workman as built the tabernacle, to make him do all the carved work and things as wanted a nice hand. And this is my way o' looking at it: there's the sperrit o' God in all things and all times—weekday as well as Sunday—and i' the great works and inventions, and i' the figuring and the mechanics. And God helps us with our headpieces and our hands as well as with our souls; and if a man does bits o' jobs out o' working hours—builds a oven for 's wife to save her from going to the bakehouse, or scrats at his bit o' garden and makes two potatoes grow istead o' one, he's doing more good, and he's just as near to God, as if he was running after some preacher and a-praying and a-groaning."

"Well done, Adam!" said Sandy Jim, who had paused from his planing to shift his planks while Adam was speaking; "that's the best sarmunt I've heared this long while. By th' same token, my wife's been a-plaguin' on me to build her a oven this twelve-mont."

3. Some of the above excerpts show obvious speech differences between the characters, particularly when one of them does not appear to exhibit any dialect traits whatsoever. What attitude on the part of the author toward his characters does this indicate? Which of the dialects seem to be more social than regional?

4. What is the present-day attitude toward dialects in litera-ture—both on the stage and in fiction? Consider this from the viewpoint of both author and his audience or reader.

BIBLIOGRAPHY

The best introduction to dialect study and linguistic geography is Raven I. McDavid, Jr., "The Dialects of American English," chapter 9 of W. Nelson Francis, *The Structure of American English* (New York: The Ronald Press Company, 1958), pp. 480–543; supplemented by the same author's "Sense and Nonsense About American Dialects," *PMLA*, LXXXI, 2 (May, 1966), 7–17. Carroll E. Reed, *Dialects of American English* (Cleveland: The World Publishing Company, 1967), is a good, relatively brief textbook introduction, well furnished with maps. A detailed discussion of worldwide dialect study is Sever Pop, *La Dialectologie: Aperçu historique et Méthodes d'enquêtes linguistiques*, Recueil de Travaux d'Histoire et de Philologie, 3ᵉ série, 38 (2 parts; Louvain: Université de Louvain, 1950). Surveying the entire field up to the time of publication, this work is especially complete for Romance languages—American dialect work, although considered to be of prime importance, is limited to pp. 914–23. British dialects are discussed in G. L. Brook, *English Dialects* (New York: Oxford University Press, 1963); and Angus McIntosh, *An Introduction to a Survey of Scottish Dialect* (Edinburgh: Thomas Nelson and Sons Ltd., 1961).

The first accomplishment of the Linguistic Atlas of the United States and Canada is Hans Kurath *et al.*, *Linguistic Atlas of New England* (3 vols. in 6 parts; Providence, R. I., 1939–1943); accompanied by Hans Kurath *et al.*, *Handbook of the Linguistic Geography of New England* (Washington: American Council of Learned Societies, 1939). This has been augmented by the following studies:

Kurath, Hans. *A Word Geography of the Eastern United States*. Ann Arbor: University of Michigan Press, 1949.

Atwood, E. Bagby. *A Survey of Verb Forms in the Eastern United States*. Ann Arbor: University of Michigan Press, 1953.

Kurath, Hans, and McDavid, Raven I. *The Pronunciation of English in the Atlantic States*. Ann Arbor: University of Michigan Press, 1961.

Atwood, E. Bagby. *The Regional Vocabulary of Texas*. Austin: University of Texas Press, 1962.

Shorter studies based upon the completed surveys in the Midwest include the following: Albert H. Marckwardt, "Principal and Subsidiary Dialect Areas in the North-Central States," *PADS*, 27 (April, 1957), 3–15; Harold B. Allen, "The Primary Dialect Areas of the Upper Midwest," in *Readings in Applied English Linguistics*, pp. 231–41; Roger W. Shuy, "The Northern-Midland Dialect Boundary in Illinois," *PADS*, 38 (November, 1962); and Clyde T. Hankey, "A Colorado Word Geography," *PADS*, 34 (November, 1960).

The best introductory study of American English is Albert H. Marckwardt, *American English* (New York: Oxford University Press, 1958). A more detailed study is H. L. Mencken, *The American Language* (4th ed.; New York: Alfred A. Knopf, Inc., 1936; supplements, 1945, 1948). This work has been brought up to date and edited in a one-volume abridgment by Raven I. McDavid, Jr. (New York: Alfred A. Knopf, Inc., 1963). A dated, but still useful study is George P. Krapp, *The English Language in America* (2 vols.; New York: Oxford University Press, 1925). A representative study of dialect in literature is Sumner Ives, "The Phonology of the Uncle Remus Stories," *PADS*, 22 (November, 1954).

Appendix: Linguistics and the Teaching of English

THE TEACHING OF ENGLISH TODAY

The entire concentration of this book has thus far been upon the English language—its forms and structure, its history, its varieties. Underlying this concentration is the fact that language itself is the object of a lifetime's work and study, requiring the specialist to work hard just to keep up with the new ideas which are continually being advanced. The basic assumption has been that the student of English, whether or not he goes on to concentrate in linguistics, must know in general terms what all this activity is about. There comes a time, however, when all but the most devoted disciple of Pure Research asks, in effect, "What good is all this? How will this help us as teachers?" The *cui bono* question is neither stupid nor smart-alecky. Postponing the discussion until now does not diminish its importance; we have to have a body of knowledge to work with first. Nor does its relegation to this appendix serve to brush it off. The following remarks are meant to suggest certain applications of language study to the teaching of English, without either vaunting linguistics as a panacea or appropriating the function of a methods course.

The first statement in this book was that the teacher of *English*, regardless of classroom level, deals with three discrete subjects—grammar, composition, and literature. Until comparatively recently, the tendency has been to maintain the separateness of these three areas, to teach them in isolation, even in courses which were supposed to combine them. Some lip service was given to the creed that a knowledge of grammar would make the student a better writer, and sometimes the student was asked to write a theme in response to literature, but in general the separation was carefully observed.

But for the past ten years, following the so-called post-Sputnik period, when the whole educational establishment came under attack, English teachers have been questioning the whole basis of their curriculum. The basic discussion has come to revolve around the following questions:

1. What can be done to make the English program sequential, rather than repetitious?
2. What changes can be made in the subject matter to make it more relevant to our students?
3. How can instruction in English grammar help us in the study of composition and literature, and which grammar should we use?

Answers are still being sought for the first two questions, which recognize two basic faults with the old program, and right now there is a good deal of experimentation going on in the development of a sequential curriculum and in curriculum materials themselves. A good deal of attention is also being given to the language problems of those euphemistically referred to as "disadvantaged youth," the children of the culturally isolated, the ghetto dwellers, and the foreign-born. Thanks to the U. S. Office of Education, the College Entrance Examination Board, and *Project English*, the first two questions are on their way to being answered.

The third question is more immediately relevant to the subject of this book. Many teachers have been bewildered by the claims and counterclaims of proponents of the competing grammatical systems. Yet the evidence is clear that school grammar, for the reasons outlined in Chapter 2, is inadequate; and if it is more realistically augmented by the descriptions of the philologists, it becomes far too detailed to be very useful. A few years ago, it was widely felt that descriptive linguistics was the answer to the teacher's problems. Although it did represent an improvement over previous methods, descriptive linguistics proved defective in the very area where it was supposed to help the most, in syntax. More recently, the specialists in both tagmemics and generative-transformational grammar have advanced some proposals in this area, particularly in the problem of writing sentences which are both well formed and stylistically pleasing. Hopefully, some kind of an amalgamation can come out of this activity which will benefit the whole profession.

It will be some time yet before we can know to what extent modern grammar theories will solve the problems which plague the teacher, particularly in composition. For one thing, the air is still full of claims and counterclaims; for another, it is almost impossible to control experimentation in this area to elicit conclusions beyond the shadow of a doubt. Writing depends upon so many factors which are not amenable to testing that it is virtually impossible to say, for instance, whether dramatic improvement in skills is due to the "new rhetoric" or to a quiet place to write and a good topic to write about. But until fuller evidence is offered, a few suggestions are tendered here about applying certain linguistic principles to composition and literature.

LINGUISTICS AND COMPOSITION

The most basic problem for teachers of composition is getting the student to recognize the written sentence consistently. Although all students know intuitively what a sentence is, once they have learned their language, they have no end of trouble practicing this knowledge on paper. Student themes abound in sentence fragments and run-on sentences, the latter category including both comma faulting and fused sentences. Yet, experience has shown that *the student himself* can detect both these weaknesses once he has had a short introduction to the suprasegmental phonemes of English, especially *pitch*.

Fragments, for instance, are easily corrected, even though they abound on paper. The commonest cause of the fragment is that the student has an afterthought which he wishes to append to a sentence, not realizing that he has already punctuated this sentence with a full stop:

> He ordered an extra-large hot fudge sundae. With lots of chopped nuts on top.

> Several tactical blunders led to Napoleon's defeat at Waterloo. One being that he committed his troops to battle piecemeal.

Later, when the student goes over his work, he often fails to catch this fragment because he reads his draft silently, checking more often for content than for form. Despite his grammar instruction, he does not as a rule check out each structure punctuated as a sentence to see that it has a complete subject and predicate.

A little time spent on the pitch patterns of basic English sentences should give the student sufficient background for reviewing his own work. All that is required of him is that he read his work *aloud* to himself or to a friend. Assuming a basic $/^{231}\searrow/$ pitch pattern, the student who wrote either of the examples above would get through the first part of each just fine, but the second part won't pass muster. Probably upon re-examination, he will notice that after *sundae* and *Waterloo* the punctuation tells him that he should read each sentence with $/^{1}\searrow/$ intonation, but his ear tells him that it should be $/^{2}\rightarrow/$. Like most fragments, these are both easily corrected by joining the fragment to the sentence it should have been punctuated with in the first place.

Run-on sentences, though related to the fragment, are a more difficult problem. They often indicate that the student lacks experience in detecting written sentence form, and even when the difficulties are discovered, they are seldom remedied best by repunctuating. The following represents a garden-variety comma fault:

> My roommate is not a particularly nice guy, for one thing, he's always borrowing my shirts.

This instance of mistaking a preposition for a conjunction can again be submitted to the reading test. The student should be able to hear that at *guy* his voice wants to go to the $/^1\searrow/$ intonation pattern, but the punctuation tells him that it should be read $/^2{\rightarrow}/$. Obviously, there's nothing wrong with his voice, so the punctuation and form need correction. In this case, probably a period after *guy* will suffice, because the second clause already has an adequate sentence transition.

Most comma faults, however, can't be remedied this easily. The temptation is to substitute a semicolon for every faulty comma, but this is based on the assumption that both clauses balance and are closely interrelated, which is seldom so. For example:

> My brother was a pretty stupid gardener, he hoed up the carrots and left the weeds standing.

Replacing the comma with a semicolon scarcely brings the statement up to the level of awkward mediocrity. There are other possibilities, but they require rewriting the clauses:

(1) My brother was a pretty stupid gardener. Once, not so long ago, he hoed up . . . .
(2) Because my brother was a pretty stupid gardener, he hoed up . . . .
(3) As a gardener, my brother was so stupid that he hoed up . . . .

Quite obviously, the rewriting depends upon the whole context of the sentences and whether the writer wishes to emphasize the stupidity or the result of the stupidity.

At this point, we begin to cross the fine line separating grammar from style. And here, grammar in its strictest sense will be of little direct help. Hopefully, some of the work being done in the "new rhetoric" will soon show how this line can be crossed, but at the moment it is still in the developmental stage. Among the problems that are currently being explored is that of the complex sentence with its variously embedded sentences, structures which frequently cause the inexperienced writer to lose his way—resulting in hopeless entanglement or in a retreat to primer-style simple sentences and choppiness.

LINGUISTICS AND LITERATURE

When anyone surveys the general field of literature, he finds that there are difficulties here of unfamiliar genres, unfamiliar or unreal subjects, *and* new and different kinds of language. For instance, virtually the only dramatic literature assigned to high school students is Shakespeare, which presents linguistic problems accumulated over a period of 350 years, as we saw in Chapter 7. In addition, any dramatic work presents its situation, delineates the characters, and advances the plot solely through the medium of dialogue, and this is a difficult thing for any student to get used to, even when there are copious stage notes in his copy of the play. These two problems come together in Shakespeare; wouldn't it therefore be simpler to take them one at a time, by first studying a contemporary play like *Our Town*, or the TV presentation of *Marty*?

Or take any of the nineteenth-century British novels which were until recently the sole "safe" fare of high school literature. In addition to the vocabulary of obsolescence (all those different kinds of buggies in *Great Expectations*), and the vocabulary of another culture (the British monetary system and the nobility), there are the problems of British regional dialect, as we noted in the last chapter, and Standard British English, which tends to differ in little details from American English. Finally, there is the fact of language change, making even nineteenth-century writing just that much more difficult, if only because it is much more formal than what the student is used to.

Even the literature of nineteenth-century America has an unfamiliar flavor for anyone who is not prepared for the cultural and linguistic changes and cannot therefore understand them. Where the problem is linguistic, it can be allayed by full, accurate instruction in the history of the English language and in its dialects. Both of these areas can be made interesting to almost any student. Further, they can be presented discretely or in conjunction with the literary work. Either way, they are both viable and valuable additions to the teaching of English. In addition, there is now a solid trend to a far greater emphasis upon the teaching of more contemporary literature.

With poetry, however, whether contemporary or not, the problem becomes more complex. Poetry, particularly modern poetry, reflects the attempt of the poet to go to the limits of language in his search for adequate expression. Except for writers like James Joyce, and to a lesser extent Faulkner, this deeply personal search for ultimate expression has no close counterpart in prose. Poetry therefore presents a linguistic problem of great complexity, one which the teacher is often ill-equipped to handle. It does little good to say that a poem is just a "story" in another form. It is even less relevant to spend time on metrics, rime schemes, and stanzaic patterns if nothing is said to suggest why the poet selected a particular pattern in the first place.

In his attempt to put an infinite concept into finite form, the poet feels the need both to express and to compress, and the result is a kind of suggesting, rather than outright telling. At the linguistic level, the reader must be aware of syntax as a connotative device. A simple example of this is in two lines from Emily Dickinson:

> The Grass so little has to do
> I wish I were a Hay—

In the last line, she placed the *nondefinite* article before the mass noun "Hay," which is clearly ungrammatical, but which permitted the poet to express at once both individuality and insignificance. When Emily Dickinson's early editors changed *a* to *the*, motivated by the desire to "correct" her usage, they practically destroyed the poem.

We also have here an example of what is too often dismissed as poetic license. The first line is unusual in its inverted word order. This can be explained away as a metrical necessity: without the inversion, the line would lack the steady iambic rhythm. But if this were the only reason, the line would be no different from doggerel. Metrical necessity becomes insignificant beside the shifting forward of "so little," with the resultant emphasis on *little*, for the entire poem is a description of the poet's envy of the lazy grass.

Rearrangement purely for meter and rime, without any other purpose, results in doggerel, the outpouring of the poetaster. Examples are legion; I will content myself with a few lines by the early eighteenth-century writer Francis Hoffman, who was so ill-advised as to try to rewrite John Bunyan's *Pilgrim's Progress* in verse. Here is the end of Worldly-Wiseman's advice to Christian:

> There empty Houses are whose Rent's not high,
> There cheap and good Provisions you may buy,
> And there with honest Neighbours safe and well
> You in good Credit may and fashion dwell.
>   *Christian* at this Advice began to pause,
> But soon concluded that if true it was,
> He must be doubtless very much unwise
> Who would not take such probable Advice.

Although Hoffman is at least in control of his basic form, everything else goes by the boards in his effort to retain control— syntax, sense, and solemnity.

The classic example of poetry stretching language to its limits is e. e. cummings' "anyone lived in a pretty how town," which is frequently anthologized. Without analyzing the whole poem, we can make some general observations. For instance, it gives some interesting problems in linguistics. In order to generalize upon the uneventful (and yet tragic) existence of his focal character, cummings chooses to call him "anyone," rather than Jones or Anderson. The basis for this is perfectly grammatical: both proper nouns and indefinite pronouns operate in the same way, and in a generative grammar of the NP, both are a possible choice at the same point in evolving the deep structure. It's just that we don't ordinarily expect to find an indefinite pronoun used to name a specific person. In the same line, we find the ambiguous "pretty how town," with the possibility of interpretation as "the town is pretty how" (*pretty* as intensifier) and "the town is pretty and how" (*pretty* as adjective). "How" is forced into service as an adjective here, explainable only as a reversal of the cliché "How pretty!", uttered by someone passing through. But the poem does not necessarily need such close linguistic analysis. A simple reading, which will point out all of the tag expressions emblematic of the cycle of years, is enough to give the general impression of the poet's intention. Close analysis, with attention to the detail, serves mainly to confirm this impression.

THE RESPONSIBILITIES OF THE TEACHER

It is undeniable, then, that the English teacher needs linguistic training as the cornerstone of his own understanding of the discipline. Grammatical proficiency is an important means of cementing the separate elements of the discipline together to make it both real and meaningful to the student. The English teacher, however, needn't give the student a complete course in grammar. Too often, the high school English teacher tries to turn his own courses into a repetition of his college work, just as the newly minted college English instructor sometimes reads his graduate seminar notes to his classes. Neither teacher has given enough thought to the needs and abilities of his students. They are trying too hard to make the course intellectually viable to themselves.

But the English teacher, like it or not, must have a thorough foundation in English grammar and linguistic theory if he hopes to develop a responsible program. Nor does his responsibility stop here. He must keep reasonably well abreast of new developments, either through institutes and summer programs or through the professional organizations and their journals. In addition to the recent linguistic-based studies of style and prosody, there are other projects which demand his attention:

1. The results of a preliminary round-table discussion on the social dialects of the urban ghettoes, based primarily on the results of dialect geography surveys.
2. Studies relating structural and transformational grammars to problems in composition.
3. The possibility of applying techniques used by teachers of English as a foreign language to native speakers of a substandard dialect of English.
4. A study, based on transformational grammar, of the grammatical structures of student writers at three different grade

levels—and generalizations on what the teachers can reasonably expect from their students.

5. The application of linguistic theory to reading instruction.

These are but a few of the materials *now available* to the English teacher. Some of them are listed in the bibliography at the end of this appendix.

There is today every indication that the English teacher is aware of the need to improve his discipline, to tie together the discrete parts of the English curriculum, to make the materials more relevant to the student. A portion of the responsibility for helping the teacher rests with the linguists, who are beginning to see that their intramural bickering over the relative merits of their special theories and hypotheses is not in the best interest of the discipline itself. But whatever the problem, and wherever the help comes from, no one should now believe that linguistics itself is a panacea for educational ills. At best, it serves in its place as one of the elements that help to improve the teaching of English. To ignore it would weaken the discipline far more than to accord it too much prominence. And it is much too late to tolerate weaknesses in American education.

BIBLIOGRAPHY

On the wave of the interest and concern about the changes in English teaching, two recent books attempt to explain what has been happening in the discipline: Michael F. Shugrue, *How the "New English" Will Help Your Child* (New York: Association Press, Family Life Library, 1966); and Neil Postman and Charles Weingartner, *Linguistics: A Revolution in Teaching* (New York: Dell Publishing Company, Inc., 1967). The first is intended for the general public; the second, for teachers of English.

As an introductory sample of possible relationships between language study and the educational process, as well as a survey of present research in the area, the following collection is excellent: Janet A. Emig, James T. Fleming, and Helen M. Popp (eds.), *Language and Learning* (New York: Harcourt, Brace & World, Inc., 1966). It is a revision and expansion of the 1964 Special Issue of the *Harvard Education Review*. The following is a brief list of articles and monographs which cover various ways in which linguistics can serve the English teacher:

Newsome, Verna L. *Structural Grammar in the Classroom.* Oshkosh: Wisconsin Council of Teachers of English, 1961.

Borgh, Enola M. *Grammatical Patterns and Composition.* Oshkosh: Wisconsin Council of Teachers of English, 1965.

Stageberg, Norman C. *Using Grammar To Improve Writing,* Educational Service Publication No. 18. Cedar Falls: University of Northern Iowa Extension Service, 1966.

Hunt, W. Kellogg. *Grammatical Structures Written at Three Grade Levels,* Research Report No. 3. Champaign, Ill.: National Council of Teachers of English, 1965.

Christensen, Francis, *Notes Toward a New Rhetoric: Six Essays for Teachers.* New York: Harper and Row, 1967.

Stewart, William A. (Ed.). *Non-Standard Speech and the Teaching of English,* Language Information Series 2. Washington: Center for Applied Linguistics, 1964.

Shuy, Roger W. (Ed.). *Social Dialects and Language Learning,* Proceedings of the Bloomington, Indiana, Conference, 1964. Champaign, Ill.: National Council of Teachers of English, 1965.

A report of the Curriculum Materials Centers and Demonstration Centers sponsored by the U. S. Office of Education, with lists and descriptions of the materials available and work projected, can be found in Michael F. Shugrue, "New Materials for the Teaching of English: The English Program of the USOE," *PMLA*, LXXXI, 4 (September, 1966), 3–38. Interim reports on Project English were printed in the same journal in the September, 1962, and September, 1963, issues.

For an excellent collection of essays which explore the possible relationships between linguistics and literature, see Seymour Chatman and Samuel R. Levin (eds.), *Essays on the Language of Literature* (Boston: Houghton Mifflin Company, 1967). The following brief list includes articles and monographs which also expand upon aspects of this subject:

Halle, Morris, and Keyser, Samuel Jay. "Chaucer and the Study of Prosody," *College English*, XXVIII, 3 (December, 1966), 187–219.

Levin, Samuel R. *Linguistic Structures in Poetry.* 'S-Gravenhage: Mouton and Company, 1962.

Epstein, Edmund L., and Hawkes, Terence. "Linguistics and English Prosody," *Studies in Linguistics*, Occasional Papers, 7 (1959).

Finally, the most interesting and provocative series of essays on the anthropological and philosophical foundations of language: John B. Carroll (ed.), *Language, Thought, and Reality: Selected Writings of Benjamin Lee Whorf* (Cambridge, Mass.: The M.I.T. Press, 1956).

Index

Abbott, E. A., 190, 194, 209
ablative case, 24
accusative case, 265
action verb, 107–108
adjective, 24, 25, 90–91
  as unknown in substantial interrogative, 122
  in Early Modern English, 195–96
  in Middle English, 232–33
  in Old English, 267
adverb, 25
  as noun phrase postmodifier, 93
  as unknown in substantial interrogative, 122–23
  categories of, 103, 104, 112
  functionally defined, 27
  in Early Modern English, 196–97
  in Middle English, 232–33
  in Old English, 267
affix, 55
  floating, 119
affix transformation, 101–102, 115
affricate sounds, 56 and n., 79
agentive noun, 133
agglutinative languages, 32
Albanian, 29n.
Alfred the Great, King of England, 252–53, 254
  translation of Boethius, 254–64
Allen, Harold B., 72, 139, 140n., 156n., 157n., 330
Allen, Robert L., 113
allomorph, 56–57, 62
allophone, 54, 56, 62, 77
allotagma, 62
alphabet, as final stage in development of writing, 144–45
  Roman, development of, 145
  chart, 146
American Bible Society, 50
American Council of Learned Societies, 279
American Dialect Society, 279
American Indian languages, 49–50

American Linguistic Atlas Project, 279–95 *passim*
Anderson, William, 215n.
Anglo-Saxon; *see* Old English
Anglo-Saxon Chronicle, 254n., 271–72
appearance verb, 107
Applied Linguistics, 140–41
Arabic, 29n.
Arabic numerals, 143
Armed Forces Language Program, 51
article, 90
  in Old English, 266
Aryan, 29n.
aspect, in verb phrase auxiliary, 101
Athabaskan, 51
Athelred ("the Unready"), King of England, 253
Athenian Mercury (1691), 37–38
attribute, 91
Atwood, E. Bagby, 277n., 330
Auxiliary (Aux), in Early Modern English, 197–98
  in Old English, 268
  in verb phrase, 99–102

Bach, Emmon, 73–74
Baltimore, Md., 285
Bantu, 50n.
base morphs, 55
Baskin, Wade, 49n.
Basque, 29n.
Baugh, Albert C., 274
be, as auxiliary element, 100–102
  as main verb option, 103
  as passive transformation element, 115–17
become, as copulative verb, 106, 108
Beowulf, 8, 179, 270n.
Berlitz schools, 51
Bible, 7, 18, 50
Bierce, Ambrose, 19–20
binary relationships, of immediate constituents, 60, 61
Bloch, Bernard, 279

345